Energetic Boundaries

Also by Cyndi Dale

The Intuition Guidebook
Kundalini: Divine Energy, Divine Life
The Everyday Clairvoyant
The Subtle Body: An Encyclopedia of Your Energetic Anatomy
The Complete Book of Chakra Healing (formerly New Chakra Healing)
Illuminating the Afterlife
Attracting Your Perfect Body Through the Chakras
Advanced Chakra Healing: Heart Disease; The Four
Pathways Approach
Advanced Chakra Healing: Cancer; The Four Pathways Approach
Advanced Chakra Healing: Energy Mapping on the Four Pathways
Attracting Prosperity Through the Chakras

Audio

Energy Clearing
Healing Across Space & Time
Advanced Chakra Wisdom
Illuminating the Afterlife
The Songbird Series

How to Stay Protected
and Connected in
Work, Love, and Life

Energetic Boundaries

Cyndi Dale

SOUNDS TRUE
Boulder, Colorado

Sounds True, Inc.
Boulder, CO 80306

Published 2011

Cover and book design by Dean Olson

Printed in Canada

Figure A © 2011 Photo Researchers, Inc. All Rights Reserved.
Figures B, C, E, and F © 2011 Richard Wehrman, MerlinWood.net

Library of Congress Cataloging-in-Publication Data

Dale, Cyndi.
    Energetic boundaries : how to stay protected and connected in work, love,
and life / by Cyndi Dale.
        p. cm.
Includes bibliographical references and index.
    ISBN 978-1-60407-561-8
1. Magnetotherapy. I. Title.
RZ422.D35 2011
612'.01421—dc22
2011010337

eBook ISBN 978-1-60407-646-2

10 9 8 7 6 5 4 3 2 1

Borders for the Bountiful Life

Though imperceptible to the naked eye, our energetic boundaries mean the difference between experiencing an enjoyable, prosperous, and loving life or suffering through a sad, limited, and unhappy existence. They separate what we need from what we don't, selectively letting into our lives only those energies, people, guidance, thoughts, situations, opportunities, and healing that bring our spiritual essence further into our real lives. They also go a step further and purposefully seek out and draw in *everything* we need to achieve our hopes and dreams.

Our energetic boundaries border our spiritual selves and promote our true nature, which is one of the reasons I often call them "spiritual borders." We long to express this inner identity, and establishing the correct energetic boundaries will help us do just that. When created and managed correctly, they make sure that our real selves—not the ideas, thoughts, and beliefs that aren't us—are in charge of our lives. And they

share information with the world, telling everyone exactly who we are, what we want, and how they can treat us.

Maybe you didn't even know you needed to craft invisible parameters to keep yourself safe and intact. As you read this book, you'll discover that not only must you have these boundaries, but also that having them improves your life dramatically. You'll come to rely on your new "force field" to the point that you won't leave home—or come home—without turning it on.

Those of us lacking these boundaries or operating with damaged boundaries often fall prey to marauders: people who, wittingly or not, take advantage of us; situations that fell us over and over; and depressing behavior patterns that leave us feeling much less happy, loved, supported, fulfilled, respected, and provided for than we deserve. Quite simply, without boundaries, we can't share who we are with the world. We won't receive the bounty the world has to provide, either.

The symptoms of energetic-boundary issues range from the irritating to the traumatic. They can include:

- Feeling overwhelmed by everyone else's feelings, moods, needs, problems, negativity, and even illnesses
- Habitual people pleasing, usually to your own detriment
- Sudden, awful attacks of negativity
- Exhaustion, anger, and frustration from carrying, and caring about, everyone else while receiving nothing in return
- Recurring monetary, relationship, and work woes
- Depressing heaviness and physical illnesses, results of absorbing external energies
- Fear and distraction caused by intrusive psychic or supernatural events or energies
- Generalized anxiety, the product of always needing to watch for unseen dangers

- Constant compulsions, which are often signs of tending others' energies and needs instead of our own
- The embarrassment of behaving in ways that don't reflect your real self and that allow you to put up with the ridiculous from others
- The nagging feeling that the universe or the Divine is present for anyone but *you*

At least two-thirds of the individuals I've seen in my intuitive-counseling practice have lacked energetic boundaries or had damaged boundaries. But by erecting and/or healing these borders, they have grown leaps and bounds.

One woman, unemployed for two years, received three job offers within a month.

A good-looking young man who hadn't been in relationship for five years met a woman within a week. He wrote me after six months and told me that they were now living together in total bliss. (Yes, bliss!)

A young mother of three autistic or attention deficit disorder (ADD)–spectrum children reported that she was able to maintain her cool, and that all three children, whom she had helped set energetic boundaries, were now attending a "normal school."

A young child who couldn't sleep was suddenly able to get a full night's sleep. Her teddy bears and "scary things under the bed" stopped talking to her.

An elderly man with amyotrophic lateral sclerosis (ALS) transformed the illness and began living symptom free.

And every person reported a greater ability to make more personally satisfying decisions; avoid or transmute bad-energy situations; establish and maintain healthier relationships; create more wealth and abundance; eliminate or mitigate addictive, depressive, or anxious tendencies; discern and follow their intuition; and enjoy life to the max.

I know that every time I generate an appropriate energetic boundary, I not only feel better, but my life also improves. People treat me better.

I'm struck with flashes of insight. The words I need flow through me. My parenting improves. I attract the money or opportunity that creates a joy out of a struggle. My health gets better, or at least I'm led to the solution for my health concern. I even make more effective stock and investment decisions, because I'm able to tune out others' negativity and stick with my own inner wisdom.

Setting healthy energetic boundaries for yourself will take some work, but the effort is well worth it. Every stage of the work increases your exposure to light and joy and decreases your exposure to sources of negativity and exhaustion. The ultimate goal is to align your spiritual borders so they more elegantly reflect your true spiritual essence. This alignment ensures that every layer and level of your being lets in supportive energy and keeps out negative energy.

Before getting to specifics, we'll briefly discuss the purpose, formation, and functions of energetic boundaries. We'll also investigate seven boundary syndromes, common conditions that result from absent or damaged energetic boundaries, and I'll help you pinpoint the ones that might be inhibiting you. This discussion will help you pinpoint the reasons you have boundary issues, so you then know how to change your boundaries for the better. Along the way, exercises will help you establish healthy spiritual borders.

By the time you are done reading this book, you will be well on your way to safely building and creating a life that's nourishing and plentiful. In the end, to create our energetic boundaries is to claim the life we always knew that we should have, the life ready to share with those we love, the life secure in the good graces of the Divine. This is the life of our dreams; this is the life we guarantee ourselves through healthy energetic boundaries.

||||||||||||||||||||||||||||||

Energy and Our Energetic Fields

Ever since we crawled out of that primordial slime, that's been our unifying cry, "More light." Sunlight. Torchlight. Candlelight. Neon, incandescent lights that banish the darkness from our caves to illuminate our roads, the insides of our refrigerators. Big floods for the night games at Soldier's Field. Little tiny flashlights for those books we read under the covers when we're supposed to be asleep. Light is more than watts and footcandles. Light is metaphor. Light is knowledge, light is life, light is light.

TELEVISION PRODUCERS AND SCREENWRITERS
DIANE FROLOV AND ANDREW SCHNEIDER

Everything in this world, from sunlight to cupcakes, is made of energy. Energy is simply information that vibrates or moves. Some energy, such as the energy composing a table or a chair, moves slowly. You can see, touch, discuss, and prove the existence of

these slow-energy objects. But most of the energy in this world can't be seen, heard, or touched through our typical five senses. It moves so fast that we can't perceive it; usually, we can notice only its effects. Is the energy transmitted by your car radio any less real than the energy that makes up the book on your coffee table? How about the microwaves that zap your food or the satellite transmissions that zip e-mails your way? You know these energies exist, even though you can't see them, yet they are vital to your life.

Trillions upon trillions of bits of energetic data are zinging around us 24/7, and our energetic boundaries, themselves composed of fast-moving, unseen energy, keep us from being overwhelmed by them all. Energy also composes our feelings, thoughts, and needs, as well as our inherent beliefs and spiritual essence.

Throughout history and across all cultures, intuitives, healers, visionaries, and shamans have been able to perceive the energetic fields that science is only now coming to comprehend and study. In fact, they have been able to see and work with the three systems that link our physical and spiritual energies and interact to form our overall energetic anatomy: **the channels,** also called the meridians; **the centers,** the most well known of which are the chakras; and **the fields,** one of which is the auric field. Other types of fields include various types of magnetic fields, morphogenetic or species-based fields, miasmic or disease-creating fields, and all sorts of other fields that link our inner self with the outer world.

The meridians spread energy throughout our body. The chakras are energy receptors or holders, located mainly inside of the body. The fields, expanding bubbles or circles of light, are found outside of our body, emanating from our skin to several feet away. These fields compose our energetic boundaries. They listen to the data in our chakras and other energy centers to determine which information to bring from outside to inside of us. The fields also communicate messages from us to the outer world. There are actually dozens, maybe even hundreds or

thousands of layers or energy boundaries extending from your body. Some hover upon your skin like a butterfly kiss; others are similar to madcap children, dashing in all directions. Some of these fields perform specific activities, ranging from protecting us from dangers to attracting people to us. (For information on the scientific research about and evidence and applications of these various energetic systems, please see my book *The Subtle Body: An Encyclopedia of Your Energetic Anatomy.*)

The most well-known field is the auric field. Many believe that our auric field is the same as our electromagnetic field, a continually emerging and fluctuating field of energy produced by the electrical currents in our bodies. Every cell in our body pulses with electricity. Electricity produces magnetism, which means that every cell and organ, as well as the entirety of your body, generates energy fields. Kirlian photography, a scientific tool in use since the 1930s, employs a special type of film to illuminate the life energy, or auric field, around plants, animals, and people (see Figure A on page 8). Kirlian images reveal that all living beings emanate a set of electromagnetic fields.

These fields are interactive; they both take in and emit energy. That's why you can sense people, or even get a read on their personalities, when they walk into your space. Our energetic fields respond to trauma and healing energies. They also react to emotions and love; when two people interrelate, their energy fields blur and merge. Science can locate the heart field from at least four to six feet away from the body, which means we're able to exchange energy with others near us, but we can also swap energy with people hundreds of miles away. As quantum physics is proving, once two particles or people have met, they remain connected forever. That's how you know what's happening to your best friend who you haven't talked with for months or how you sense the exact moment a faraway loved one dies.

Even more startling, human energetic fields invite energy-information exchanges between people who have never met, between the living and the dead, and between people from the future and present day. And this

Figure A. *Even a plant has energetic boundaries. Look at the auric field on this plant and see its electromagnetic, or EMF, fields emanating from it. This photograph, taken with a specialized film used in Kirlian photography, underscores the existence of energetic boundaries. You wouldn't be able to see the leaf's field with your naked eye, but it is there.*

Kirlian photography is now being used to measure the energetic fields of people, plants, and animals in order to diagnose diseases (including cancer), preserve foods, prove the effectiveness of spiritual healing, explain the strange phenomenon of love and intimacy, and discover nature's mysteries, such as why dew collects in certain areas of a leaf and not others.[1]

He said she surely just dreamt that she was able to fly.
The baby stood her ground like an angel.
She said she knew she was able to fly
because when she came down she always had dust on her fingers
from touching the light bulbs.

J. D. SALINGER, *RAISE HIGH THE ROOF BEAM, CARPENTERS*

To Michael, Gabriel, and Katie,
the three young adults whose
quests for truth have spurred my own.

Contents

||||||||||||||||||||||||||||

process isn't limited to people. We can also converse energetically with plants, animals, and even inanimate objects.

No matter which scientific instruments we employ, we can take pictures of only a few of the many known energetic fields. Dozens of other scientifically proven energies, such as high-level infrared, ultraviolet, and gamma waves, as well as microwaves, expand farther than and stretch under visible light, the tiny spectrum of color we're used to working with. Every physical cell and organ actually generates its own magnetic or auric field. Furthermore, your body is 70 percent water, and each water molecule in your body spawns its own energetic field, because water molecules have north and south poles and conduct electricity.[2] With so many individual components of our body generating their own energetic fields, it's almost impossible to figure out how many energy fields each of us actually has.

Most images of the auric fields depict them as rippling bands of light. This is because electromagnetic energy *is* light. The electromagnetic spectrum is really a band of different speeds and temperatures of radiating energy or light. At the measurable end of this spectrum are radio waves, which, with their long wavelengths and low frequencies, are considered low energy, or not very powerful. On the other end are gamma rays, which feature short wavelengths and high frequencies, and are high in energy, or very intense. Somewhere in the middle is the relatively small band of energy called visible light, the range of rainbow colors we're actually able to see.

These various electromagnetic energies are not really different from each other. They are all made of photons, the unit of energy that creates light. This means that everything composed of electromagnetic energy is light, including your energetic fields—and you yourself. Research such as that conducted by Hal Puthoff, and discussed by Lynne McTaggart in her book *The Field,* is showing that we are actually made of and surrounded by photons. Our DNA is, in fact, a biophoton machine, a mechanism responding to the light outside and inside of us.[3]

Not only are we made of light, but we also generate light. That personal, literal light radiates from deep within our bodies. It also streams right through from outside to the inside of us, not stopping for skin or clothing. Because we consist of light, our energetic boundaries are nothing more or less than light.

Our auric field actually consists of twelve different bands of light, as shown on Figure B. Each band operates at a different frequency in the electromagnetic spectrum. For instance, most intuitives and Kirlian photographers see the band closest to our skin as red. We are born with each layer intact, but each becomes active at different points in our lives, from conception all the way to our elder years. As shown in Figure C, the bands become colored in, or tuned to a specific frequency, with our life experiences.

||||||||||||||||||||||||||||||||||||||||||||||||||||||||||||||||||||||||||

Measuring the Miracles of Your Energy Field

Decades ago, only mystics and madmen believed that there was an energy field around all living beings. Now science has actually proven that series of fields exists and that the sum total is much stronger and more potent than ever imagined. In fact, research done on this field is yielding a rich base for everything from diagnosing illness to enhancing food to creating prosperity—all of which we'll examine throughout this book.

The new science started in 1963, when Gerhard Baule and Richard McFee of Syracuse University detected a biomagnetic field around the human heart. The prefix *bio* stands for biology, or the chemical processes that create life. Magnetism is the energy produced by electricity, although it can also generate on its own under certain conditions. In the 1970s, researcher David Cohen of the Massachusetts

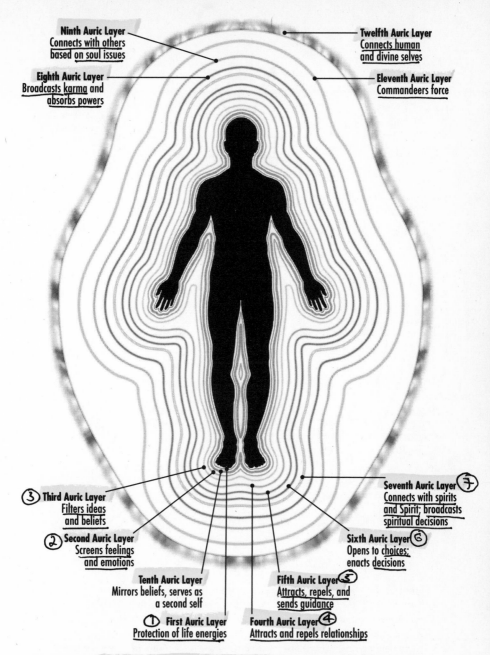

Ninth Auric Layer
Connects with others based on soul issues

Eighth Auric Layer
Broadcasts karma and absorbs powers

Twelfth Auric Layer
Connects human and divine selves

Eleventh Auric Layer
Commandeers force

③ **Third Auric Layer**
Filters ideas and beliefs

② **Second Auric Layer**
Screens feelings and emotions

Tenth Auric Layer
Mirrors beliefs, serves as a second self

① **First Auric Layer**
Protection of life energies

Fourth Auric Layer ④
Attracts and repels relationships

Fifth Auric Layer ⑤
Attracts, repels, and sends guidance

Sixth Auric Layer ⑥
Opens to choices; enacts decisions

Seventh Auric Layer ⑦
Connects with spirits and Spirit; broadcasts spiritual decisions

Figure B. *Our energetic boundaries circle our body as bands of light or energy. There are many energetic boundaries. The most well known is the auric field, shown here with twelve layers, each of which filters a specific type of information-energy that we send out into or take in from the world.*

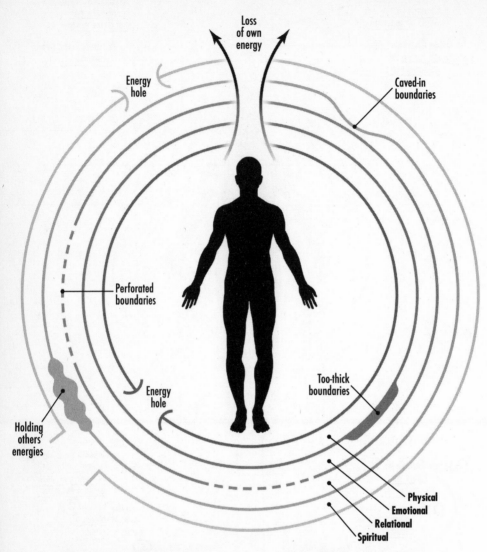

Figure C. *When we are conceived, all of our energetic boundaries are present, but not all are active. At the first sign of life, our physical and spiritual borders start filling in. These borders expand with our spiritual essence, but they also respond to events in our environment.*

As we mature, the various layers activate and are colored in with our universal and spiritual truths, or programs, as well as our responses to life and others' energies. Unfortunately, the unsuitable programs often outweigh our own spiritual or suitable programs, as we seek to fit in. Every boundary operating from unsuitable or insufficient programming becomes susceptible to boundary violations.

Institute of Technology (MIT) used a SQUID (superconducting quantum interference device) magnetometer, a means of measuring magnetism, to confirm Baule and McFee's results and measure the magnetic fields surrounding the human head and produced by brain activities.

Science has since started using the magnetocardiogram and magnetoencephalogram to measure magnetism from the heart and head, respectively. The magnetic fields detected by these instruments are so strong that we can analyze them for signs of disease before disease shows up in traditional medical tests. Illness alters the biomagnetic field, and the "sick area" of a field can be tracked to the related part of the body. Even more importantly, changing the biomagnetic field changes the body, which means that pulsing magnetic fields into the body can stimulate healing.

For almost five centuries, healers across the world have used the energy of their own bodies to help others heal, to detect events before they happen, and to transform physical matter. Eastern medicine is based on these concepts, as are most shamanic methods from the Western world. It's pretty amazing that science is now showing how these practices work in physical reality, and research is revealing the potential of these long revered, ancient practices.

For instance, in 1992, Japanese researchers studied practitioners of various martial arts and healing practices. Many of these systems are based on the idea that a natural energy called qi (chi), prana, mana, orgone, life energy, kundalini, or other names flows through the body and regulates health. These researchers discovered that the qi emission from hands is so powerful that it can be detected with a simple magnetometer consisting of two coils with 80,000 turns of wire. Since then, a number of studies of qi gong, a well-respected energy-balancing method, have measured the sound, light, and thermal fields emitted by its practitioners.

Particularly important is that the frequencies of these emanations, which often pulse, vary from moment to moment. Medical researchers creating pulsating magnetic-field therapies are discovering that these same frequencies can actually initiate healing in soft and hard tissues, even in patients who have gone unhealed for as long as forty years.[4]

Other research is just as exciting. Bioengineering professor Henry Lai of the University of Washington, along with three colleagues, used weak magnetic fields to eliminate and heal malaria bacteria. In the study of magnetism, researchers found 33 to 70 percent fewer parasites in the exposed versus unexposed samples.[5]

These dances into the scientific prove what ancient wisdom has already known: if you paint your world with every color of the rainbow, the world will smile back.

||||||||||||||||||||||||||||||||||||||||||||||||||||||||||||||||||||||||

Exercise: Finding Your Field

Want to see your energy field with your eyes? Find a private place with low or soft lights. You want to be as relaxed as possible, so you might want to sit in a comfortable chair or lie on your bed. You don't need much light—a candle in the corner, light seeping under your door, or the moon or streetlights shining through your bedroom window.

As your eyes become accustomed to the relative dark, hold out your hands and gaze at them. Your eyes should be glazed; you might want to actually peer just beyond your hands and keep your hands in your peripheral vision.

Now move your fingertips so both hands are touching, finger to finger. Breathe deeply, sensing the spiritual flame inside your heart. Consciously invite this flame to emanate from your heart, down your arms, through your hands, and into your fingertips. After you can feel the exchange of this spirit-flame between your fingertips, examine the outside rim of both hands. You might see a hazy, rather dim corona of light. Now move your fingertips slightly apart and gaze at the electrical charge that continues to connect them.

If you want, consciously send this energetic electricity from one fingertip to another and then move this glowing blaze over your skin, up and down your fingers, and over your hands. What happens? Can you perceive a shift in the hazy white you previously perceived?

You can play with this energy as long as you desire. When you are done, gently release your fingers from their position and draw the energy back into your heart. Breathe deeply and return to everyday consciousness.

Chapter 2

The Border Patrols:
Our Four Energetic
Boundaries

"No" is a complete sentence.

ANNE LAMOTT

Think of our energetic boundaries as the border patrol. These guards are our internal programs, and they serve three basic functions:

- **Providing protection.** They keep out the energies that fail to support our spiritual essence.
- **Filtering.** They let in the energies that enhance our spiritual essence, keep in the energy we need, and let out the energy or information that sustains us in the world.
- **Magnetizing.** They draw what we need to us, including healing, information, guidance, people, events, jobs, money, healthy relationships, life lessons, and more.

As explained in chapter 1, there are many types of energetic boundaries around our body, but the main one is the auric field. As we grow up, our spirit activates the age-appropriate auric layer or energetic boundary, enlightening it with the spiritual truths or programs explicitly and elegantly suited to our unique self. Unfortunately, our spirit isn't the only influence on these boundaries. Our parents, relatives, ancestors, schools, religious institutions, friends, enemies, coworkers, bosses, news sources, and the culture at large also have their say—for our good or ill. Life events, from the chronically negative to one-time traumas, can also keep our boundaries from developing or staying in harmony with our true spiritual essence.

When our boundaries are violated, there are three basic repercussions, energetically:

- **Our boundaries become rigid or immobilized.** Think of an icy wall. Getting near it makes us and others feel cold and shut down. Rigid energy boundaries have the same effect. People stay away, perceiving us as unavailable or disinterested in them. Immobile boundaries also repel potentially positive events or opportunities: investments, promotions or new jobs, healing energies, referrals to the right health-care professional, friendships that might warm our hearts, the loving and trusting touch of our child. When such positive people and experiences are constantly turned aside, we end up feeling isolated and alienated.
- **Our boundaries become permeable.** A permeable boundary is loose and flaccid. Picture going to war with a limp rag instead of a sword. You'll last—what?—about ten seconds on a battlefield. People with permeable boundaries are pushovers. They are easily swept aside, ignored, used, taken advantage of, or unrewarded.
- **Our boundaries are sliced, diced, and cut full of holes.** Gaps in our energy boundaries leave gaps in our lives, doorways through which anything and anyone can walk. We easily absorb

others' energies, from diseases to poverty issues, and lose our own life force. The more disturbing the issues in our lives, the greater the possibility that we have holes in our energy fields.

Any of these situations can contribute any of the seven energetic syndromes we'll discuss in chapter 3.

Each of our twelve auric layers carries out a different function and is important for our health and well-being. For example, the innermost layer, closest to our skin, regulates our relationship with sex, money, career success, and your basic safety and security needs. The green band, which corresponds to our relational field and centers, is tied to love, change, and heart concerns. One of the outer layers, which I see as gold, stretches to the very heavens, ushering spiritual manna into our everyday lives.

Based on my studies, professional practice, and personal life, I've grouped the twelve layers or boundaries into four types, based on their jobs or functions, and I associate each type with a particular color:

- Physical (red) boundaries
- Emotional (orange) boundaries
- Relational (green) boundaries
- Spiritual (white) boundaries

Within each of these boundaries are subsets of other colorations. For instance, gold and silver are members of the white family, while yellow belongs to the emotional. I'll discuss the specific layers and their functions in chapter 4. For now, let's walk the rainbow road to find out what happens within each category of energetic boundary, how our lives would look if each were healthy, and what compromises each.

Your Physical Energy Boundaries: Red at the Crossings

What do you think of when you concentrate on the color red? Life, love, excitement, valentines, blood, fire, racing cars, wounds. Red is associated with physicality, the richness of being a physical being and the ups and downs associated with it.

The job of our red boundaries is to assure our physical safety and motivate us toward physical success. It's to screen out the situations that might endanger our security and potential triumphs, and to enhance or draw positive situations to us. Our red boundaries enhance our physical welfare by enhancing all our basic needs, including our health. They ensure that we have a safe, homey place to live; clothing that suits our lifestyle and goals; and fresh air, clean water, and healing foods. They promise us partnership, which can include a spousal relationship that is romantic, sustaining, sexually fulfilling, and sweet.

Our red boundaries guarantee that we have money and financial stability. Real financial security, however, isn't only about having enough money to pay the bills, with a little extra thrown in. It involves knowing that our money is the tail on the kite of a fulfilling career or job. We are here to make a contribution to this world. We *are* a contribution to this world. Financial remuneration is only one part of the formula. We deserve to make a difference through our efforts and to be recognized for doing so.

We can't enjoy relationships or money, careers or sexuality, or even fun foods and dream houses, if we aren't physically safe. Being physically safe means we and our loved ones are protected from and, as much as possible, free from severe disease, abuse, addictions, or threats to our material and bodily well-being. Physical safety and security is one of the most important blessings of our red boundaries, because without it, we cannot enjoy the other blessings.

Even if we have strong physical borders, however, life will have its perils and problems. We always have lessons to learn, such as that security is fundamentally an inner, not outer, achievement. Good energetic boundaries, however, make sure that when life hands out the ups and downs, we're not always on the falling end of the teeter-totter.

What Compromises Our Physical Energy Boundaries?

Unfortunately, many situations and conditions impose on our physical energetic boundaries. Each carries its own laundry list of energetic problems and can lead to any of the seven syndromes introduced in the next chapter. A few of the injuries that lead to rigid, permeable, or gaping boundaries and physical energy problems are:

- physical violations or injuries (or witnessing others experiencing these things)
- physical abuse or addictions (or witnessing others experiencing these things)
- illness (our own or witnessing someone important to us experiencing illness)
- neglect; basic needs going unmet
- exposure to severe financial problems or work issues, such as being shunned or unfairly blamed
- being unwanted, abandoned, or constantly shamed
- our mother attempting to abort us before we were born or giving us up for adoption after our birth
- inherited family issues, beliefs, and genetics
- epigenetics, the ancestral programs and memories encoded in the chemical soup around our genes; these inherited recollections can cause all the situations listed above to adversely affect our physical energetic boundaries, even though the events originated in our ancestors' histories
- microchimerism, the inheritance of our mother's cells from pregnancy
- spiritual invasions

Topping the list are physical violations, such as being involved in an accident or suffering an injury. A blow to the body produces an immediate effect in our energetic boundary. These boundary injuries can heal, but they don't always. Although we may suffer long-term bodily effects from an injury—a car accident can leave us without a limb, a sports injury can cost us full use of a leg—we will not attract further consequences, such as other injuries or wounds, if our energetic boundary fully repairs itself. If our energetic boundary remains ruptured, however, we can experience any of the seven syndromes.

For instance, one of my clients experienced a severe car accident when she was sixteen. She was driving the family car, with her mother and sister as passengers, when they were blindsided by a drunk driver. My client's mother was killed instantly, and her sister was paralyzed from the waist down. My client escaped the accident with only a small twist of the neck, the results of which didn't even show up on X-rays. She called me when she was thirty-six. She was desperate, having consulted with doctor after doctor and healer after healer. Every time she thought about doing something good for herself, such as asking for a raise or taking a vacation, her neck would spasm so horribly that she would have to cancel her plans. Not only that, but every time someone asked her for a favor, she would feel the same excruciating pain unless she performed the task, even if she didn't want to do it. Her father was especially good at getting her to obey his orders, from cleaning his home to making dinner for him and his new wife.

My client's guilt over the car accident made her feel like she not only had to constantly atone, but also deny herself grace and goodness. This lack of self-forgiveness was like a wedge that kept her physical energetic boundary from closing. Unfortunately, others, especially her father, learned how to slip in through this hole and demand that she meet their needs at the expense of her own. As my client learned how to close this hole and open her heart to herself, the energetic boundary filled in and her neck aches stopped completely. She also learned that responsibility starts with taking care of herself.

Being abused—sexually, physically, emotionally, and/or mentally—sets us up for a life of pain, which is only exacerbated by the resulting permutations in our physical energy field. I've worked with probably 20,000 clients who received horrific treatment as children, were raped or abused as adults, or helplessly witnessed the same being inflicted on others. Any abuse—whether it happens to us once or repeatedly, whether it happens to us or we see it happening to others—punches holes in the physical energetic field, which can lead to any or all of the syndromes discussed in the next chapter. It will also affect the other three boundaries, making them rigid, permeable, or full of holes. Chapters 5 through 8 discuss ways to heal the energetic issues caused by abuse.

People often think that *they* weren't really injured if they only witnessed abuse. Since they didn't experience the abuse themselves, how could they have the same problems as those they saw being abused? The reasons are largely energetic.

Children are usually unable to distinguish themselves from others. They can't tell where their personal boundaries start and others' boundaries stop. So they personalize what someone else is experiencing. For instance, if children see someone being physically struck, they will energetically absorb the force of the blow. If it happens only once, their injured physical energetic boundary will probably recover. Repetitive occurrences, however, will permanently damage children's physical energy boundaries. As a result, they will later attract partners who want to get rid of their energy by hitting others, or the children themselves will grow into adults that free themselves from negative energy by hitting someone else.

Children are especially vulnerable to anything their mothers go through. One reason is that they are energetically linked to their mothers via an umbilical-like energy cord until they are at least three years old. Mom's experiences pass almost straight through the cord to her child. So does any energy of any issues that Mom disowns or won't deal with, like her abuse, illnesses, and addictions. This energy can also include problematic emotions, thoughts, and spiritual beliefs, which can damage her child's other three boundaries.

One of the reasons children's energetic boundaries absorb the energies of others is that children are innocent. They love. They haven't yet renounced their hearts, the part of our body that generates the largest energetic field. Children don't soak up others' negativity to hurt themselves; they do it because they love and want to help their loved ones.

Bottom line, hurtful forces are actual energies that can produce physical effects, and they can remain stuck in our energetic boundaries forever—or at least, until they are gently removed through therapeutic and energetic means. The gap they create in the physical energetic boundary can't help but invite the same treatment that we experienced during the initial abuse.

Do you think that illness can't be caught energetically? Think again. Experiencing our own or another's long-term illness can leave us vulnerable to taking on others' illnesses and predicaments—that is, until we close down the vulnerable gap in our physical energy border. One of my clients had been diagnosed with thirty diseases during her lifetime, from leukemia to shingles. Guess what? Her mother had been sick the entire time she was growing up. My client's pattern of illness cleared up after she closed down the physical energetic borders.

Any traumatic physical, emotional, or relational violation—such as being abandoned, unwanted, neglected, overworked, or exposed to long-term poverty—can injure our physical energy boundaries. One of my clients, for example, lost her mother at an early age. My client became a shopaholic, but interestingly, she bought only red clothes. It turned out her mother loved the color red and had been wearing a red dress when she was killed in a car crash. After my client dealt with her abandonment issues, her spending sprees ended.

I also worked with a fifteen-year-old girl whose mother had tried to abort her seven times. The girl's physical energetic boundaries had been punctured so many times by the attempted abortions that she had no physical energy borders of any sort. This girl did absolutely everything anyone asked her. If friends tried cocaine, she did. If others cut classes, she did. If someone wanted to have her do his or her homework, she did it. By the age of fifteen, she was sneaking around and having sex for money to buy drugs for her friends. She had been working with a therapist, but nothing changed until I had her carry around a doll for a week. Her job was to dress this doll in red clothes and take care of it. After a week of toting around the doll, my client said no to sex with her latest boyfriend. She moved to her aunt's house, transferred a different school, and began working hard to get straight A's.

Even spiritual violations can damage our physical energy boundaries. For instance, I've worked with a client who was tortured by the spirit of an ancestor. This ancestor had been addicted to gin while alive, and now his spirit came to my client as a voice and forced him to drink every night against his will, so it could feel the drunken high through my client's drinking binges. This spirit took advantage of my client's upbringing and original trauma, which had involved being beaten by his own drunk dad, and entered the resulting hole in my client's physical energetic field. We sent the spirit away and sealed up the hole. And presto, no more compulsion!

An emerging field called epigenetics is revealing another way of looking at our physical energetics. Epigenetics is the study of the chemical "soup" surrounding our genes. This soup contains memories and imprints of our ancestors. If our great-grandfather lost the family farm and decided he was a failure, we can literally inherit his failure syndrome. What one generation experiences, from poverty to mental illness, can be passed on and determine which genes are toggled or turned off or on.[1] Information transfers across generations, and this information changes not only the genes, but also, I propose, the fields of energy emanating from our DNA and cells. That means that through the fields of our individual cells, our ancestors might be telling people how to respond to us.

Yet another important field of study, called microchimerism, has proven that our mother's cells live within us long after we disconnect from her placenta; in fact, many remain our entire lives. If these cells get along with our own, they can bolster our immune system, keeping us from getting everything from diabetes to cancer. If these cells don't jibe with our own, our body attacks them, setting us up for a multitude of diseases.[2] I believe that mother cells, like all cells, also emanate their own energetic fields, which create physical responses within us.

In short, all types of physical invasions cause problems by initiating or furthering damage done to our physical selves and by damaging our physical energetic fields. Any or all of the seven syndromes can evolve from the cracks left in our physical energetic fields.

Your Emotional Energy Boundaries: Orange You Glad You're Happy?

Orange is the color of our emotionally charged boundaries, the ones that steer us toward joyous opportunities and away from unhappiness. They enable us to transform so-called negative feelings, such as fear, sadness, disgust, and anger, into joy. They prompt us to adopt attitudes and actions that mature us through all of our life experiences, the good, bad, and ugly.

Emotions are beliefs joined with feelings. They can be described as orange because in the energy system, red represents deep sensations or feelings and yellow represents our thoughts. Put those two together and you have orange, the marriage of two interdependent ways of knowing and experiencing.

A belief is a perception about reality. A feeling is a message from our body. Beliefs tell us what feelings we should feel, and our feelings tell us what to do with our beliefs. When we're in reactive mode, it's pretty hard to figure out which starts the process, but all of life is easier if we have fully functioning, healthy emotional energy boundaries. At the very least, they buy us the time we need to feel our feelings, discern the vital messages our feelings are providing, and think through our reactions. This emotional buffering ensures that our responses to life's stimulations are life enhancing and not destructive to ourselves or others.

For instance, imagine that your mother tells you that you can't bring your significant other to a holiday dinner. You feel angry and disrespected. Because you have strong emotional energy boundaries, you know the anger you're feeling isn't your mother's; it is your own. You know that her action says more about her than you. Instead of overreacting, you are able to respect the message of your anger, which is telling you that you need protective boundaries, or space, to make a decision based on your own value system, rather than your mother's issues. Your anger also alerts you to your own sense of value, telling you that you deserve respect. In response, maybe you tell your mother that you'd love to come for dinner—as long as your partner can also. Or maybe you propose that your mother come to your house, where you, she, and your significant other can celebrate together.

Rigid, permeable, or gaping emotional boundaries will muddle your feelings and thinking, however. Instead of allowing yourself to feel angry about Mom's prohibition, you will most likely have one of the three fear-based reactions locked in by damaged boundaries: freezing, fighting, or fleeing.

Perhaps you tell yourself you have no right to feel anger toward anyone, especially your mom, so you freeze, telling yourself you'll go along with Mom's request in order to keep the peace. You could justify your cop out by thinking your significant other shouldn't have a place at her holiday dinner table, because cooking for one more person would be a burden, or holidays are a time for just family, no outsiders, or just "Well, Mom always knows best." Maybe you'll mumble some excuse to your significant other, pretending to be sick during the holidays so you can sneak off to your mother's. Your own guilt will subsequently cause you to blow up at your partner at some point. At an energetic level, this explosion dumps the anger you should have directed at your mother onto your loved one.

On the other hand, maybe you'll fight and tell your mother you'll never to speak to her again. This knee-jerk reaction is an unhealthy substitute for feeling and explaining your own feelings and needs.

The other typical response is to flee. It's time to book that ticket to Cancun and leave both your significant other and mother behind, right? Wrong. Reacting in fear, instead of feeling and then making a decision, only increases our agitation and renews our energetic boundaries' injuries. These reactions don't serve anyone, including you.

What Compromises Our Emotional Energetic Boundaries?

What damages our emotional boundaries? The main causes are having our feelings discounted, absorbing others' feelings, and holding immature beliefs. These situations can leave us with rigid emotional energetics, the type that make us feel alone in the world and out of touch with ourselves; permeable boundaries, which cause us to have feelings of craziness and erratic emotions; and gaping boundaries, which can leave us emotionally overwhelmed and exhausted.

"Discounted feelings" means that our feelings aren't being counted or noticed, by others or ourselves, when they should be. This experience, especially if it's chronic, leaves us feeling like we don't count and as if we have no value. Most of the time, we can write off someone's disregard for our feelings, with no permanent damage to our hearts or emotional energy boundaries. If a bank teller doesn't smile at us, we can assume she's having a bad day or is just impolite. Whatever is keeping a smile from her face is not about us. But some disregard creates wounds that go deeper and last longer. It's hard to value our feelings or ourselves if others, especially our loved ones, don't.

Consistent cruelty, ridicule, shaming, blaming, "guilting," or neglect also force our energetic boundaries to respond. They might turn into thick walls to protect us or permeable membranes to hide our injured feelings. Or they might not be able to keep up with repairing the huge, gaping holes caused by incoming negativity simply because that negativity never stops battering them.

Our emotional energetic boundaries become damaged if we spend too much time around people who don't and won't deal with their own feelings. Sometimes others deny their own feelings, leaving us to pick up and experience those emotions so they don't have to. Worse, some individuals energetically jam their emotions into us, penetrating our energetic boundaries and leaving us overwhelmed and confused.

I often see emotional energy body damage play out between men and women in a primary relationship. Most frequently, the man's feelings were never validated or counted when he was growing up. As a result, he felt hurt or sad. But showing that hurt or sadness isn't seen as a masculine thing to do; it's easier and much more acceptable for him to be angry. The anger builds up, and it doesn't feel good. The energy needs somewhere to go, and eventually, it breaks out of the man's own emotional energy boundaries, creating a gaping hole or escaping through an outlet already present. Typically, the outer result is a stream of hurtful words or even physical violence, although sometimes men invert their anger, turning it into passive-aggressive behaviors. For instance, they might agree to help their spouse with a project, but fail to remember the due date, or promise to pick up a child from daycare and then get "too busy" at work. In both cases, their significant other is forced to deal with the crisis. The further he gets from his real feelings, such as sadness, hurt, or disappointment, the harder it becomes for him to listen to his true emotions and respond honestly, rather than reactively, to situations. The short- and long-term consequences include illnesses and stress (caused by built-up emotions), poor decision-making, and wounded or dissolved relationships.

Too often, the man's female partner absorbs the anger into her own emotional energy boundary. Women are often raised to take care of others' needs. Others' emotions penetrate their own shields when they are young, creating either holes or permeable membranes. Without knowing it, their energetic boundary is announcing, "Here, here! I can care for your anger." So in comes the anger, which the woman experiences as pain or hurt, and out goes her loving energy.

In the body, psychic or subtle energies can transform into physical energies through the chakras, which are able to convert physical energy into psychic energy *and* vice versa. What starts as a psychic toxin turns into a physical toxin, which creates or enhances inflammation, the cause of dozens of various disease states, including chronic fatigue syndrome, arthritis, heart problems, and even cancer. The shame of ignoring her feelings and carrying someone else's emotions can also increase a woman's already-existing self-disgust or low self-worth. Having a poor self-image can lead to further issues, including anorexia, overeating, and addictions or compulsions, such as overdrinking or excessive shopping. These issues could also include many less intense addictions, such as dependence on religion or spirituality, and codependency, the caring for others at the expense of the self.

I saw this pattern completely end with one couple when the woman refused to continue taking on her husband's anger and battened up the hatches, so to speak. This client's husband was always angry. He lost his temper often and without thought of the consequences. She would acquiesce to his angry demands. If he yelled that the pot roast wasn't cooked enough, she would fix him a steak. If he screamed that she wasn't giving him enough sex, she would put on a negligee and act sexual. Internally, however, she was both hurt and seething. Every time she gave in to his demands, she would sequester herself in the utility room and eat massive amounts of chocolate-chip cookies or Twinkies. This habit led to a weight issue, which in turn resulted in self-shame, aches, and pains—and persistent criticism from her husband. She was about to leave him when she asked me if we could patch up her emotional energetic boundaries. We did.

The immediate outcome wasn't pleasant. Her husband stormed and ranted even more, until he saw that he wasn't getting any result. Then, one night, he burst into tears and asked if she would help him get help. Apparently, he had been sexually abused as a child and had never told anyone.

Although I most often see men shoving the energies of their uncomfortable emotions into women's overly receptive energetic boundary, it can just as easily happen the other way around. People can also act out this pattern with their same-sex partners, their friends, or their children. Anyone is capable of pushing away negative emotional energies, and anyone with permeable or gaping energy boundaries is susceptible to absorbing them.

Many of us grew up in dysfunctional families, such as those characterized by alcoholism or other forms of substance abuse or by various types of neglect, sexual issues, or emotional or verbal abuse. These dysfunctional behaviors often lay the groundwork for unhealthy emotional energetic boundaries.

For example, my own parents were both alcoholics, although my father took the lead. Night after night, he sat and drank martinis to avoid dealing with his feelings. Because I loved him, I would absorb the feelings he was refusing to feel, like his sadness, fears, and anger. I'd also pick up the emotions of everyone else in my family. I knew who was sad and who was glad, who hated his or her job (like my dad did) and who didn't. Subsequently, I was constantly full of tangled emotions and feelings I couldn't figure out. I couldn't sort my own feelings from everyone else's. Not only did I lack the emotional energetics necessary to screen out others' feelings, but other violations at home also set me up to take on everyone's everything, including their thoughts, needs, dreams, and responsibilities.

Lack of emotional energetics can make it hard to stand on our own legs. Emotions are power. They are the energy in motion, or energy that moves us along in life. If we absorb others' emotions, we'll become drained and unmotivated because we lack the fuel of our own emotions.

I once worked with a young woman who was so emotionally damaged that she couldn't even make a decision by herself. Her mother was an extremely wealthy woman, but she was also a helicopter mom, hovering over her daughter to such an extent that she pulled her out of thirteen schools in ten years because she didn't like how her daughter was treated. The truth was that every time her daughter got a little gumption, her mother would lash out at her, rage around the house, and pull her out of the school, teaching her how to be insolent in the process. The daughter had almost no personality and had become extraordinarily lazy. Why try to do anything when it's just going to hurt your mother's feelings? Any friends she made treated her exactly the same way her mother did, pulling the stuffing right out of her. She began reacting to any changes in the environment, from sunspots to the slightest bloom of flowers to changes in the feelings of her one close friend, her dog. The emotional abuse was so critical that the girl's boundaries were a complete, flopping mess. Fortunately, she responded to some of the techniques I taught her, and she became bold enough to begin therapy when she was in college.

Emotional injuries can occur from almost any situation, but they always accompany physical violations. An adult who was sexually abused as a child, for instance, will have not only degenerated physical energetic boundaries, but also damaged emotional energetic boundaries. So will an adult who, while ill as a child, was ignored for long amounts of time during recovery or never visited in the hospital after surgery.

As an example, I once worked with a woman who had stage two intestinal cancer. The mass in her abdomen was as big as a basketball. She had undergone treatment for years, yet the mass kept growing. Then she remembered that when she was a child, her father used to hit her in her stomach whenever he was drunk. Hurting her made him feel better. Her father had literally pummeled his malignancy into her stomach, creating a malignancy in her body. He had violated her physical energy boundaries, but the fact that no one cared—that her mother and uncle, who lived with them, never stopped him—also hurt her feelings and her emotional energetic boundaries. Upon remembering the abuse, she began to cry, and she continued crying for an entire week.

I taught her a few of the techniques we'll cover in chapter 4, and her emotional energy boundaries began to heal. So did her body. Remembering the abuse and healing its energetic effects transformed the malignant mass into a benign tumor small enough to be removed.

Abuse is an attempt to get rid of one's own negative or unwanted energy and steal someone else's positive energy. The abuser's inner self thinks, "Why should I hang on to this bad-feeling energy when someone else can carry it for me?" Rape, shaming statements, passive-aggressive behavior, and other types of dysfunction punch holes in another's emotional energetic layer so the undesirable feelings can be deposited into the other person's energetic system. Meanwhile, through those same holes, the abuser can also extract energy from the victim. "Why not help myself to what I want? Look at all this beautiful energy!" thinks the abuser's inner self. And out goes the shocked victim's resources—the very resources he or she needs to respond to the abuse. The emotional effects of abuse are often a factor in illnesses, mood disorders, or any extreme condition.

The other component of emotional energetic challenges is the beliefs involved. Beliefs are perceptions that help us make decisions. They are basically thoughts. Emotional mistreatment and the resulting boundary malfunctions lock in thoughts that keep us believing that we are unworthy, undeserving, or have no value. Because thoughts are energetic, just like feelings are, our thoughts can poke holes in our boundaries, erase good feelings, formulate rigid walls around our hearts, and transform our life into a nightmare.

We have 50,000 to 70,000 thoughts a day. Of these, 40,000 to 56,000 are negative, and we're aware of only 100 to 300 of these debilitating beliefs. According to Dr. Deepak Chopra, about 95 percent of these thoughts are the same, day after day.[3] The Institute of HeartMath, a research organization in California, has studied the power of negative emotions and concluded that negative thoughts affect our heart's field, leading to minor and major dysfunctions and diseases, including hypertension, heart attacks, digestive disorders, fatigue, and sleep disorders. Conversely, positive emotions create better health, social communities, and prosperity.[4] The underlined phrase is the "heart's field," the electromagnetic (EMF) energetics that pulse from our heart around our bodies, creating the opportunity for us to share all good things—and those not so good—with the people around us.

Emotional boundaries are, by their very nature, tied into our relational boundaries, the next step on our staircase to heaven.

Your Relational Boundaries: Greening the World

Green is the shade of new life, mowed grass, young leaves, freshness, and the dreams of life. Green is the combination of the yellow of the sun and the blue of the celestial realms. It also represents your relational boundaries, the energetic fields that link all parts of you to yourself, the Divine, and the rest of the world.

Good relationships promote justice, fairness, honor, courage, and the other high virtues. They flourish through accurate and loving communication, care, and compassion. Relationships also require appropriate relational boundaries—boundaries that distinguish us from others, but also invite bonding with others. Ideally, these energy borders turn away the riffraff and certainly any dangers, but set out the welcome mat for joyful friends, partners, and all other sorts of companions, even companion animals.

We've all experienced less-than-perfect relationships. Sometimes it may have felt like we didn't choose to be in those relationships. And maybe we didn't. We aren't in charge of whom a company assigns to be our boss. We don't get to pick our relatives or even our children—at least, not in the sense of ordering what we want out of a catalogue.

But we do choose how to respond to people, unless there's something crooked or distorted about our relational boundaries.

Having strong yet fluid relational boundaries is like wearing the zipper of our hearts on the inside rather than on the outside of us. Our true self is able to decide when to open our hearts and let someone in, or when we're open to stepping out and mingling. If we're tired or need a little time alone, we can close ourselves up a little bit or zip up entirely to get the rest we need.

Healthy relational boundaries attract people who will support our spiritual mission and core personality. Such boundaries will deter, if not totally repel, individuals who might hurt, harm, ridicule, or demean us. When someone unappealing or harmful does enter our energy field, we'll go on high alert. Our intuitive senses will turn on. If the person is a little negative, we'll get a twinge, a sensation, a bad feeling, maybe even a skip of our heart or a slight headache. If he or she is downright horrific, our internal signal pulls out all the stops. Our heart will hammer; our body will shake. Objects might even knock over in our presence without us touching them, because our boundaries are sending such strong energetic signals. We could receive predictive dreams that show us what could go wrong if we let this person into our lives, or the Divine might speak to us directly or through a friend.

Our relational boundaries are able to protect and alert us through one particular bodily organ and its emanating fields: the heart. This, the most electrical and magnetic organ in your body, is the key to establishing the energetic borders you need to ensure that you have supportive relationships and to save you from disasters.

The power of the heart is well documented. Its magnetic component generates a field that is 5,000 times greater than the magnetic field produced by your brain, while its electrical field is sixty times greater than that of your brain. The heart's magnetic field can be measured from several feet away from your body. This small, fist-size organ is highly affected by different emotions and relationships, and the most positive relationships produce measurable and healthy results in every area of your body and mind. Furthermore, the heart's electromagnetic field, which we'll call your relationship field, interacts with the heart fields of other people, transferring feelings and even synchronizing heartbeats, even if those other people are not present.[5]

The Institute of HeartMath has proven the electromagnetic field generated by the heart permeates every cell of the body, actually synchronizing every cell to each other. The rhythm of your heart, in fact, creates "fields within fields" that are so intense that they can alter the cells and DNA of a baby inside its mother's womb.[6]

Positive relational boundaries ensure us a joyful social life, a loving community, and good friends. It's a well known fact that people with an affectionate community live longer, are happier, and are more prosperous than people who are alienated. They also have less heart disease and are healthier overall. When centered in love, the heart produces hormones and other chemicals that support our optimum health at every level. All this is possible because the heart is a field, not only an organ. When people touch, are close to one another, or even think of each other, one person's heart signal can affect the other's brain rhythms and moods. This means that our cardiac field or relational energy field carries vital relational information. In fact, the information emanating from your heart energetically tells people how to treat you.[7]

If, as the ancient philosopher Sophocles once said, the word *love* "frees us from all the weight of the world and the pain of life," then without warm, encompassing relational boundaries, we are doomed to the opposite.

What Compromises Our Relational Boundaries?

I once dated a man who seemed really nice, but in my heart, something about him just didn't sit right. He knew a number of my other friends, and I couldn't see any logical reason to sense a problem. Then one day, one of his best friends came to see me.

"Cyndi, I want to warn you," he said. "He's not a good guy."

My friend had no proof, but had long suspected the man I was dating could be mean or cruel. The advice felt right, so I broke up with the new boyfriend that evening.

My heart had known something was off from the start, but when I hadn't immediately listened, my heart field had pulled in a messenger to force me to listen. Suitable relational boundaries will show us the true nature of another person or a group, and if we fail to listen, they will draw help to us. The problem is that our relational borders aren't always in fail-safe condition. We might be too isolated, as in the case of inflexible boundaries; too confused, as happens when our borders are wishy-washy; or simply broken, as occurs when we have holes or slashes in our field.

Any or all of these situations set us up for problems. Perhaps we meet and marry the same man or woman over and over, or always have a nasty boss. Maybe we'll constantly attract needy people, who love to have us fix their lives, but offer little in return. Maybe we'll be overwhelmed with activity and productivity while everyone else in our lives is sipping colas on vacation. If psychically sensitive, we'll be aware of every mood, activity, or need of the living and the dead, yet have no one taking care of us. Healers are often the worst off, because the world is full of people happy to deposit their problems in someone else's energy field and steal love in return. And those of us sensitive to the environment will feel for every living being everywhere, but lack the power to help the great or the small.

Lacking healthy relational boundaries, we'll fall into at least one energetic speed trap, and then every detail in life becomes one to question. On the most mundane of levels, we won't even be able to accurately assess the truthfulness of another person or a group's words, gestures, or thoughts. We won't know who or what to trust or when.

We've all sat next to someone and listened to him or her wax poetically about us, perhaps complimenting us about how great we look or what a terrific job we did on a project. What if you couldn't tell if that person were telling the truth or pulling your leg? What if you make the wrong assessment because your relational fields are warped? You could make a friend who sets you up to lose your job, marry someone who steals all your money, or trust your child to a babysitter who is abusive.

What injures our relational boundaries to the extent that we would attract or suffer difficult, hurtful relationships rather than enjoyable, supportive ones? The list of heart-damaging complaints is too long to even start on, which is a tragedy unto itself. We've only to watch the evening news to see children with limbs blown off and bloated bellies, women who've been raped while walking to the store or ostracized for wanting a say in their lives, and men being used as money-making machines or foot soldiers. In our own homes, exposure to addictions, shaming, emotional or physical abuse, greed, manipulation, racism, or even continual coldness sets up our relational boundaries to expect less than love. We are born with our hearts intact, but few of us survive childhood, much less life, with whole hearts.

If we were to reduce the causes of heart strain and relational-boundaries damage to one word, it would be *negativity.*

As already discussed, the Institute of HeartMath has shown that negativity is the basis for much of our stress, which is itself the cause of most of our ills, from heart disease to anxiety.[8] Even at work, negativity is one of the core reasons for dissatisfaction and the stress that leads to everything from major illnesses to relational breakdowns, as show in a recent groundbreaking study by Steven P. Brown and Thomas V. Leigh, published in the *Journal of Applied Psychology* in 1996. When people are treated poorly, such as when they are subjected to caustic humor and suspicion, they become anxious, fearful, intolerant, and despairing.[9]

If we were abused as children, raised or schooled in a negative environment, or felt forced to work in the same, our relational energy boundaries have been violated. I believe we all have relational-boundary wounds because we naturally need relationships to survive and thrive, yet negative relationships are inescapable.

The good news is that we are designed to respond to love, which means we can repair and recover from our relationship wounds. But always, we have to be willing to return to love, and doing so is the focus of our relationship work in chapter 8.

Your Spiritual Boundaries: Peace on Earth

We are spiritual beings here to experience physical reality, and isn't that a grand event to celebrate? Unfortunately, most of us are taught that the everyday world is less holy than the one located in the heavens. The truth is, all of earth is an altar to goodness, but the path to living in a sacred and joyful manner must be chosen with wisdom. And wisdom is often hard earned.

Our spiritual energetic boundaries are equally a protection and a goal, the key to awakening our ability to see all things, not just some, as spiritual, no matter their appearances. Transparent white in coloration, this grouping of energy fields surrounds all other energetic boundaries. You could consider it your first guard, the layer of defense that asks, "Does this incoming energy match my spiritual self or not?" Accompanying this query is another: "Are the energetic messages arising from within me communicating my truth to the world or not?"

If healthy, our spiritual boundaries reflect our ever-enlightening spiritual essence, letting in that which will highlight our spiritual powers and gifts and disseminating love to the world. In many ways, these are the most important of all the boundaries, for they illuminate who we really are and help us become the self we are meant to be.

Many religions believe that we become closest to the Divine within a designated place of worship, but we aren't supposed to be filled with spirit—our own or a greater one—only in church or when we're being watched. We are heavenly beings here to transform this world into the slice of heaven it was created to become. There's no right or wrong way to do this, only loving or unloving paths. There are not just a few, limited doorways to the Absolute, but so many of us believe there are. Our spiritual borders are, therefore, both stairways to the paradise we are creating and membranes that keep us safe while we are learning about ourselves.

If our spiritual boundaries are intact, we will know ourselves as spiritual beings, no matter the condition of our lives. Whether we are sick or in good health, depressed or happy, in a primary relationship or alone, we will know ourselves as part of the spiritual family of the living and the passed, the visible and invisible, the natural and the supernatural. We will be assured of grace, the optimum goal of life, or peace in the midst of anything.

On the practical level, we will also embrace the fact that we are here on this planet on this time for a specific purpose, a spiritual mission that is ours alone to fulfill. Our purpose doesn't have to look majestic in the eyes of the world. Neither must we appear imposing or religious. Our spiritual tasks might include mothering or fathering our children or the inner children within our clients. We might make our living counting figures or carving gravestones. Purposeful expression isn't really even about what we do for a living. It's about how we become what we can become.

As we strive to live our purpose through the everyday, we come to know the Divine more personally. We awaken our intuitive faculties and learn to master all things human, from containing a bad temper to paying our bills on time.

What Compromises Our Spiritual Boundaries?

Broken or injured spiritual energy boundaries can produce almost any type of negative result in life, including illness (physical and mental), poverty, debt, depression, anxiety, and phobias. The most common spiritual-boundary violations include:

- religious guilt and shaming; for instance, being a woman raised in a church that allows women no voice
- spiritual intolerance; for instance, being told that your views are ungodly or that views unlike those held in your place of worship are sinful
- inhumane spiritual standards; for instance, being told you are a sinner if you commit a natural and/or humane human act, such as talking to someone outside of your religious group or having sex within your marriage
- cult organization and brainwashing, such as when a religious leader has the power to make decisions for others' well-being
- ritual abuse, such as that which occurs in Satanic—and actually many fundamentalist—organizations
- doctrines of terrorism, killing, ostracism, or coercion, especially when such things are said to be done in the name of God or virtue
- discrimination, such as hearing that God only loves men, but not women, or whites, not blacks
- political pressure, such as being told you need to be a Christian to join a particular political party or that you aren't a Christian if you belong to a certain political party
- any message or manipulation that insists that, for some reason, you are and should be separate from the Divine
- messages inflicting the deep sense of shame, unworthiness, a lack of value, powerlessness, or badness
- ancestral spirits or entities that control humans through the intuitive realms

Personally, I've found that clearing the physical, emotional, and relational boundaries is most quickly and effectively done in combination with healing spiritual boundaries. This is because the source of our truest healing is spiritual. Our truest healing lies in the center of our being and in the planes of heaven that surround us all.

I've experienced days when, as a healer, I do absolutely nothing but take phone call after phone call from people needing to heal spiritual boundaries. They might not know that's why they are calling or the type of healing they need.

One woman was plagued with voices and had been deemed schizophrenic. Now, schizophrenia is an actual condition and must be taken seriously in terms of seeking and following a physician's care. But the fact that a psychiatrist had referred this client to me made me believe that she was experiencing more than a chemical imbalance. As a child, she had been raised in a very fundamentalist Christian society. Women could hold no positions of authority; only men could talk in church. Intuitive abilities were seen as evil, and anyone who "rebelled" against the church doctrine would go to hell.

My client had been psychically sensitive since birth. For as long as she could remember, she could see ghosts and colors around people. She could hear the voices of angels and the deceased. She knew what family members thought and felt. And she was told that because she could sense these things, she was evil. The judgment and pressures from her family and the church had crashed her spiritual boundaries, which only heightened her psychic sensitivity to the point where it was harmful. Hormones often exacerbate our boundary issues, and during puberty, my client began hearing new voices—different voices, too many voices—and felt overwhelmed by them. Eventually, she was put on a host of pills for schizophrenia.

Once I taught her how to create spiritual borders, the voices stopped talking. She is now completely free of the schizophrenia and free of prescription medicines, except for sleeping pills at night. She uses her intuitive gifts as an energy healer and has a very successful practice.

Yet another client had severe osteoporosis, and her prescription medicine for it wasn't working. She was losing weight, and her overall health was sliding downhill. After speaking with her, I learned that she had been raised in the Ukraine and within a church that promoted the idea of sacrifice. Her interpretation of that message was that to be good and loved, she needed to work, work, work, often with little financial reward and very little assistance from the people around her. Not only did she give her energy away to every living person she met, but she also gave it away to the dead. Every night, she was plagued with vivid images of "the saints," as she called them. They'd parade before her, hands outstretched, seeking supplication and blessing. Guess what she gave them? The very marrow of her bones.

Because she was energetically depleted in many life areas, it made sense that her body was also depleted. Her deep sense of unworthiness had established a harmful energetic pattern. As soon as we shifted her spiritual boundaries, using a technique covered in chapter 4, she began to recover from both her osteoporosis *and* the sense that she did not deserve love unless she first gave herself away.

Much of healing is about releasing ourselves from the burden of unworthiness so that we can own our true place in this world. We can be victims of any repetitive disorder, from depression to ritual abuse. We might be plagued by people who pull on our spiritual gifts and abilities and give nothing back. We can be convinced we have to serve something or someone other than ourselves, no matter what. Our job is to sacrifice and perform; that's the road to heaven.

Psychic sensitives, individuals who are too exposed to the invisible dimensions and others' subtle energies, often suffer the most from spiritual-boundary issues. Lacking spiritual boundaries, psychic sensitives are prey to any or all of the dark forces that seek to penetrate their world. A similar condition exists for those with no boundaries at all; they lose their energy while taking on the spiritual flotsam and jetsam of this world and the supernatural worlds. The results I see most often include conditions others might call mood disorders, attention deficit disorder (ADD), autism, schizophrenia, and bipolar disorder. Healers with damaged or permeable spiritual boundaries are often propelled into constant duty by spiritual misperceptions such as, "It's good to help others" or "Helping other is noble work, and I am noble for doing it." But helping others to the point of having no life or energy of your own isn't good or noble. The environmentally sensitive, linked with the beings and forces of nature, often find that all their energy is drained to support the needs of the natural world.

All in all, our spiritual borders are key to becoming our true selves, but also in maintaining ourselves in a world that has little understanding of things spiritual.

The Four Boundaries Pulled Together

Many, if not most, life conditions involve two or more energetic boundaries. Weight issues, for instance, most typically require work on all four boundaries. Most individuals with serious weight issues have extremely loose or permeable physical boundaries, which is why their bodies showcase their issues—and, quite often, others' issues, too. These individuals' own feelings are often subverted in favor of others' feelings, which is an emotional energy issue, and they often find it challenging to express their true selves, which is a relational issue. In addition, they usually don't believe that they really matter, which is a spiritual-boundary issue, and as a result, they hold onto too much physical matter. Complicating the diagnosis and energetic treatment of weight issues is the fact that they can stem from any or all of the syndromes described in the following chapter.

Logically, we have to wonder how we're supposed to consciously regulate all four types of energetic fields to create safety and happiness. Well, we don't have to. We simply need to generate *coherency*, which exists when everything that makes us is held together and working in harmony on our behalf. If we are truly coherent or consistent, we are able to invite everything that isn't us into the same game, so that no matter what, we're able to formulate more and more goodness and love.

Exercise: Coloring Your World

Want to experiment with the color frequencies of your energetic fields, and see how they color not only your world, but also your life?

Pick four days of the week for which you can stylize your wardrobe. On the first day, you'll be wearing a lot of red (if not as your outer clothing, then at least under it, such as red underwear or socks). On another day, you'll wear orange, then green, and—you guessed it—white.

As you put on the clothing color of the day, revisit the information about the affiliated energetic boundary. Now give permission for your inner spirit to activate the related energy boundaries all day long. Pay attention to how you feel, how your body reacts, and how the people around you react. Do you respond differently? Are there changes you'd like to make permanently? If so, ask your inner self to hold these changes in place for you.

Chapter 3

Spiritual Syndromes: Specific Energetic-Boundary Issues

I heard my name associated with the Peter Pan syndrome
more than once. But really, what's so wrong with Peter Pan?
Peter Pan flies. He is a metaphor for dreams and faith.

TELEVISION PRODUCER MARK BURNETT

How many of us end our workdays feeling uplifted, fulfilled, and connected, rather than drained, uninspired, and too exhausted to enjoy our leisure time? Worse, how many of us feel like we slave away, only to have to dig to the bottom of our purse, under the sofa cushion, or in the cup holder of the car to find two coins to press together?

Are our relationships flourishing? Or are there people that leave us feeling used, overwhelmed, or, as my dad used to say, "tuckered out?" Do we go through the day with a spring in our step, smelling the flowers and giving distance to the thorns, or do we keep getting suckered into giving away our roses in exchange for someone else's thorns?

Do we enjoy and thrive climbing and moving forward, or do we long to get to the end of a rope, that rope being a chronic illness, long-term addiction, parenting dilemmas, sensitive children, or maybe even the stranger stuff of the otherworldly?

Poor energetic boundaries, the spiritual borders that enable us to thrive in every aspect of life, can create nearly any struggle. Lacking spiritual boundaries, having too rigid or too flexible boundaries, or having boundaries with holes in them is an invitation for trouble, even when we're not looking for it. We'll be susceptible to at least one of the seven major energetic syndromes, as I call them.

You probably don't have to read far to start relating to some of the symptoms. Pay attention to how many grab at you and which situations they might apply to. Some people have one syndrome all the time; others report that they exhibit different syndromes in different settings. Still others exhibit all syndromes all the time.

But you can learn how to find the gifts within these spiritual syndromes. The lessons you learn from overcoming energetic challenges can be worthwhile, when what once caused grief now calls forth compassion, when what had been exhausting encourages nourishment, and when that which was stolen returns through grace. As suggested in the quote starting this chapter, sometimes our issues are what we make of them. Get ready to transform your gifts into wings—and fly!

The Paper Doll Syndrome: Can We Ever Get Out of Here?

My client stared at me with her big brown eyes.

"I can't believe it," she cried. "I met Harold *again!*"

After spending years of therapy and thousands of dollars on dating services, Katie had just suffered through a tortuous evening with yet another version of the man she had married right after high school, a deadbeat alcoholic who lied and cheated—and who was more than a little like Dad.

Katie was afflicted with one of the main types of energetic disturbances caused by poor energetic boundaries. I call it the *Paper Doll
Syndrome,* because it is reminiscent of the childhood exercise where you
create a row of identical paper dolls. You fold blank white paper over
and over and then cut out a doll shape, leaving two corners connected.
Open the creases, and presto, you have a string of linked, indistinguish-
able people, each one joined at the hands and feet with the next. You
could color in the images to try to make them look different from each
other, but all of them will still have the same basic shape.

Those troubled with the Paper Doll Syndrome can't seem to break
the chain of sameness that plagues at least one area of their lives. The
cycle might center on an addiction, activity, health challenge, or a recurring relationship or work pattern. Those with the Paper Doll Syndrome
seem doomed to attract the same undesirable situations—in Katie's case,
the same mean mate—over and over.

I can't tell you how many of my clients report that they are stuck
going through a pattern, no matter how much therapy they go through,
how many Twelve Step programs they attend, or how far from home
they wander. One client told me that no matter how many times he
tried to date a woman different than his mother, "she" would show up.
Once he even deliberately arranged a date with a blonde because his
mother was a brunette. Guess what? His date dyed her hair the night
before and showed up to dinner as a brunette.

Another client reported that no matter how hard he worked at his
issues, he kept smoking marijuana. He'd quit and go through drug
treatment, and when he was clean, the first person he'd meet back on
the job or in his friendship circle would offer him the drug. He couldn't
shake the sense of being cursed. His energetic boundaries simply kept
blaring, "I want marijuana" to the world. And the world listened.

Yet another client had been laid off from every job she'd ever had, even
though she usually received glowing reviews. And another had been in
fourteen car accidents in his lifetime. I've met clients who can't seem

to quit drinking, smoking, or engaging in dangerous sexual activities no matter how many different ways they approach the problem. I've worked with others who just can't obtain a job position equal to their true gifts or talents. Others can't get out of debt no matter how much money they make, or they end up with the same type of friends no matter where they go to meet people. Yet others can't relieve themselves of a chronic illness or an unexplained pain.

There can be many factors involved in the Paper Doll Syndrome, but at least one of them is energetic. If you relate to this syndrome, most likely something difficult or traumatic occurred to trap you in a repetitive energetic pattern. Your energetic boundaries might have become so rigid that they won't open to allow in the person, opportunity, idea, or event that might interrupt the cycle. Or the original event may have created a hole or permeable section in one of your boundaries. Your boundaries are supposed to act like a bar bouncer, a huge muscle man that is supposed to throw out the riffraff and let in only the classy clientele. The problem is, your bouncer has mixed up his instructions. He's actively recruiting anything and anyone that will keep you stuck, while at the same time, he is "bouncing out" the good guys.

Do you think you've been hurt by the Paper Doll Syndrome? Signs can include the following:

- You're stuck in repetitive patterns that won't go away or be changed no matter what you do.
- You are treated in negative or harmful ways by others, either universally or in specific areas of your life.
- You inflict negative or harmful treatment on yourself and aren't able to stop, no matter how many times you get help.
- You feel powerless to change recurring cycles.
- You feel frustrated, hurt, and angry because your patterns keep you going round and round without getting anywhere, like a hamster on a wheel.

How might the Paper Doll Syndrome play out in different life areas? When affecting our health, it manifests any chronic or recurring condition or illness. Your job or work situation—including the problems and the people—will be consistently the same, no matter how you change your behavior, no matter where you work or what your job duties are. Or you always feel the same way around certain people, groups, or situations, regardless of how you approach them.

Active in your financial life, this syndrome can have you making the same financial error over and over or snared by the same money dilemma again and again. This pattern might continually challenge your financial survival or even your life. Maybe you maintain certain feelings or beliefs linked to money, or you get stuck in financial ruts, like always spending money on the same useless things while neglecting basic needs.

In your relationships, you may experience the same physical or sexual trauma in every major relationship. You might be always used by your lovers, or you might flee every good potential mate and select only unhealthy partners. Maybe family members always betray you or friends consistently abandon you. You might get stuck in repetitive emotional patterns, such as constantly responding to your loved ones with anger. You might repeatedly select the same type of mate, parent, or even best friend, or even feel like you're reliving a relationship from another lifetime.

In your spiritual life, rigidly adhering, consciously or unconsciously, to particular spiritual beliefs could threaten your health, safety, or prosperity. Perhaps you believe that you don't need to take any common-sense safety precautions because God will protect you, that you should stay in an abusive relationship because divorce is a sin, or that you must capitulate to your mother's every dictate because the Bible says to honor your elders.

The Vampire Syndrome: Anyone Want to Suck My Energy?

My client really did look like she had wrestled with a vampire—and the vampire had won.

"I just can't keep going," she complained. "I'm a dental hygienist. Every day, I go to the office ready to do my job, and by my fourth patient, I can hardly move. It's so bad I keep a stash of jellybeans under the bathroom sink and pop them for energy in between patients. By the time I'm on my last patient of the day, I should be super-gluing my eyes open. There's nothing left of me."

I immediately knew I was talking to a vampire victim, one of the super-kind, special individuals who are exhausted because other people drain them of their life energy. Some people, like my hygienist client, are unwittingly robbed by almost everyone. They go to work and pour their hearts' energy into their coworkers, clients, customers, or other contacts. When friends or relatives have concerns, they know all they have to do is call or see their victim, and they'll feel renewed, stronger, and filled up with energy.

My hygienist client's energetic boundaries were making a victim of such energy vampires because they were tuned to the frequency of an underlying belief. She had been raised to believe that her entire life had to be about work and that you should do *anything* to please the people you serve. This included giving them her own vital, positive energy. After identifying that belief, she used some of the tips provided in chapter 4 and 6 to keep her clients from stealing her energy. Previously, her field had holes in some areas and been porous in others. The holes were allowing her energy, goodness, and kindness to leak out. The permeable boundaries, like half-asleep security guards, would sometimes cave in, allowing my client's life energy to escape and others' energies to take up residence. Within a week of healing these boundary issues, my client had enough energy to join a yoga class after work instead of leaving the dental office completely drained.

Some vampire victims fall prey to only one or a few individuals. I worked with one man who always woke up more tired than when he'd gone to bed. He couldn't even open his eyes in the morning and experienced chills.

"I feel like my wife puts a hose in me," he yawned. "I can literally feel all my energy flowing from me to her during the night." Aware that he was losing energy to her, he felt used and angry.

My client and his wife had established an unconscious pattern in which he gave and she took. It operated only when they were in close physical proximity, because when he slept apart from her, he felt absolutely fine. Was his wife a bad person? Was he a dupe? No; in fact, his wife was very sweet. She wasn't intentionally or consciously stealing his energy, but his weakened energetic boundaries made him susceptible to energy vampirism. He and I tracked his susceptibility back to his mother. Every time his mom had a problem, she would relate all her woes to him. He felt trapped and hemmed in, yet was unable to do anything but support his mother. My client suddenly understood that he was carrying out the same energetic pattern with his wife. (So he was suffering from both Paper Doll and Vampire Syndromes.)

It took awhile for him to shift his pattern. He didn't believe his wife could survive without his energy any more than he had thought his mother could survive. But eventually, he was able to heal and strengthen his energetic boundaries to the point that he could sleep with his wife and wake up in the morning energized.

The key signs of being a vampire victim are:

- You lose energy around certain (or even all) people or circumstances; you can almost feel the energy bleeding out of you.
- You experience overwhelming exhaustion, a sense of emptiness, and/or difficulty motivating yourself after contact with the vampire or vampiric system.
- You feel a building sense of rage or frustration; you're tired of being used.
- Every so often, you feel dead, like you're a walking zombie.
- You get the chills, feel cold, and lose body heat when in contact with the vampire(s).

- Your energy decreases when you're with the vampire(s), but increases when you're not.
- You sense there is an invisible force that steals energy from you.
- You believe it's your job to give or supply your energy to another, even if doing so is to your detriment.
- You think another will be harmed if you fail to perform your duty; conversely, you think you will somehow be punished, hurt, or abandoned if you don't.

The loss of vital life energy you experience as a Vampire Syndrome victim puts you at risk for many health problems, most notably a compromised immune system. Or no matter what you do, you can't sustain or build up your physical stamina, either in general or only in specific situations (such as at work) or around certain people (your one friend, your boss). You notice that others' physical energies spiral upward when they're around you, while yours plummets downward. Especially during sex and sleep, you might feel your life energy being sucked right out of you.

Emotionally, you might be less feeling or thoughtful than you should or want to be. You definitely can't feel joy. You are constantly buttering or cheering others up, only to feel drained and lifeless yourself, or others steal your thoughts, ideas, or words and claim them for themselves.

On a financial level, money could seem to be draining from your bank account because of certain people or circumstances that seem out of your control. You might feel as if others plug into you to make *their* money. You believe you're obligated to emotionally support others on their financial paths, but you never receive assistance in return. At work, this syndrome often manifests as being paid less than your coworkers or others in your field.

A spiritual belief, such as "It's better to give than receive," when misapplied, might cause you to feel guilty or bad if you don't give away your energy or resources to others.

A Spooky Vampire Story

My new client, Betty, was particularly unlikable. Her abrasive attitude immediately set me on edge, but I knew in my heart that she was self-protecting. She was living like an agoraphobic, remaining in her house week after week. For days, she'd see no one but a delivery person; even he would have to leave her food outside of the door, ring the doorbell, and walk away before she'd open the door.

What was underneath her extreme loneliness? What would drive someone to such an empty existence?

When I intuitively checked Betty's energetic boundaries, I noticed a dark stain around her neck. I perceived an energy link, which to me appeared like a long, garden-hose-like cord, between Betty's neck and a looming, shadowy figure. This figure, which I would call an entity or a fallen angel, seemed to be drinking in Betty's energy through what passed for its mouth. The life energy that could and should be pulsing through Betty, establishing the magnetic force field and layers of her aura to protect her, were getting sucked up by this being.

Even though dealing with weird, otherworldly things is part of my job, I never like to bring up such matters with clients, especially as most of my clients are mainstream folks—accountants, homemakers, mechanical engineers, executives, nurses, doctors, and secretaries. I certainly hate presenting information that might frighten more than inspire. Nonetheless, of the 35,000-plus sessions I've given, I'd say at least 20 percent have included sharing information about otherworldly interference. You know what? Not *one client* has protested. In fact, most say, "I'm so glad you said that! I've suspected the same thing, but thought I was crazy."

Sharing my observations with Betty, I felt a huge sense of empathy when she began crying.

"The entity has been with me my entire life," she sobbed. "In fact, I remember it attaching to me during birth, when the doctor cut me out of my mother's belly two months early, to save my mother's life. I could see it passing from my mother to me, but there was nothing I could do."

She added, "I believed that this creature has been with me to keep me alive, but all it's really doing is vampirizing me."

The presence of a disturbing energy filled in some of the puzzle pieces, but not all of them.

"I can understand why you are too tired to participate in community," I observed, "but not why you won't see *anyone.*"

Betty paused.

"Everyone I get close to dies," she whispered. "Everyone."

She recounted the deaths of seven or eight close friends, all of whom were unexpectedly killed in accidents or through sudden illnesses after they'd initiated a deep relationship with her.

Now I understood why Betty was so caustic. She didn't want to hurt anyone else with her "curse." The vampirish demon clearly wanted her all to itself.

I first suggested to Betty that this penetrating, interfering dark figure let her connect only with people who were going to die. (I crossed my fingers on that one.) I then helped her release the beliefs and energetic bindings underlying her susceptibility to this figure. We then asked the Divine to fill in all energetic holes and expand her energetic field.

Finally, I helped Betty surrender to a greater power, one that immediately began to shower her with all the love and grace that this interfering entity had convinced her was unavailable. At this point, so much divine energy emanated from and around Betty that the dark figure screeched off. Both Betty and I felt it leave, and it was as if a bag of ice had been removed from our souls.

After a few more sessions with me, Betty moved and formed close friendships with a spiritual community. She now runs her own healing practice and shines as brightly as the golden sun. Not one of her friends since then has passed away, either.

I've thousands of stories like this, and they usually end with an immediate release of whatever conditions are plaguing the victim, including cancer, back problems, abusive stalkers, and infertility issues. If you are being vampirized by marauding spirits, know that it is possible to become free. Freedom is a happy ending to what might otherwise be a challenging life story.

||||||||||||||||||||||||||||||||||||||||||||||||||||||||||||||||||||||||

The Mule Syndrome: Is There Any Work For Me to Do?

One of the phrases I most frequently use at home is, "Am I the maid?" God help the child who would ever reply, "Yes."

Actually, my kids have been well trained to take responsibility for their own feelings, homework, and life challenges. The three dogs (not to mention the boyfriend) are still in training. But they're not really the ones with the obedience issues—I am.

You see, I grew up as the family mule. My dad went to work and left my mom at home. She spent a great deal of time in bed, depressed, leaving a house to be cleaned, dinners to be cooked, and a large garden to be tended. Oh, and sisters to be dressed and cared for.

The true stress, however, was the burden I incurred energetically. If there was a free-floating feeling, I took it on and tried to work it out. If someone in the family had an allergy, illness, money problem, worry, or concern, I ended up with it in my body and mind. I was constantly trying to solve problems for others, to the point where I had to go double-time to doctors, therapists, and healers just to cope.

Later, when I took my first job, I noticed that most of the extra work automatically ended up with me. My boss would take off, and I would write her news articles. Worse, I would feel guilty if I didn't get her assignments done on time, even if they took me all night. (Funnily enough, she never felt guilty.)

The Mule Syndrome stems from the belief that if there is work to be done—emotionally, mentally, spiritually, or physically—someone has to do it. And that someone has to be *you*. Energy has no boundaries; neither does our ability to respond energetically. The energy of whatever people won't deal with, feel, or do is pushed out from their bodies and literally floats around the room. The mule, the person who has been elected most capable and responsible, ends up with the energy of these issues and usually responds by working overtime to get through them. The mule will be the most responsible person in a system that encourages this tendency. If you're the mule, you'll be the one working for the bacon, buying the bacon, and cooking the bacon. Even if you're a vegetarian, you'll make sure those who aren't get their bacon! Anything extra to do? Guess who's on it!

On the inside, you won't feel as competent as you appear externally. You'll feel like a ball of worry. Will you get to everything? What if you don't get everything done? How will you deal with the guilt and shame of not being prepared or perfect? General and specific anxieties float around your body and mind, along with the fear of letting others down.

If you could stop the whirring for a minute, you'd be able to feel others' work and issues penetrating your body. Different types of work and issues enter different parts of the body: physical, including tending to physical needs or making money, ends up in the hips; emotional work or issues are drawn to your abdomen; duties, tasks, and time-tables gravitate to your stomach; relational problems enter your heart; issues or work involving communication or sharing information lodge in the throat; problems or work involved with meeting long-term goals (usually others' goals) end up in your forehead; spiritual needs and obligations land within the top of your head.

But doing others' work for them, even emotional work, robs them of the right to feel their feelings and heal their own pain and issues. *We can only learn from our own problems; we can heal only issues that are our own.*

Think about how different you'd feel if you were free of all those *shoulds* and instead focused on your own *coulds*. That's the goal of establishing the correct energetic boundaries.

What are the signs and symptoms of being energetically available as the mule?

- Your ceaseless and endless activity is characterized by work, work, work. (Many service-oriented individuals, especially, operate on assumptions that keep them working all the time.)
- Work flows from others to you, but no further, and never back to them.
- You are plagued by the nagging thought there is more that needs to be done—always.
- You feel responsible for completing not only others' tasks, but also handling their emotions, needs, and worries—to the point of working on these issues for them.
- You feel lots and lots of anxiety, both general and specific.
- There are different pains in different parts of the body, which can reflect the places others' energetic work has lodged in your energy system.
- You experience a combination of physical and mental exhaustion, or even depression.

Absorbing others' subtle energies is hard on your body, mind, and soul. The Mule Syndrome affects your health by ramping up our stress a thousand fold, which can lead to a wide array of diseases, illnesses, and conditions. Because you are taking in and trying to process everyone else's feelings or thoughts, you might end up overemotional, full of illogical feelings, thoughts, anxieties, and worries that just won't quit. I worked with one woman who was so overwhelmed by her family's emotions she ended up in the psychiatric ward several times. She felt immediate and long-lasting relief after we helped her block others' energies and heal her energetic fields.

At work, you, the mule, are the one still sitting at your desk (or at your kitchen table or in your lab or in your classroom) when everyone else has gone home. Even when you say no or are busy, you somehow end up responsible for accomplishing others' goals. Your to-do list is always longer than anyone else's.

When it comes to money, mules work harder than everyone else, yet usually aren't paid more and don't get any credit. You might feel guilty if you aren't always working to make or save money. You might shoulder others' monetary obligations, only to feel taken advantage of or angry and resentful that no one ever helps you out financially.

In relationships, you're the one doing all the work—perhaps overall or perhaps only in one arena, such as monitoring the finances, initiating sex, doing housework, child-rearing, or planning outings or vacations. You call your friends, but they don't call you; you take care of your adult children, and they don't even remember your birthday. Or maybe your friends and children contact you only when they need something, from money to a shoulder to wail on.

You might believe that you must sacrifice your time and money to undertake spiritual work. Spiritual ideals often result in a service mentality—one that views it as noble to assist others, even at (or sometimes because of) the cost of our own good. I often find gender-based religious ideals to be the culprit of the Mule Syndrome. Such ideals can result in women doing all the work in the home and/or men having to provide all the income for a family. They are also taken to lethal extremes in certain cultures. For instance, in Africa women can't refuse sex, even with a man with AIDS. In many Muslim communities, a woman is murdered if she has sex with a man not her husband, even if she was raped. These are all indications of an awry Mule Syndrome.

||||||||||||||||||||||||||||||||||||||||||||||||||||||||||||||||||||||||

Cords, Curses, and Bindings: Inhibiting Contracts

Throughout this book, I suggest examining your energetic boundaries for energetic contracts or constraints that result in lost energy, the acceptance of others' toxic energy, and harmful connections. Many types of energetic influences can create these negative effects. Here is a list of these restrictions and what they look like psychically. These can all be healed through the processes described for cord work in this book.

Cords are energetic contracts or connections that appear like garden hoses. The older and more limiting the cord, the thicker the tubing. Energy flows through the middle of these cords. If you read this energy, you can interpret the nature of the contract. Yellow energy, for instance, means exchange of beliefs; orange might indicate that feelings are being swapped. You know you have an energy cord if you can't detach from a certain person, group, or system no matter how hard you try.

Life-energy cords look a lot like regular energetic cords, but are psychically red or orange in color because the energy flowing through is basic life energy. These cords can exist between parts of the self, such as current life and a past-life self, or between a person and any other individual or group. Life-energy cords work like wires running off a mainframe to deliver electricity to different end users, thus splitting your basic life energy into several streams going to several outlets. Energy depletion, chronic or severe illnesses, chronic fatigue, and adrenal problems usually stem from life-energy cords.

Codependent contracts or bargains are unique cords usually formed between a parent and child to engender a two-way flow of energy. We create these in order to ensure our survival while in the womb or during our infancy.

Unconsciously perceiving a security threat, we believe we have to bargain for our life. This might be an accurate assessment. At some level, we figure out that Mom, Dad, or both parents don't want us or aren't capable of fully taking care of us. We then reason that if we energetically assist our parent(s), they will then better provide for us. So we establish an energetic bargain, which usually involves taking on parental problems or responsibilities and giving away our own vital, creative juices. From the child's point of view, common bargains are these: "I will give you my life energy and take on your pain," or "I will give you my spiritual gifts, and you will keep me alive." While we achieve a short-term benefit—now Mom feels pain free enough to get up in the middle of the night and feed us— the long-term results are devastating. In this case, Mom's pain continues to flow into us long after our infancy. We'll become sick, achy, and miserable. Mom, on the other hand, will continue to receive infusions of our energy, which prevents her from facing her inner issues and leads to a dependency on us.

Even worse, the codependent cords have established a structure within our energetic boundaries (and at least one chakra) that serves as a template for all other primary relationships. We'll not only keep feeding Mom and taking on her pain; we'll do the same with anyone in primary relationship with us.

Curses look like tubules of thick, dark filaments bound together. They, too, can run between a person and any other individual or group. Curses are not empty at the center; the energy is bound in the tubes themselves. Curses hold many diseases or sexual and monetary disorders in place.

Bindings are elastic-like bands that connect at least two beings. A binding keeps the beings stuck together, usually lifetime after lifetime. Unlike cords, they might not involve an exchange of energy, merely a gluing together of two or more souls.

An **energy marker** looks like a clump of counterclockwise, swirling charges forming a symbol. This symbol will instruct others how to treat the marked. An energy marker on one field will affect all other fields. For instance, if you're always treated disrespectfully, no matter your behavior, you might have an energy marker.

If someone's life is stuck, I look for **holds,** energy restrictions placed by one person on another. A lot of parents put holds on their children, usually to keep them safe, but sometimes to ensure themselves a steady diet of basic life energy. Very immature and overly mature (bored) individuals are often the product of holds.

A **miasm** is an energetic field that programs a group of souls or family members; miasms often create disease patterns within family systems. To check for a miasm, look for brown areas in the red physical boundaries. These areas will have a cross-stitch pattern and a cord that travels

time to an ancestor or an event that occurred
;o.

re energy strands that connect pathways or
realities. Many healers move filaments and, by
doing so, open an entryway for the energy or forces of a
previously unexposed pathway.

Energy contracts disappear only after you determine
their *payoff,* or the reason you are holding onto your end.
Traditional therapy can be extremely helpful for figuring
out payoffs, as can asking yourself these questions:

1. Am I one of the original creators of this contract, or is
   something or someone else?
2. If I did not create it, how did I receive it? Is there
   something I must do, say, understand, or express to
   release myself from this contract?
3. If I did enter this agreement, when did I do so? For
   what reason?
4. What is the nature of the contractual agreement? What
   am I giving? What am I receiving?
5. How is this contract affecting me? How is it affecting
   the others around me or in the contract? Which
   syndrome or set of syndromes is it causing? Which
   energetic boundaries is it affecting?
6. What do I need to know to release myself from,
   to change, or to better use this contract? What
   feelings must I understand or express? What beliefs
   must I accept? What energy must I release or
   accept? What power or gift must I be willing to
   accept or use?
7. What forgiveness or grace must I allow myself or the
   other(s) involved?

8. Am I now ready for this healing? If not, why or when will I be?

9. Am I prepared to release the related syndrome so I can be my true self?

10. Am I ready to accept full protection so I can safely live my purpose in this world?

If you work through these questions and find yourself willing to release the contract, I suggest using a *healing stream of grace,* which is an ever-present reflection of Divine love. If you were to look at the world through "God glasses," you would perceive streams of unconditional love pouring down upon us from the heavens. Healers throughout the ages, including myself, have detected these bands of light, noting that they flow around—but not into—individuals who are experiencing illness or challenges. When a stream is attached, especially to the bodily or energetic area in trouble, healing occurs.

You can call for a healing stream of grace to shift an issue, including energetic bondage. The following exercise can help you do this.

1. When you are absolutely willing to release the contract or cord, ask the Divine to substitute a healing stream of grace for it.

2. Accept the gift of this stream of grace, acknowledging it as perfect for you.

3. Ask the Divine to cleanse you of any remnants or effects of the cord.

4. Ask the Divine to provide a healing stream of grace for all others concerned in this contract.

5. Ask the Divine to now heal you internally and to

restore your energetic boundaries so you can now live freely and in harmony with Divine will.

6. Feel the gratitude that accompanies this life change.

Throughout this book, there are also several guided meditations for releasing cords from the various energetic fields and for specific life concerns.

|||||||||||||||||||||||||||||||||||||||||||||||||||||||||||||||||||||||

The Psychic-Sensitive Syndrome: Knowing Too Much

If there's a ghost around, it's going to talk to you and no one else but you. If there's something no one but you can see, you'll see it; a being no one else can hear, you'll hear it; a sensation, feeling, knowing, or idea that's totally imperceptible to others, you'll still be tuned in.

You're the person awash in the invisible, inaudible, and inexplicable—in the psychic. You hear a boss tell you one thing, but your gut insists he's lying. You listen to a neighbor's husband swear that he didn't cheat on his wife, but those pictures in your head tell another story. Your child's doctor insists that your little girl only has a cold, but you know there's something much worse going on. Who are you going to get to believe you?

Who *ever* believes you?

Being a psychic sensitive is a lot like being a no-boundary person, described later in this chapter, except that you are actually able to hear, see, sense, feel, and understand the energetic data coming into you. And data it is—a whole truckload of information, driven by a maniac that obviously can't even read stop signs, much less a road map. You're run over, day and night, by information that you'd usually rather not have.

The trouble is, you know this information might help someone else. The tug of your heart suggests that you really should be open to the predictive dreams, the ones that might save someone's life or keep someone from making a big mistake. Your concern for others keeps you picking up all this information, even though knowing it leaves you feeling responsible for doing something helpful with it. Your feeling of being overwhelmed and having to maintain your vigilance is now matched by a gnawing sense of overresponsibility. What if you don't get all the information right? What if it's wrong? What if you share it, and people get hurt because of what you say? What if you don't share it, and someone is harmed?

Many psychic sensitives suffer from other syndromes at the same time, most commonly the Mule or Healer's Syndromes. Since you are able to absorb others' issues, why not pile on their work, as well? If you're able to sense others' needs, it's easy to take the next step into a full-fledged Healer's Syndrome, owning another's problems while sending him or her a solution. Violations to one energy boundary affect all other energy boundaries. In addition, one condition often overlaps another, and not only for psychic sensitives. Any syndrome can interlock with another syndrome, creating a truly mingled mess.

For the psychic sensitive, there are a few particular issues blocking a healing. Even if you wanted to close down the flow of psychic information, would you be able to? Very few people are trained in dealing with psychic phenomena. Those that are usually teach people how to be more, rather than less, psychic. (I'm one of the few I know who emphasizes the need for boundaries, the subject of this book and another, *The Intuition Guidebook*.) Moreover, would you *want* to reduce the amount of psychic information you receive? Many psychic sensitives perceive their condition as both a curse and a gift. On one side is the constant exposure to overwhelming and sometimes even dangerous information and energies. On the other side is the sense of satisfaction gained by being uniquely insightful. One more inch, and this contentment can lead to feeling special. If we lack self-worth, it's easy to use our psychic sensitivity for ego gratification rather than let it go and be a "normal" person.

I've been overly psychic my entire life and can testify to the confusion, tiredness, idiocy, and fright that accompanies this condition. There tends to be a psychic sensitive in every generation of my family. My dad's mother could see ghosts. The family wouldn't talk about her odd gift, and they also ignored me when I started to point to an area in the garage where I knew a woman had hung herself. My youngest son has inherited the trait. One day, I was releasing some negative energy during a therapy session, only to receive a startling phone call from my son's teacher a few minutes later. Apparently Gabe had thrown out his back while just sitting in his seat. Because this was pretty much a physical impossibility, I knew without a doubt that my son had picked up the pain I had sent away. A week later I took him to my therapist to work on his own energetic boundaries!

Symptoms of a Psychic-Sensitive Syndrome are colorful, confusing, and multidimensional, because there are at least twelve different types of psychic gifts. Here are a handful of signs that you might be a psychic sensitive:

• Beings, entities, energies, or visitors from the various planes of existence (meaning they aren't alive, as we now define physical life) constantly bother you.
• Invisible spirits or beings call on you to perform tasks or deliver messages.
• You feel like a psychic sponge, continually absorbing others' physical illnesses or conditions, emotions, thoughts, needs, or problems.
• You constantly experience déjà vu regarding your own life or others' lives, or you receive predictions about the future.
• You know what others are going through (or might go through) even when you aren't with them.
• You experience a constant influx of psychic data that usually doesn't pertain to you.
• You are often anxious and have a hard time going to sleep or staying asleep; after all, you don't know who or what is going to visit you in the night.

- You're scared of your gift, but also scared to turn it off.
- You have a sense of being different, crazy, and not like other people.

The Psychic-Sensitive Syndrome can have a huge impact on our health. Psychic energies—which we can pick up from the living, the dead, the spiritual and natural realms, and elsewhere—transform into physical energies through our chakras, and our immune system then attacks the physical toxins. We simply can't process energies that don't match our own unique blueprint. So our body, considering these intrusive energies to be marauders, increases its own antibodies.

The major sign of the Psychic-Sensitive Syndrome is that no matter what you do, every ache, pain, illness, addiction, or compulsion of those around you is absorbed into your body. You catch every bug that goes around. If your sister in Maine brushes against poison ivy, your arm will start to itch, even though you're in Minnesota. You might even absorb others' physical likes and dislikes. Seeing someone order a martini makes you feel like drinking one, even though you hate gin.

Because you absorb others' issues, you're unable to distinguish which of the myriad feelings, ideas, or goals inside of you are really your own. You don't know what might make you happy because you can't differentiate what brings you joy from what brings others joy. You might be absolutely overwhelmed with your loved ones' emotions. They, on the other hand, probably think you're crazy, wonder at the voices you hear, and believe you should get therapy when the truth is that you are feeling their feelings, acting out their beliefs, or reacting to their private memories and dreams.

At work, you may be distracted because you know *everything* that's happening with everyone around you. Jimmy in the mailroom is having an affair with Suzie in Accounting. The bank clerk feels underappreciated. The bus driver is worried about paying the bills and hopes her alimony will arrive on time this month. Your coworker is crafting a resignation letter.

You might even experience the presence of entities or spirits, whether ghostly or ancestral. Some of my clients are visited by entities that prey on them sexually; others tell of having out-of-body sex. You might receive messages about other people and feel compelled to deliver them.

This syndrome often begins with teachings that support a lack of spiritual boundaries. Churches, including the Pentecostal, several Hindu sects, and even mystical Jewish religions, often recognize spiritual gifts that are psychic in orientation. Yet they call or label psychic activity evil, or they encourage the development of these gifts while providing no training.

The Healer's Syndrome: A Heart as Big as the World (but the World Doesn't Include Yourself)

Are you tired of being everyone's healer?

Usually that's the only question I need to ask a person to get a resounding, "Yes!" If you're the healer personality, you'll know it.

You're the first person everyone turns to when they feel tired, anxious, or depressed; the one whose kindness and compassion flows infinitely; the one who gives and gives and gives, often to the point of wipeout. You're the one who can literally feel your heart energy pouring out, constantly, and not just dripping out like water from a leaky kitchen sink. Your energetic faucets are always turned fully on. By the time you are done taking care of others, they are as happy and loved as can be. You're the one that feels dried up.

The Healer's Syndrome is like a combination of the Vampire and the Mule Syndromes. Like the vampire victim, you are constantly losing energy to those seeking solace, those who would prefer to steal their assistance rather than obtain it in a straightforward way. But like people with the Mule Syndrome, you also take on others' issues, often to the point of sheer exhaustion. As a healer, your higher intention is just that: helping and healing others. The problem is you end up with others' illnesses and problems, while they get all the energy required for you to live a healthy life.

The healing forces go out, and what replaces them but the energy that others are trying to get rid of. Out goes the energetic cure for the other person's cold, and chances are, in comes the energy of cold itself. Out goes your compassion and wisdom, and in comes the other person's depression and confusion. The hardest part of being a healer isn't that you are helping; you like helping. It's that you become burdened with the problems you are fixing.

Because I work in the healing field, I constantly meet individuals with the Healer's Syndrome. It's natural for individuals who love healing to join the ranks of doctors, nurses, medics, hands-on healers, or other healing professionals. Unfortunately, many of these same folks also join the private club of "healers with the Healer's Syndrome."

And it isn't just professional healers who can be members of this club; anyone who cares about others to the point of having tragically flawed energetic boundaries can qualify. One of the most affected individuals I ever worked with was a mailman. He never finished his route on time because he could always sense when one of his "clients," as he called the people on his delivery route, needed care. A spiritual individual, he would stand at the door and send prayers into the houses of the needy. He'd end his day when the sun went down, absolutely exhausted and flabbergasted that his energy never rebounded. In fact, he often felt the same aches and pains he prayed to relieve in his clients.

"I'm doing good," he said. "So why do I always feel so bad?"

Then he added, "What makes me feel really bad is that I'm doing God's work. So why isn't God helping a little more?"

The mailman thought he was sharing divine energy, but what he was really giving away was *his own* energy.

The law of physics is pretty clear. Nature abhors a vacuum, so when something goes out, something else must come in. This formula works if healers give away their energy and then replace it by, say, drinking in the nectar from the gods, the dew from the flowers, or at least a strong tonic. But no, healers' boundaries are usually programmed to let in the needy person's problems. If the needy person is a family member, this exchange most likely is the result of an energetic agreement established between the two during the healer's childhood. Why would loved ones just let in the brilliant love of a healer when they could also rid themselves of the source of their dissatisfaction at the same time?

How might you distinguish the healer from the mule, energetically? This is how I describe it: The mule's energetic boundaries look like a door that opens from the outside to the inside. People on the outside throw their stuff through the door and, if they're smart, slam it shut and run away. They know the mule will work on it for them. The healer's boundaries, on the other hand, resemble a door that swings both ways. The healer tosses the healing into the needy person, and the needy tosses his or her problems back into the healer. Neither syndrome leaves the healer or the mule feeling good or able to lead the good life he or she deserves.

If you're afflicted with the Healer's Syndrome, you might experience any of the following:

- You constantly exhibit concern, care, love, compassion, and kindness, but don't receive these in return.
- Healing energy flows from you to another, but only sick or problematic energy comes back to you.
- You're plagued by aches, pains, emotions, problems, and even illnesses that appeared in others. You didn't display the symptoms before you helped or were in contact with others, and they no longer experience those symptoms themselves.
- You feel guilty if you take time for yourself when someone else has a need.
- You feel like you wear an invisible sign that says, "Available 24/7. Need a nursemaid? A heartmate? A little love? A listening ear? Here I am!" (Notice the absence of a fee.)
- You're tired of everyone telling you how kind you are.

- You feel bushed, fatigued, worn out, and used after interacting with others.
- You're uncomfortable when someone tries to do something nice for you.
- There is physical dissonance in your heart, lungs, or breasts, after you give too much.
- You feel refreshed when you're alone or after you eat a lot of carbohydrates or sugars.

The Healer's Syndrome can underlie any health disorder. As explained in the Psychic-Sensitive Syndrome section, any external energy that enters your energetic fields can transform into a physical toxin in your body. Compounding this influx of overwhelming poisons is the loss of your own vital energy. You'll take on others' work, illnesses, issues, drives, addictions, and needs, and in return, you lose physical energy, stamina, and health. You will feel sicker, heavier, and more physically ill than vampire victims, whose energy is "merely" sucked away, because you are also taking in noxious energies. Most likely, no doctor in the world will be able to really diagnose what's happening to you; either that, or your diagnosis will keep changing.

If stricken with the Healer's Syndrome, you are often everyone's darling, the fix-it queen or king, the loving therapist who always has time for others. It might seem like all your money goes to support those you love, who in turn, dump debt and bills on you without saying thank you. You might feel responsible for providing for your loved ones' needs and taking care of their problems—physical, financial, work-related, relational, emotional, behavioral, sexual, or otherwise. You are the giver. Your mothering/fathering compulsion causes you to give away your time, attention, care, and compassion, but all you get in exchange are other people's issues and emotions. Your loved ones are guaranteed that their heart's desires will be met, because you make sure they are; unfortunately, your desires won't be, because you're exhausted from carrying their burdens.

You might feel that achieving success or getting love depends on healing all of everyone else's issues. You feel good, and maybe even think you *are* good, only when you are helping or giving to others. After all, isn't it better to serve others than be selfish? We are often spiritually trained to not only give unto others, but also take their problems unto ourselves. This is an extraordinarily common syndrome among women and any persons working in a spiritual discipline.

If you've ever thought, "That's it! I'm so tired of taking care of everyone!" you're likely struggling with the Healer's Syndrome.

The No-Boundary Syndrome: Where, Oh Where, Did Those Boundaries Go?

I stared at my friend. When did he ever stop? Okay, so I struggle with boundaries too, but really!

He started the day by getting up late and overeating, then he biked ten miles (maybe to wear off the calories he'd consumed). Tired out, he then snoozed, which meant he didn't get to his work project. From experience, I knew that meant he'd be up all night (as he was every night) in order to complete his responsibilities. Next, he was on the phone with three people at once (a technological feat) before flying off to pick up his son from school—late.

I didn't feel like talking to him about it. We'd probably cover three topics in two minutes flat, and I'd be completely bushed.

I know what you're thinking: maybe he has ADHD—and perhaps more than that. Some individuals have so few energetic boundaries that they actually might be diagnosed with attention and/or hyperactivity disorder, or even autism or Asperger's spectrums. Then again, they might be considered just anxious, hypervigilant, overwrought, always worried, or manic, or, if they're being complimented, just really busy and good at multitasking. (I vote the latter, as I fit into this category myself.)

We are all born with certain biochemical predispositions, but the energetics of our surroundings determine if these tendencies will be an asset or a liability. If someone's energetic boundaries are punctured or so full of holes they resemble a slice of swiss cheese, any natural inclinations are going to be harmful, not beneficial. Such is the case of the no-boundary person.

No-boundary people are just that: individuals with such thin or transparent boundaries that they let everything in and everything out, and the people can't get their bearings no matter how hard they try. As energetic as some of these individuals appear, they are often completely worn out and depressed. Some might even seem so flat that they appear to lack in empathy or emotion altogether. The truth is that they have taken into themselves the emotions that others deny. Because it is impossible for them to process feelings that aren't their own, these internalized feelings sit inside no-boundary people like balls of glue. Their insides are so sticky that they can't feel their own feelings or show that they can relate to those of others.

Sometimes it's hard to convince a no-boundary person, especially the hyperactive victim, that forming energetic boundaries will be helpful. Think of it this way. You're raised in the tropics and spend your entire life running around naked, feeling the balmy breeze, licking the coconut juice off your fingertips, and baking in the hot sand. I come along and tell you that you'll now have to cover up, or wear at least a sarong and thongs. At first, the most meager of wraps will make you feel like you are smothered in Inuit garb. You might not even feel like you can walk anymore!

If you're used to being full of others' feelings, you've also become accustomed to not having to feel your own. Personally, I'd much rather skip feeling my feelings. Why not just hold onto other's energies, constantly replenishing the bolus, so you can avoid your own pesky sensations?

Though it's not easy to convince a no-boundary person to add boundaries, my no-boundary clients that flesh out their spiritual borders, to the one, report having more satisfying relationships (and their partners are also often quite pleased at the substantial changes), greater prosperity (because their bosses can actually find them), and better health (as they actually get three square meals a day plus a full night's sleep). They are also less attracted to addictive substances and exhibit fewer compulsive behaviors, partially because they no longer need to smother the stressful energy that plagues them. By keeping out what frightens us, energetic boundaries help us feel safe in our own homes, including our bodies, the houses of our souls.

Here are some indications of the No-Boundary Syndrome:

- You're hyperactive and/or constantly overwhelmed, which results in exhaustion. But you can't stop. You don't know why, but you can't.
- You're hypervigilant, feeling that you are endangered or threatened, even though there's no current reason for your paranoia.
- If anyone lives life in the fast lane, it's you—and that's the only speed you know.
- You have a history of addictive and compulsive behaviors.
- You experience insomnia or can't really rest and relax, while at the same time you follow a bizarrely abnormal schedule.
- You can't figure out or express your true feelings. You may display feelings, but others find them inauthentic or implausible.
- You tend to blame others for your personal problems.
- You engage in desperate displays of bravado, yet have a sense of inner emptiness, terror, and a fear of abandonment.

A no-boundary person is "all over the board," afflicted with so many problems and symptoms that it's almost impossible to arrive at a single or simple diagnosis. On a health level, No-Boundary Syndrome might manifest as attention-deficit/hyperactivity disorder (ADHD), Asperger's syndrome, addictions, abuse issues, borderline syndromes, and more.

You may well look and feel like an out-of-control child. On speed. With no brake control. You walk into a work meeting, and soon you are tapping your pencil, jiggling your feet, getting everyone coffee, passing out papers, opening and shutting the blinds. At home, one second you might explode at your spouse, and the next you're crying on the bathroom floor. Another minute might find you laughing, and the next, fretting over a vicious to-do list.

Because you are distracted by other tasks, drives, and situations, you might let money matters slide entirely. You might act as if there are no monetary limits. You could be the person who just takes out a new credit card when you hit your limit on your old card, or blows an entire paycheck on friends to make sure they love you. Somewhere along the line, you might have internally decided that emotional happiness comes from pleasing others.

When it comes to emotions, you are similar to the psychic sensitive, minus the common sense. On the outside, your emotional behavior will appear flagrant and inconsistent. You'll have wide mood swings, periods of coldness, and then seeming moments of warmth. On the inside, you'll feel lost, unable to get to your own feelings and needs. Because your feelings and ideas are so tangled up with those of others, you'll be unable to discern sound actions or behaviors from unsound ones. Without even knowing it, you act out absolutely every desire, compulsion, or need emanating from everyone around you. This syndrome can get you into extra trouble if you act out others' irrational, unethical, or illegal fantasies.

You might exhibit signs of sex, love, or physical addiction and can't feel good unless you are being touched or in a relationship. Yet no matter how much physical love you get, you don't experience true love or loving energy. In relationships, you probably act like you can get by with anything. Unfortunately, your relationship partners most likely enable this attitude. Low self-love or self-respect indicates a lack of boundaries. If we struggle to keep ethical relationship boundaries, we most likely feel unlovable.

You'll often be vulnerable to the types of spiritual beliefs that leave you unable to make your own decisions. You'll be susceptible to any religion or spiritual system that says you're supposed to just follow the rules and not think for yourself, even though adhering to the rules might not be in your best interest.

Environ Syndrome: What's This World Coming to? (And Why Does It Always Come into *Me?)*

I once worked with a Canadian woman who had been consulting with doctor after doctor and healer after healer for twelve years, trying to get a fitting diagnosis. She'd experience bouts of flulike symptoms, including nausea and a low-grade headache, with occasional diarrhea. These might clear up, only to be replaced by an inconsistent heartbeat, shallow breathing, and a general weakness. She almost always felt anxious. None of her symptoms added up to a clear medical diagnosis, and medical tests never showed anything wrong.

When working with her, I kept getting intuitive images of a dumpsite. My client insisted that she didn't live near a toxic dumpsite and never had. Nonetheless, I continued to receive the same images until finally, I asked where she was born.

"Holland," she reported. "On a farm."

It turned out that her home farm had been turned into a chemical dumpsite, and the soil was now full of barium, a toxic heavy metal. My client's symptoms matched those of barium poisoning. But how could that be? She hadn't set foot on the family farm for decades and certainly not since it had become a toxic-waste site.

People with Environ Syndrome don't have to be anywhere near an environmental pollutant to experience the symptoms of toxic poisoning. Because their spiritual borders are so permeable, they can pick environmental poisons or energies out of thin air. They've only to drive near a forest that's been recently logged to feel the pain of the felled trees. They can walk near a recently revamped office at work and swell up from the toxins in the new paint or carpet. They might also toss and turn all night in a hotel room because they can sense the leftover energy of an argument the previous occupants had, or they can drive their partners silly searching through the kitchen cupboards because "there's an injured mouse in here that needs to be helped, I just know it." Perhaps they'll never even make it to the kitchen, because the sixth planet in the Orion belt suddenly shifts in orbit, making them so dizzy that they can't move!

Can someone really be this sensitive? Ask my Dutch-Canadian client, whose symptoms relieved within a week once we corrected her energetic boundaries—with no other treatment. Because they lack certain energetic boundaries, such individuals are incredibly vulnerable to energies within their environments.

The kindest souls on this planet are those who can feel what nature is going through, who can sense both the plight of the dolphins and the healing powers of their songs, who can uphold the rights of the trees while teaching others about the trees' curative properties, who can sense the turn of a planet and inform the rest of us how to best access the resulting energy to achieve our destinies. Like all syndromes, this one really can be shaped and formed to produce beauty and joy, not only heartache and trouble.

A few of the myriad signs of being an environmental sensitive include the following:

- You sense or pick up on what has recently occurred in the environment or a room.
- You have a strong connection to nature, to the point of feeling what's occurring in an animal, plant, tree, or object of nature.
- You're unusually sensitive to changes in climate, geography, or land masses, here on earth or elsewhere—even what occurs in the stars.
- You experience physical sensations before a natural event, such as an impending volcanic eruption, hurricane, or earthquake. You

might also feel the terror or physical pain of the living beings affected by the event.

• You're sensitive to environmental and geo-physical shifts or toxins.
• You're susceptible to diseases or stressors that come from shifts in nature, such as an influx of mold or lead poisoning in the land or seas.
• You have extreme allergic reactions to natural substances or human-made, artificial ones.

If you're affected by Environ Syndrome, you might feel physically depleted around power lines, cell phones, appliances, and computers. Radiation and even natural energies, including sunspots, ley lines (natural energies in the earth), and cosmic influences (such as the movement of the moon or planets) penetrate your electromagnetic fields and cause everything from mental illness and learning disabilities to cancer and heart disease.

Does just walking into a certain building or room make you sick and tired? Does turning on your computer drain away your physical energy? Do you begin to wheeze and sneeze when the walls are being painted, the floors are being recarpeted, or the bathroom is being cleaned? Oversensitivity to your physical surroundings is a hallmark of Environ Syndrome. It's as if you are allergic to just about everything, or as if manmade and natural objects are sucking out your energy.

In addition to being a magnet for every illness going around, you might only have to touch someone's pencil to flash into his thoughts or sit in someone's chair to know how she felt earlier that day. Even residual emotions left on objects, such as walls or pillows, affect you. The free-floating emotions of any natural beings—whether it is a strong sensation from your guinea pig or the groans of the tree bending under an ice storm—are guaranteed to intrude on your own emotions.

In relationships, you might see it as your job to guarantee your loved ones, human or animal, a pleasing environment, no matter what or how much it costs.

You constantly sense your relationship with nature. You easily sense the emotions of any and all natural beings around you. Some individuals sense exactly what is happening within or to their companions of nature—from their pets to their houseplants. Others have only to touch a tree to feel its scream at having been hacked by the gardener. I have one client who won't travel to cities because she can sense the cry of the water exposed to pollution. Affected by the toxicity, including emotional poisons, of the environment, you can't think straight about your own needs.

You might over-bond with their animals or pets, exchanging emotions so frequently it's challenging to separate their needs from your own. I've worked with several clients whose main relationships have been with natural beings, especially pets.

You might be susceptible to the influences of the negative natural forces. Like the Psychic-Sensitive Syndrome, this syndrome also exposes us to entities or beings. Whereas the psychic sensitive can pick up on all entities, human or not, the environmentally sensitive will read mainly the needs of natural and supernatural beings. You might also be susceptible to ancestral interference, the lingering presence of your ancestors, whose spiritual thoughts intrude on your own.

Similarities and Differences between All Syndromes

Some syndromes share several common factors. Both the healer and the mule work on others' problems, while the vampire victim, healer, and the psychic sensitive are great at absorbing energies not their own. The psychic sensitive and the environ are overly attuned to the psychic data around them.

There are differences between all seven syndromes, however. As pointed out, the healer takes *and* gives, while the mule mainly takes on energy. Healers absorb the illnesses or problems of those they're healing, the environ takes on energies relating to the world of nature or the cosmos, and the psychic sensitive actively sponges all types of psychic data.

As suggested earlier, you might have more than one type of syndrome. I know that I do. That's why it's important to fix up all of your energetic boundaries, not just a select few. To do this, it's important to know more about the four main types of energetic boundaries, how they are formed, and what damages them. Knowledge is power. Comprehending what's going on will not only help you set strong, appropriate boundaries, but also transform your energetic issues into gifts that can help you improve your life.

Exercise: What Kind of Syndrome Do I Have?
The Journal Strategy

Do you have a sense which syndrome affects you the most often, or which ones strike you when, where, and with whom? The purpose of this exercise is to better help you define your boundary challenges so you can shift them to work for rather than against you.

Start by reviewing the seven basic syndromes:

• Paper Doll
• Vampire
• Mule
• Psychic-Sensitive
• Healer's
• No-Boundary
• Environ

Which ones immediately strike you as best describing you, your daily challenges, and/or specific situations? Jot down notes about which syndromes suit you and under what circumstances.

To test your initial assessments and begin to figure out what—or who—might be under some of your energetic-boundary problems, try the following journal exercise.

Buy a journal, a special one, dedicated only to deciphering your energetic-boundary issues. It's important that you value yourself and this process enough to select a journal that reflects your intention and your real self.

Commit to carrying this journal with you wherever you can during the next week and keeping it near your bedside at night. For right now, keep this journal private. It represents a conversation between your conscious self (the self with the syndrome) and your spiritual or true self. Chances are these bonds have been overshadowed by others' energies. All relationships prosper when we dedicate time to them. Talking only with your true self on your journal pages will restore or empower what has probably been a weak link.

Evenly divide the journal into seven parts, one for each syndrome.

To initiate this exercise, clear a few minutes of your time and sequester yourself in a room that has a mirror. Standing before the mirror, concentrate on your right eye, which represents your everyday, conscious self—the self you've become as you've adapted to your environment. Unfortunately, fitting in and surviving probably required weakening or damaging your energetic boundaries.

With compassion and care, gaze into this eye, the self who has been wounded by the need to respond to the world in ways that have proven harmful. As you fall into the pools deep below the surface, give yourself permission to start to feel the pain caused by living with fractured energetic boundaries. Now ask this self if he or she is willing to point out every time he or she feels the effects of an energetic syndrome. Promise that you, the conscious self, will stay alert and record these occurrences.

Now switch your focus to your left eye and gaze into its depths. This eye reflects your soul and inner spirit, the higher part of you that hasn't had to change to suit the world. Instead, he or she carries the codes for your original boundaries. Ask that this self begins the process of healing the injured boundaries as you become aware of them, or at the least tells you how to begin the repair process. Again, promise that you, the conscious self, will record these insights.

Now peer into both your eyes at once, joining your conscious self with both your left-side, spiritual self and your right-side, adapting self. With these two selves unified, you will be able to undertake your assignment for the week.

From this point on, you will be aware of every syndrome you fall into or operate from. When you have time and space, take note in your journal of the syndrome, the signs you exhibited, and the situations involved. Describe who was involved and how you felt. If you awaken at night with a bad dream or some other indication of a boundary invasion, you will be able to immediately register what occurred, writing it in your log, and then fall back asleep.

Once a day, take a few extra minutes to close your eyes and ask to see or perceive the past situation, person, relationship, event, teaching, or trauma that formed the beliefs that led to a damaged energetic boundary. Record these insights or observations, too, in your journal.

At the end of the week, review your journal and spend a few minutes writing down your conclusions. Congratulate yourself for caring enough about yourself to analyze your energetic boundaries and what might be causing disarray. How are you going to reward yourself?

||||||||||||||||||||||||||||

Chapter 4

Shoring Up the Borders: Tips and Techniques for Energizing Your Boundaries

I'm not afraid of storms, for I'm learning how to sail my ship.

LOUISA MAY ALCOTT

O*nce upon a time, there was a small island on the coast of Nowhere. People there were warned of an imminent hurricane, and so they gathered at the seaside in front of their village, each toting great sacks of sand, ready to shore up the beach that led to their homes.*

But one man remained behind, in his small cottage. The other villagers felt angry, if not alarmed. "Who does he think he is?" "He lives here, why isn't he helping?" "Can we survive unless every hand is helping?"

A crew left their work and stumbled through this man's front door, about to ask these very questions. But when they saw him, they stopped, mouths agape.

There the man sat, stitching burlap sacks.

"Ah," he said, his eyes breaking out in a smile. "You are in need of more sacks. It is hard to shore against the seas without something to hold the sand!"

We have to shore up our energetic boundaries to survive the storms of life. Who doesn't want protection against life's weathering squalls and a filter system that allows in just enough sunshine to warm us, but not burn us? Before we address healing techniques for specific life areas, here are a few basic, but powerful general techniques for healing all of your energetic boundaries. The following processes can be used to shift any of your energetic boundaries, no matter which of the syndromes might afflict you. You'll be using them throughout chapters 5 to 8 to grow in health, wealth, love, and purpose.

Setting an Intention

Intention is focused commitment. We use it to declare our objective and to alert the universe that we are serious about changing our patterns. Setting an intention is a critical step in healing our protective boundaries.

The most powerful intentions are created with the full cooperation of both our invisible and visible selves. "Setting our energy" is equivalent to blowing a whistle on a football field. The sound assembles not only the players, but also the referees, fans, and popcorn sellers. In short, we want to set an intention so strongly and intensely that everything and everyone inside and outside of us holds hands and joins in the game. That includes that 90 percent of ourselves that isn't us—those quirky little microbes and fluids that aren't marked by our own DNA. It also encompasses other people and beings—tangible and intangible—that long to assist us, even if they don't know it yet! From an energetic perspective, intention programs or charges every cell, subatomic particle, thought, emotion, and energetic field so they all work together.

Dr. Dean Radin, a pioneer in the consciousness movement, tells us there are at least 1,000 published studies on the power of intention. These originate from institutions such as Harvard, Princeton, and Duke Universities; the U.S. military; the Max Planck Institute; and the

University of Edinburgh.[1] These studies point to intention as a critical force for shaping reality, from inviting healing to bolstering prosperity.

Even mechanical objects respond to the forces of intention, as Lynne McTaggart examines in her book *The Intention Experiment*. Consider a series of studies conducted over twenty-five years by Princeton University researchers Brenda Dunne and Robert Jahn, who studied the effects of the mind and intention on machines called random-event generators. These machines should produce an equal number of positive and negative pulses, and they did when no one was trying to influence them. In over 2.5 million trials, however, when humans concentrated on creating a certain outcome without touching the machines, the results added up to a significantly statistical deviation from chance expectation. In other words, human intention controlled the machines.[2] Sixty-eight other independent investigators replicated these outcomes.

After setting an intention, we might reiterate it—every day or every hour, for instance—to maintain our decision, or we might just set it once and get on with our business. We can also use the five steps of setting an intention as part of the techniques that will clear, heal, and strengthen our energetic boundaries.

We can lock an intention into any substance, such as food, water, gemstones, colors, shapes, clothing, our surroundings, and more. For instance, holding a rock and wishing upon a star isn't going to do a lot for you. Holding a rock and sending an energy intention into that rock charges or blesses it. Your intention actually alters the molecular content and structure of that rock. Afterward, every time you hold that rock, your intention is played back for you, like a recorded energetic message, to help you reach your goals.

I've first provided the basic steps for setting any energetic intention, then included an example of how to program an intention into a gemstone, so you can see how to program an actual substance with your intention.

Setting an Intention: Five Basic Steps

1. Release guilt, shame, and blame. At some level, our energy boundaries were violated and are vulnerable because we inadvertently decided it would be safer to have them that way. But guess what? We wouldn't have unconsciously altered our boundaries if someone or something were not hurting us. Most likely, any people involved were also stuck in bad patterns and hurting us because they had been hurt.

We want to stop the cycle of sharing the resulting guilt, shame, and blame by forgiving others and ourselves. To forgive isn't to forget. Neither is it to allow a transgression to continue. Rather, it is to say that it's time to leave the past in the past and look for a new future.

To take this step, take a few deep breaths and focus on your heart. Sense, see, and feel the damages caused by the current energetic pattern. Allow yourself to feel any guilt or shame you hold about unconsciously creating or continuing this pattern and any anger or blame you have toward others for forcing you into it. Feel the heaviness of this guilt and shame, the burden of the anger and blame. Are you ready to let all of that go? It's so unnecessary, isn't it? Allow the light of your own spirit and the higher spirit to sweep these judgments away.

Know that these old emotions might come up again or even lead you into memories that need to be faced and healed. You can further work on the unresolved issues through the exercise "Uncovering Your Storyline" or by working with a therapist.

2. Clear out current intentions. Our energetic boundaries are off because we unconsciously believe the distortion is helpful. It might have been, at some time, but it isn't any longer. Decide to eliminate the programs that have been holding you in the past, and they can begin to unwind.

After releasing the guilt, shame, anger, and blame covering up the formerly important intention, ask your spirit or the Divine to help you better understand the original intention behind or purpose of the boundary distortion.

Did you unconsciously retain a boundary shift, build an armored fortress, retain gaps or holes, or remain too fluid, in order to adapt to the surrounding environment or to appease a particular person or set of events? Did someone else threaten or coerce you to the point that you felt you had to remain wounded in order to survive? You had a good reason to energetically respond to the world the way that you did. Your boundaries became unhealthy in order to provide some sense of safety. Acknowledge the original intent and then make a different decision. Let the light of your own spirit and all things divine wash clean the old intentions and decisions. This releases everything you internalized from others and your personal rationales for maintaining weakened boundaries.

More information and memories might trigger after this phase. You can use the exercise "Uncovering Your Storyline" or work with a trusted therapist or healer to continue cleansing yourself of the past.

3. Establish a new intention. We don't have to phrase or frame our new goals perfectly. We can state or visualize them. What's really important is to set this intention in and through our heart.

You might want to spend some time creating a new intention. Enjoy the process of deciding how you'd like your life to really look, feel, and operate. What is of physical importance to you? Emotional? How would you like to feel in your relationships? How would you like to relate with the Divine? Are you ready to accept your spiritual purpose or destiny and be guided into it daily?

Now spend a little time coming up with statements that will universalize these life dreams on the energetic level, such as, "I now enjoy energetic boundaries that enable a fulfillment of love" or "I am now able to care and share safely and lovingly with all people in my life."

4. Ask for support. We will fall. We will slip. As soon as we establish a new energy boundary, something or someone will come along to test it. That's just how it works. But you know what? We get to ask for support—from others, from our own inner spirit, from the Divine—and not only once, but over and over again.

This step deserves to be mulled over and pulled apart as one might a treasure chest, searching for all the gold you can find. When you get up in the morning, ask the Divine to support your boundaries in a way that provides the spiritual guidance you need. When you feel yourself slipping into or triggering an energetic slide, call a friend. Ask for help. Be willing to keep learning what you need to do and/or receive from others to maintain your healthy boundaries.

5. Believe. To believe is to know in our hearts that what we are requesting is already true or that we already have it. We are simply following a path to make that reality concrete in the material world. I suggest affirming daily how deeply the Divine believes in you. Open to this assurance, and you find it easier to believe in yourself.

Using Intention to Bless an Object

Intention underlies the blessing of stones, water, food, and all other substances, as well as energetic changes in thoughts, feelings, colors, shapes, and borders, to support our resolve to become safe and healthy. The following is an adaptation of the five intention steps for blessing a simple gemstone to clear and heal our energetic boundaries.

1. Hold or think about the stone you are going to use.
2. Clear your mind of everything you've been thinking about.
3. Center in your heart.
4. Sense any feelings, thoughts, experiences, people, resentments, or obstacles that have been compromising your energetic boundaries. Concentrate especially on guilt, shame, anger, and blame.
5. Release these factors, allowing your own spirit or the Divine to flush them out of your system and your spiritual borders.

6. Now ask the Divine to completely cleanse you and this stone of all intentions, decisions, or energies that might keep you mired in an unhealthy pattern.

7. Reflect on the new intention you would like to set. Sense, feel, embrace, visualize, or otherwise fully experience this new intention.

8. Create a ball of light in your mind's eye and visualize this intention, along with the full sensation of it, being inserted into the stone. Feel this new intention flow from your heart down through your arms and hands and into the stone.

9. Acknowledge that this stone now carries the energy of your intention and that holding, stroking, carrying, or thinking about the stone will reenergize your new intention.

10. Believe that the Divine will continue to reach you through this stone, and in all other areas of your life, as you begin living your newly established commitment.

Uncovering Your Storyline

Your storyline is the sequence of events that led to distorted boundaries. Some of these events are concrete, but most of them—the most important—are invisible, consisting of your inner reactions and unconscious decisions.

This particular exercise is designed to help you dig down to the internal and external experiences that led to the current state of energetic affairs and to create a better way to meet your safety needs. Sometimes boundaries shift with knowledge of the storyline. Whatever occurs for you is what is meant to happen for you.

There are five elements involved in uncovering the sequence of events that led to your current energetic problems:

1. Your imprisoned self. If a trauma was really big or hurtful, the energy of it locks us into the age we were when we experienced it.

That part of us never gets to grow up, to stretch, grow, and fly. She or he is incarcerated in the energetic fibers created by the people or situation that injured us. We must rescue this hidden, trapped self in order to release the negative energies keeping him or her in prison.

2. **The safety violation.** This refers to the nature of the event, attitude, person, or chronic situation that threatened our survival.

3. **Your security decision.** In order to survive the situation, you had to quickly decide what to do—maybe so quickly that you weren't even thinking when you decided (unconsciously) how to energetically protect yourself. What did you decide that you had to do in order to survive?

4. **The syndrome.** Inevitably, your survival-based decision locked up your development and impacted your energetic boundaries. What syndrome or set of them did you develop because of this decision? How did this decision affect you short and long term? How is it still affecting you today?

5. **The need.** What was supposed to happen? How should you have been treated, if you had been loved, protected, and valued? Here is your work; herein lays the answers to the question of how to fix your energetic boundaries.

Are you ready to discover a pertinent storyline? The easiest way to perform this exercise on your own is to take out a pen and paper and conduct a guided meditation much like the following.

The meditation I have designed involves asking your spirit questions about the storyline. We each are a spirit, and this spirit is also our wise self. This process asks you to see, experience, hear, or sense your wise self as a being separate from you. This is so you can obtain the necessary answers and healing that is buried within your subconscious. At the end, you will reintegrate this wise self so your healing can continue.

Secure yourself in a quiet place and make sure you won't be disturbed for a while. As calmly as possible, settle into a comfortable position and breathe deeply, guiding yourself into your heart.

Now ask that your own inner spirit, or wise self, appear on your mind's inner screen. Take a moment and engage with this wise self. What does he or she look like? How is your wise self dressed or clothed? Does he or she hold any objects of power or talismans?

Ask this wise self if there is a name you should use when consulting him or her and, if so, to share the meaning of this name. Also ask if your wise self is willing to help you journey back to the origin of the problem you are experiencing.

If he or she says yes, prepare to travel, and with your wise self as a guide, slip backward in time.

You soon find yourself in an earlier time and place. You are able to observe what occurred back then. Noticing the persons or people involved in the damaging event, you are able to completely reexperience everything that occurred, including your emotional responses. You are also able to perceive the changes that occurred in your energetic field as a reaction to the trauma.

Pencil and paper in hand, you now turn to the wise one at your side and ask his or her opinion about the following. You are able to write down what you hear or are shown, even as you are listening:

- I was traumatized by this experience because:
- Because of this experience, I decided to believe:
- Because of this belief, I felt:
- I decided that, to protect myself, I needed to:
- To further protect myself, my energetic boundaries became like this:
- Whenever I am in an experience that makes me feel the same way, my energetic boundaries do this:
- And my boundaries create the following syndromes or problems for me:
- What I *really needed* to happen during and after the trauma was:
- What I *really need* in order to heal is:
- In order to be truly protected in my life now, my energetic boundaries should be formed like this:
- I can remain both safe and loved by doing this:

After you ask additional questions of your own, you and your wise self look at the you who was injured by this past experience. Together, you reach out your arms and hearts and hold this younger you. You reassure your younger self that everything is being put right. Embracing this self even tighter, your current, wise, and younger selves all merge together, the wise one transforming all wounds into wings of joy and all injuries into gifts of grace.

Take a few deep breaths, and record anything else you feel drawn to write down. Then return to a state of full consciousness. Know that you can engage your wise self for further information and healing any time you want.

Spirit-to-Spirit

I developed this exercise to use during sessions with clients, but have gone on to employ it in every area of my life. At workshops, I teach it to professional healers, doctors, nurses, therapists, or intuitives, and afterward, most of them say, "This is the only technique I really need—for *anything!*"

"Spirit-to-Spirit" is a three-step process for establishing the spiritual borders we need to engage in any activity with another person. It ensures clean and pure boundaries, leaving us able to receive highly accurate, clear information, guidance, directives, or healing for ourselves or to offer to someone else.

I suggest you use this technique whenever you are engaged with a person who is triggering one of the energetic syndromes. It will immediately shift your energetic boundaries, disengage unhealthy connections, support loving bonds, and call in the assistance of a greater presence.

1. Affirm that you are a full, powerful, and loving spiritual being. Breathe into your heart while making this affirmation, and feel the resulting shifts in your energetic fields.
2. Affirm that the other person is also a fully developed and loving spiritual being. Sense the presence of his or her spirit inside and

engage with it. Feel how the unhealthy connections release and only love remains. (This step can also be done between you and an entire group of people, such as your family or business community, or even between you and an animal.)

3. Call upon the presence of the Divine, which immediately shifts the situation into whatever it is supposed to be, while providing you with any necessary insight, protection, healing, or act of grace.

You can use the above exercise when engaging with *any* person or group—not just those causing you problems. For instance, I use this technique when working with clients. I first affirm my own internal spirit, then the essence of my client. Lastly, I call upon the assistance of the Divine, which, in turn, supports my client through a transformation and me as the witness to the process. I also use this technique when I simply want to connect with friends, inserting their spirit or spirits into step two. Because of its universal nature you can use this technique for all intents and purposes, for it furthers only divine will.

What if you're alone and want to shift a situation involving a harmful person or group? Can you still use this process? Absolutely. A person does not need to be present—or even alive—to be acknowledged through step two. For instance, imagine that someone who has disappeared from your life or the spirit of a deceased person has violated your boundaries. As before, affirm your immortal self in step one and simply link with the divine essence of the absent person in step two. Energy cannot separate; a thought links us immediately, even through the ethers of time and the veils of death. Then conduct step three by confirming the presence of the Divine and await the unfolding transformation.

I also use Spirit-to-Spirit to connect with spiritual guides. As I meditate, I affirm the presence of a guide, angel, or master who is there to love and assist me. I most often use Christ. Several of my clients call upon the Virgin Mother Mary; others affirm a quality of the Divine, and still others connect with the Buddha, the goddess Kwan Yin, or a guardian angel. If in doubt, ask for the Divine to attend you in step two as well as in step three.

Working with Color

One of the easiest and most fun ways to evaluate, cleanse, and establish our energetic boundaries is to work with color. Using our ability to perceive psychic images, we can evaluate our energetic boundaries by sensing their colors, and we can employ different colors for healing purposes.

How do you get pictures in your mind? I recommend entering a meditative state and breathing deeply. Use the Spirit-to-Spirit process and ask the Divine to open your visioning faculty. You can also employ the exercise "Finding Your Fields" in chapter 1 to see your energetic boundaries.

Color healing consists of (1) diagnosing, (2) cleansing, and (3) repairing.

To diagnose is to check for correct coloration. We know that we need to see reds near our skin, because red relates to our physical energetic boundary. *Red* is a vast term. Hues of red can include brown, russet, auburn, rose, or apple red. Likewise, our orange band will include ranges of yellows and oranges; our green will include green's kissing cousins, blues and indigos, and our whites will incorporate purple, but also stretch into silver, gray, black, pink, and gold.

When diagnosing, we're basically making sure the right colors are where they are supposed to be. If we see off-kilter, blotchy, low, dark colors; missing hues; gaping holes; or cords, which look like garden hoses leading between our energy field and something or someone else, we can begin to figure out what might be off with our fields.

When checking, you can peruse every field at once to see which one grabs your attention, or you can concentrate on a specific field, if you already have a sense of which is distorted. For instance, let's say you are low in money. You might guess there's a problem with your physical energetic boundary, which regulates material matters. If you intuitively perceive a glowing, cherry red energy throughout your physical energetic field, right where it's supposed to be, you can rest assured that this boundary is doing its job. Then you might check the other three fields. If, instead, the red border is dark and blotchy, there's most likely an intrusive energy mingling with that boundary. If the red is dim, you're lacking life energy and passion. If the red is wavy and irregular, your physical boundary is confused and sending mixed messages to the world. Do you spy gaping holes? If so, you are losing energy. Do you see a garden-hose shape coming out of the red boundary? That's a cord. You might want to visually follow it and determine who has been enjoying your life energy—and, therefore, your money—while you're struggling.

Perceiving colors that aren't supposed to be in this boundary tells you that you're mixing up your energy—such as that of your feelings, thoughts, and beliefs—or perhaps carrying others' energy. These energies are negatively affecting the strength of your boundary; conversely, your energetic boundary might be off and, therefore, creating this mess. Seeing off yellow in your boundary where you're supposed to have red, for instance, suggests that negative thoughts have intruded on your physical well-being—thoughts that aren't helpful, but harmful.

Often, to repair the boundary problem once and for all, we have to find and address the issue underlying the problem. To do this, we can use exercises such as "Uncovering Your Storyline." But for a short-term fix, we can use color as a salve and solution.

No matter what you spot in a boundary—too-light or too-dark hues, holes, or interference—you need to cleanse it. To cleanse is to purify or wash clean. The best way to cleanse an energetic boundary is imagine a streaming waterfall of one of these three colors, depending on your purpose:

• **Pink** equates to love. If you are affected by a cord or another's
  energies, pink will return that energy to the other person with care
  and concern. It actually sends the intrusions back to the other's
  higher self, which can then deal with the real-world self or soul
  according to divine will.

- **Gold** equals power. If you are really frightened by what you see or if you feel gripped by something scary, such as a dark angel or manipulative pattern, gold produces immediate change. It's the "God power" that transforms.
- **White** equals innocence. If the problem in your field makes you feel guilty, embarrassed, or shameful, white will return you and all other persons involved to their natural state of purity.

Your final step is to repair. Making repairs is actually the easiest step of the process. Ask the Divine or your own higher self to help you picture this boundary as healthy. Notice the coloration, shape, form, and relative thickness. Check the permeability. Notice the prescribed color and its tint.

Ask also if there needs to be a different color on the inside of the field than the outside. Sometimes we are safer when we present one hue to the world and a different one to ourselves. Cushioning the part of a field nearest us with pink, for instance, comforts us with love, while putting silver on the outside deflects lies and untruth. If we have a problem with lying, however, we might require silver on the part of a field closest to us, to assist us with our truth-telling. Then we might want pink on the outside, so love flows from us to others as a way of making amends for our earlier deceptions.

The center of a field should always remain the correct color. If we're using pink internally and silver externally for our physical boundary, for instance, the middle of the field will be red.

What Do Your Colors (and Those Odd Intrusions) Mean?

Here are brief descriptions of what the basic colors mean in regard to your fields. First, I describe the healthy colors as related to the four main boundaries. I also suggest what might be occurring if that color is too dim or pale or too dark; you want to strengthen the too dim colors and lighten the too dark colors. At the end of this outline, I've also listed different types of intrusive energies and described various ways they might appear psychically, in addition to their negative effects.

Physical Energetics: The Reds

Red: passion, power, vitality, life energy, sexuality, physicality, primary needs, pleasure.

Pale Red: lack of passion, power, money, work, or sexual connection; poor physical health and/or sense of identity. Something or someone else might be draining your life energy.

Dark Red: violence, abuse, addictions, lust, rage, materialism. You might be infected by others' physical energies. Cords might be creating physical issues.

Brown: grounded, anchored, practical, down-to-earth, sustained, nourished, connected to nature.

Pale Brown: ungrounded, undernourished, spacey, airy. Something or someone, such as an ancestor, is stealing your bodily energy.

Dark Brown: repressed toxins, psychic or physical; avarice, greed. Family or other ancestral energies, nature-based interference or toxins, or cords to nature or ancestors are disrupting your physical boundary.

Emotional Energetics: The Oranges

Orange: feelings, creativity, childlike ability to play, joy, fun, sensuality, expression, dynamism.

Pale Orange: lack of joy or play, repressed feelings, inability to feel feelings, lost creativity, fear of feelings. Someone else is holding your feelings or creative urges hostage.

Dark Orange: unfelt feelings, bitterness, shame, disgust, guilt. Others' feelings are present; cords are creating emotional loss.

Yellow: mental activity, personal power, work success, optimism, ability to sense psychic information, ability to digest and interpret information.

Pale Yellow: lack of thoughtfulness, lack of intuitive information flow. Your thoughts are elsewhere—literally; someone or something else is holding or has captured them.

Dark Yellow: suspicion, prejudice, discrimination, criticism, covetousness. You are holding others' mental issues, thoughts, and beliefs; emotional cords are present.

Relational Energetics: The Greens

Green: healing, relational love, balance, harmony, connection, calm, adaptability.

Pale Green: lack of love, need for healing, weak self-love, missing connections. Someone else is holding your relational and healing energy.

Dark Green: Deceit, envy, jealousy. You are holding others' relationship energies; relational cords are present.

Blue: communication, both verbal and intuitive, celestial guidance, logical thinking, sharing, listening, truth.

Pale Blue: repressed knowledge or wisdom, hidden truth, missing truth, unshared thoughts. Someone else is controlling your communication.

Dark Blue: too much analytical thinking, overuse of knowledge instead of heart truth or higher principles, depressed views, resentment. You are holding others' truth or knowledge; cords are feeding another's relational information into you.

Indigo: You are operating from higher truth and principles, inspired wisdom, and devotion to truth. You are linking relationship with spirituality. (This color is either present or not; there are no negatives associated with it.)

Spiritual Energetics: The Whites

Purple: vision, strategy, the future, mystical understanding, cosmic possibilities.

Pale Purple: lack of vision; confusion about self-image, purpose, future, direction, and goals. Others might be blocking your destiny.

Dark Purple: striving too hard, multiple and mixed directions and goals, trying to please too many people, body- or self-image problems. You might be holding others' views of your self or reality; cords are pulling you in wrong direction or making you serve others instead of your self and the Divine.

White: purity, spiritual purpose, enlightenment, innocence, spirit light, connection to the Divine.

Pale White: You don't accept divine love; you lack knowledge of your personal destiny and an avenue for expressing your prophetic gifts. Others might be controlling your spiritual life.

Dark White: You are under the sway or control of others or an entity, cord, or other binding, in relation to your spiritual purpose or spiritual walk.

(See also gray, silver, pink, gold, or black, as well as the descriptions of cords, bindings, and attachments in chapter 3.)

Other Colors

The following colors have several meanings and can appear anywhere in your field. I describe both the positive and, if applicable, negative affects of these energies.

Pink: love, connectivity, selflessness, gentleness. Pink cannot be negative—only more or less intense in hue and, therefore, strength. For instance, if you are sharing pink energy with someone, the deeper the color, the more romantic the love. The lighter the color, the friendlier the love.

Silver: deflects negativity, opens higher communication, conveys divine truths. Silver is only negative when it's used against you. For instance, certain people or entities might hold silver around you, so that it acts like a mirror, keeping your gifts, thoughts, emotions, and relational needs reflecting back to you. If these aren't shared with the world, your needs won't be met. Likewise certain negative entities will establish mirrors that deflect your spiritual light, gifts, or love to them, thereby stealing this energy from you and keeping it from reaching the desired source.

Gray: hidden, occult, cloudy. Gray is not bad. When spun through our energetic boundaries, it can hide us from predators or others who wish us ill. Too much gray can indicate that we are trying to hide something or that someone is hiding something from us.

Black: absorbs, depresses, oppresses. On the positive side, black will hide us and provide us room and space to breathe, think, and be. It is a magical color, cancelling out previous thoughts and events so we can exist solely in the present. Black also erases, cancels outs, and makes secret. But manipulative entities or people might wrap us in black to keep us under wraps, unable to access our power.

Negative Dark Green: This is a unique green known to the ancient Egyptians. Despite being called *negative* dark green, it is a positive color. It is a spiritual carrier wave, able to convey information and healing energy from the spiritual realms into this one. To call it, simply focus on the Divine and the angelic messengers that bring all good things.

Gold: "God power," higher good, harmony, idealism. Gold creates necessary changes instantly. It is always good. It is the divine color of creation, transmutation, alchemy, and transformation. But be wary. If we use it, we must be ready for divine will to assert and our own to take a back seat.

Centerfield: The Chakras and Your Energetic Boundaries

Your energetic boundaries, or auric fields, are only one of three parts of your energetic anatomy, the subtle or spiritual body that composes the reality underneath the obvious physical reality. The others are your energy channels (or meridians) and your chakras. The latter are closely related to your auric fields and, hence, your energetic boundaries.

Chakras are energy centers that manage the inside of your body. Although some of the chakras extend into your energetic fields, they are located primarily within your body, and each chakra locks into the body through a major endocrine gland. Because the chakras regulate different physical, emotional, mental, and spiritual concerns, they often hold issues that affect your boundaries.

Each chakra is partnered with a specific layer of the auric field, which responds to a chakra's messages to determine what energies can come into your energetic system and which must stay out. Your boundaries, therefore, reflect what's occurring in your chakras, which is why it can be helpful to track an energetic-boundary issue back to its related chakra or chakra region. This section covers the basics about the chakras and provides a few powerful techniques for diagnosing, cleansing, and repairing your boundaries via these energy centers.

I work with a twelve-chakra system, which, like your energetic boundaries, can be divided into four categories: physical, emotional, mental, and spiritual. Organized according to these levels, the following list gives each chakras by name, color, location (both physical area and ruling endocrine gland), the bodily functions and other life functions it governs, and age at which it develops and locks in beliefs, programs, and patterns. All of these details can help you work with and heal your energetic boundaries.

The spiritual chakras include the two main spiritual chakras located within the body, the sixth and seventh, as well as four of the

Category	Number	Color	Body area/endocrine gland	Primary functions	Age of development
Physical Chakras	1st	Red	Hips/adrenals	Physical safety, security, sexuality, primary needs, money, excretory organs, genitals, hips, physical intuitions	Womb to 6 months
	10th	Brown	Underground/bones	Connection to nature, genes linking to ancestors, feet, legs, environmental intuition	Preconception and 35 to 42 years
Emotional Chakras	2nd	Orange	Abdomen/testes and ovaries	Feelings, creativity, mercy, intestines, sexual organs, feeling empathy	6 months to 2½ years
	3rd	Yellow	Solar plexus/pancreas	Thoughts, beliefs, power, work success, digestive health, mental empathy	2½ to 4½ years
Relational Chakras	4th	Green	Heart/heart	Love, relationships, care, healing, heart, lungs, chest, breasts, relational empathy	4½ to 6½ years
	5th	Blue	Throat/thyroid	Communication, truth, guidance, speaking, throat, jaws, teeth, verbal empathy, channeling	6½ to 8½ years
Spiritual Chakras	6th	Purple	Forehead/pituitary	Vision, strategy, futuring, eyes, body image, clairvoyance	8½ to 14 years
	7th	White	Top of head/pineal	Spirituality, purpose, link to the Divine, enlightenment, higher learning, sleep, moods, prophecy	14 to 21 years
	8th	Black and silver	1 inch over head/thymus	Shamanism, time travel, access to the Akashic Records, soul issues, immune system	21 to 28 years
	9th	Gold	1 foot over head/diaphragm	Harmony, soul programs, the path to loving power, breath	28 to 35 years, preconception
	11th	Rose	Around body, connective tissue	Command of natural and supernatural forces	42 to 49 years
	12th	Clear	Around entire auric field	Reflects personal spirit and spiritual gifts and in 32 secondary points within the body	49 to 56 years

Centerfield: *The Chakras and Your Energetic Boundaries* five out-of-body chakras that link our spiritual and physical natures. The other out-of-body chakra, the tenth, is primarily physical in its effects and, thus, one of the physical chakras.

When we reach age fifty-six, the chakra development begins recycling. We revisit the first chakra between ages fifty-six and sixty-three, the second chakra between sixty-three and seventy, the third chakra between seventy and seventy-seven, and the fourth chakra between seventy-seven and eighty-four.

There are thousands of ways you can use chakra knowledge to create and heal your energetic boundaries. Here are a few of the most useful, powerful, and easy ways.

For diagnosing. Most of us seek assistance because we're experiencing challenging symptoms, and we want to create better lives. To figure out which energetic boundary to work on, psychically examine your chakras to select which one hosts the problem. Having money problems? That's a first-chakra issue. As this chakra lies within the physical energetic domain, you can simultaneously work on your first chakra and physical boundaries. Dealing with feet issues? That's a tenth-chakra issue, which is also related to your physical boundaries.

For cleansing. The same techniques for clearing your energetic boundaries will work on your chakras. If you're working on money issues, you can use the tips provided in the physical-energetic-boundary section of chapter 7 and work directly on the first chakra. For instance, you can set an intention to cleanse your first chakra of others' money issues and program this intention into a stone.

For healing. Healing the related chakra gets to the heart of the issue affecting an energetic boundary. Use the "Uncovering Your Storyline" technique to find the reason this chakra and its related boundary are distorted. Searching for that moment or experience that explains the problem? Look at the column listing the age at which each chakra develops. Money issues? You might need to traipse through time to your in-utero experience or early infancy. Relationship issues? Walk into your heart and those first school days, and you might discover your answer. Again, the same healing processes that apply to the related energetic boundary will help heal your chakras.

Working with Sound, Shapes, and Numbers

For thousands of years, healers around the globe have understood that we are made of vibrating frequencies. Sounds, shapes, and numbers represent or hold vibrations that can help cleanse and heal any of our four energetic fields.

Ideally, we want to expose ourselves to frequencies that attune to our personal harmonic, the essence of our spirit. Our energetic boundaries should welcome the vibrations that suit us and deflect or transmute those that don't. If our energetic boundaries are healthy, they'll let in the energies that create work, monetary, relational, and physical ease. Energies that suit our true selves provide nourishment and healing through a process called resonance. If our boundaries are distorted, they'll keep out the positive harmonic energies and let in the discordant ones. This is the formula for dis-ease in any or all areas of our life.

I want to introduce you to the basics of using sound, shapes, and numbers to create boundary wellness. Many of the boundary-enhancing techniques described in chapters 5 through 9 will incorporate this information.

Sound Healing: The Songs of the Gods

Sound, considered a mechanical wave, is able to penetrate the fields around us and produce near-instant effects in the body. Sounds that resonate with our true selves support our spiritual path and everyday life.

Conversely, sounds that fail to attune to our real selves detract from our lives and can even create disease.

There is considerable research proving the healing benefit of sound. One particular article, "The Healing Power of Sound," by Lia Scallon, does a splendid job summarizing research by well-known authors, including Don Campbell, Dr. John Beaulieu, Chris Neill, David Hulse, Steven Halpern, and others.[3] One of the primary sound researchers, Scallon notes, was French physician Dr. Alfred Tomatis, who figured out that the ear is the first organ to link with our brain's developing neurological systems and that we can hear by our second trimester in utero. Interference in the development of this connection—and, conceivably, exposure to the negative or cruel thoughts or words of our parents or others outside our mother's womb—can create listening, learning, and emotional disabilities later in life. Tomatis also discovered that the two sound experiences that provided our in-utero selves with the most joy and subsequent health were the higher pitches of mother's voice and the music of Mozart. The latter, as shown by researcher Don Campbell, stimulates the creative and motivation sections of the brain.

One of the problems with modern life is that we are constantly subjected to lower tones, which create dissonance in our bodies and cause stress and disease. The high vibrations of nature can counteract these disturbing vibrations, stimulating a field around our head that resonates at eight cycles per second, which matches the electromagnetic frequency of the earth itself. This hertzian state is the same as the state achieved during deep relaxation or meditation.

These and other discoveries tell us that music is a vital instrument for building our energetic fields. Any maternal and loving song, sound, or tone stirs instant healing within our body and helps sustain our energetic fields. The music of Mozart, Bach, Brahms, Chopin, and other classical composers has been shown to improve our social, emotional, mental, and physical well-being. As it enters our energetic field, it nourishes these important spiritual borders. As well, exposing ourselves

Boundary	Chakra/Field	Hindu Syllable	Octave/Note	Boundary Shift Results
Physical	1st	Lam (pronounced "lum")	C	Promotes physical health; encourages the release of addictions; attracts money, work, positive primary relationships, and patience
Emotional	2nd	Vam (pronounced "vum")	D	Helps us feel our feelings, release them from our body, and mature them toward joy; promotes sensuality and creativity; promotes intestinal and sexual health; enhances the vibration of purity and a "return to innocence"
	3rd	Ram (pronounced "rum")	E	Enhances mental clarity; promotes success; increases mental and personal power; improves digestion; increases spiritual radiance and self-confidence
Relational	4th	Yam (pronounced "yum")	F	Attracts love and positive relationships; improves breast, lung, and heart health; increases contentment
	5th	Ham (pronounced "hum")	G	Enhances communication ability and the ability to speak our truth; attracts guidance; improves thyroid health; enhances hearing; enables control of eating and promotes healthy food choices; activates the power of unity in all life areas
Spiritual	6th	Om (pronounced with a long "o" sound)	A	Enhances vision and eye health; improves our connection with our higher self; enables us to see the future and possibilities; improves self-image; builds spiritual foundation for all parts of life, physical and otherwise
	7th	None	B	Helps us find and connect with our purpose; enhances our connection with the Divine; brings balance to all life areas; enhances higher brain functions, such as learning and thinking; encourages embodiment of our spirit in everyday life

Sound Healing: *The Songs of the Gods*

to natural sounds enhances our connection with the electromagnetic field of the earth, bolsters our energetic fields, and stimulates relaxing brain waves.

Different parts of the body and different energy fields respond to different sounds. The ancients often linked particular tones and syllables to the chakras. As explained under "Centerfield: The Chakras and Your Energetic Boundaries," when you nurture a chakra vibrationally, you nourish its related energy field, or energetic boundary.

The facing list matches the seven in-body chakras and their related energetic fields with two different sounds you can chant, tone, think, or hum to produce boundary shifts. One sound is the Hindu syllable associated with that chakra. The other sound is the octave tone most typically associated with that chakra. Also provided is the shift you can expect in the related boundary by using these sounds, including the virtue that is added. (I have provided considerable tips on using these sounds for physical healing; know that you can employ the same techniques for all life areas.)

Using Shapes to Reshape Boundaries

In the fifth century BC, Pythagoras insisted that sound produces geometry, that in between all shapes lies music, and that music creates shape and form.[4] In 1787, Ernst Chladni produced visible structures from sound waves, a phenomenon furthered centuries later by Dr. Hans Jenny, who oscillated pulses that, in turn, formed beautiful shapes on sand.

This process of transforming sound to shape is now called cymatics. It is the basis for research by Japanese physicist Masaru Emoto, who sent positive and negative messages into water and then photographed the way the water's molecular crystals changed in response. He found that positive words, such as love and faith; positive messages; and beautiful, harmonious music, such as a Mozart symphony, transform water crystals into lovely, hexagonal shapes, while negative messages, such as

"You make me sick," warp the structure of a water molecule. Based on his research, Emoto believes that water crystals in their highest form create hexagonal shapes, and they create these shapes when they are attuned with nature or spiritual truths. When exposed to lower sounds or ideas, they are literally out of tune and, therefore, appear shapeless and ugly. (To see Emoto's photographs documenting the water crystals' changed appearance, check out either of his books, *The Hidden Messages of Water* and *The Miracle of Water*, or his website, Welcome to the World of Water, hado.net.)

Cymatics and Emoto's research show that sounds and shapes are intimately connected. Like sounds, shapes can produce healing effects in our energetic fields. A shape is a pattern. The shape regulates the energy flow around and within a boundary and tells your body's electrical energy how to respond to stimuli. By shifting the energy of your field, you change the energy and health of your body and mind.

Research conducted by Egyptian architect Dr. Ibrahim Karim over thirty years has demonstrated the amazing effects of geometrical shapes. One study, led by the Egyptian National Research Centre, showed that simple shapes could stop the replication of bacteria. Most frequently, he surrounded the subjects of his experiments with materials formed into various shapes, such as triangles, squares, or circles; he has also created an extensive index of thought-provoking shapes that integrate other shapes, such as spirals and lines, each of which promotes different changes, such as the healing of heart disease or the growth of new cells in the body. Another project, evaluated by the Egyptian Department of Agriculture, found that chickens grew healthier and faster in an environment energy balanced by Karim's methods, which included the use of shapes, than they did when antibiotics and growth hormones were given to the birds. And Professor Peter Mols of Wageningen Agriculture University in Holland discovered that Karim's methods, labeled as BioGeometry™ energy methods, could be used in place of pesticides and artificial fertilizers to grow healthy organic crops.[5]

You can empower any of your four boundaries by visualizing a shape around it. You can also meditate on and/or psychically view the shape of your overall field and the shapes within your field. Then you can visualize shapes being inserted into your energy fields for various outcomes. Wearing clothes that incorporate specific shapes can produce desired effects in your physical energetic field, as can hanging pictures or decorating your space with items that are or use the applicable shape. Various other techniques for using shapes to help our energy boundaries will be described in chapters 5 through 9.

Though there are hundreds of different shapes in this world, there are three basic ones. Through my studies years ago with four teachers—two Siberian shamans, one of whom was a medical doctor; a Peruvian shaman; and Serge King, a Hawaiian kahuna—I learned these three basic shapes and their meanings.

Square. A square is the symbol of stability and strength. The corners contain the most active energy and stimulate reactions when they touch something (or someone). If you want to manifest something, visualize a square with the request within it and the outside corners touching all parts of that bigger image. For instance, I recently needed an additional $25,000 to help finance my son's college education. My desire to help was matched with an equal desire to encourage him to take responsibility for paying the money back, which qualifies as a boundary issue. I also wanted to make sure I held my boundaries with his father, so I didn't do all the work. (I'm well aware that I'm a good mule.)

I imagined a positive outcome in my mind without picturing the process. For a few days, I went to bed picturing the money at the school, with both myself and my son's father as the conduits for it getting there, but my son's name as the note-holder on a loan. I viewed this image inside of a box and pictured the edges of the box reaching outer space. I knew the Divine would have to create the path; I wasn't innovative enough to do so. Within a few days, an entirely unexpected outcome emerged. A well-off, kind friend of my son's father helped, as did my mother, and my son signed a loan. All of my needs were met.

Inserting a square (or a rectangle) into an energetic field will protect, ground, and stabilize you. If, when you psychically examine your field, you find a small square lodged within it, see if there is a substance within the shape; whatever you find within the square is something that you are storing, repressing, or hiding. We often conceal feelings, beliefs, memories, others' energies, parts of our soul, and dreams. Repress enough feelings, and you'll create depression.

Gifts and abilities are often stored inside or near the chakra that reflects them. Are you constantly shy of money? You may have repressed a manifesting gift in your first chakra. Do you have a hard time achieving success at work? You might need to access your third-chakra gift of channeling the power necessary to establish and maintain your boundaries.

In a nutshell, the chakra gifts are these: manifesting (first chakra); creativity and compassion (second chakra); administrative abilities and mental acuity (third chakra); healing and relating with others (fourth chakra); communicating, including orating, writing, and musicality (fifth chakra); visioning and strategy (sixth chakra); creating good out of bad and ministering to others (seventh chakra); shamanic healing and mystical journeying (eighth chakra); creating harmony where there is dissension (ninth chakra); applying natural elements and forces for good, such as nature-based healing (tenth chakra); commanding natural and supernatural forces, and serving as a leader (eleventh chakra). Your twelfth chakra contains gifts personal to you.

Warped squares, or those with broken sides or cut-off corners, signify incomplete protection or boundary violations. We need to repair these squares so they will resume their correct purpose.

I often visualize a square around my house or car, adding an extra blessing of protection.

Circle. A circle promotes relationships, harmony, and connection. A circle envisioned between two or more people (or living beings) invites an exchange of energy. Check the energy. If it's bright and loving, the swap is positive. If it's negative or dark, the exchange is hurting you and creating a syndrome.

Establishing a circle around ourselves, through any or all of the energetic boundaries, will emphasize wholeness and send an energy of love to others. It will also create a "sacred circle," a protected space that only love can enter. You can also psychically draw a circle around a part of you, such as an inner child or an idea, and keep it secure.

If you constantly pick up energy from others or the environment, go a step further and imagine a circle (a silver one is best) drawn under your feet and moving everywhere you move. This circle will cleanse the ground you walk on and shimmer upward through your entire field, deflecting negative energies.

A broken circle sandwiched in your energy field or extending between you and someone else indicates a broken relationship and, potentially, betrayal or heartache for you. If you fix the circle, you fix the relationship. But before you do, make sure you want the relationship back; it might be in both your and the other person's best interest to dissolve the circle entirely.

Smaller circles within a field or in the body might be holding your relationship issues, your true feelings about a relationship, or a part of you that you don't want to reveal. If you find a circle within an energy boundary, check to see what substances or energies are inside.

A spiral is a form of a circle. Counterclockwise spirals bring energy out, so they can be used to take energies away from our field. Clockwise spirals bring energy in, so they can be used to attach us to sources of positive energies.

Triangle. Related to the pyramid, a triangle represents creativity, mental activity, and connection with the Divine. A triangle will intensify or amplify energy, so be careful about what you energetically put into it. It can increase debt or abundance, disease or healing.

Use a triangle around your body to promote activity and growth. Say you want to write a book or a report. Take the nugget of your idea, insert it in a triangle, and watch your creativity explode.

Triangles can be inserted into any boundary or place within it that needs healing to promote change and transformation. A broken or spotted triangle indicates a misfiring, a place where you're not thinking logically or appropriately. A broken triangle connecting you and someone else, a job, your finances, or a project can indicate that you aren't accurately perceiving what's occurring or that your interactions are off and need to be fixed.

Cross or X: An X is a form of a cross, symbolizing the magical properties of a crossroads. When seen in a cross form, such as in a T shape, the cross represents protection. An X also obstructs or blocks. It bars the doorway to negativity and protects from marauders, visible and invisible. Depending on the reason it's present, it can also block wisdom, truth, and love.

Consider the use of the swastika in Nazi Germany. By reversing the flow of the cross and making it more an X than a T, the Nazis erased their followers' free will and inserted a message in their energetic boundaries. When I see an X on or in someone's energy field, I know that they have an energy marker telling the world to mistreat them in some way. These imprints can keep us from meeting a mate, making money, getting a job, or healing. They often indicate the presence of a syndrome, because energy markers uphold repetitive energetic patterns. It's important to erase these energy markers to free yourself from old patterns.

Transforming Your World with Numbers

The most learned of the ancients believed that numbers represented the fundamental principles of the universe, providing the only true explanations of the enigmas of reality. Today, many scientists are drawing upon the workings of mathematics, frequencies, geometry, and other numerically based approaches to explain healing, create new therapeutic modalities, and solve the puzzles of medicine. This concept is part of an esoteric and mystical lore called numerology, which is the study of numbers for practical application. Cultures across time and space have reduced reality to numerical equations. Even today, practitioners derive numerical formulas using birth dates, astrological figures, the letters in names, and other ideas to explain personalities, life lessons, soul purposes, health problems and solutions, and relationship and partnership potential, as well as to forecast future events.

I love working with numbers in relation to boundaries. The most helpful way of applying numbers to boundaries is to visualize a chosen number imprinted on the outside of a weak or distorted boundary or in the area most affected by a syndrome. This number will now infuse the field with its frequency and effect a change. For instance, if you keep taking on others' feelings, inserting a 1 into your emotional boundary will help you put yourself first.

Following are some of the meanings of the numbers 1 through 10, plus some powerful numbers above 10:

1: Initiates and begins; invokes the Creator; brings your needs to a conclusion and puts yourself first.

2: Represents pairing and duality; balances relationships; creates healthy liaisons; shares power.

3: Reflects optimism; the number of creation, it brings a beginning and an end together; ends chaos.

4: Signifies foundation and stability; provides grounding; achieves balance.

5: Promotes and progresses; creates a space for decision-making; provides the ability to go in any direction at will.

6: The number of service; indicates the presence of light and dark, good and evil, and the choices made between these.

7: Represents the divine principle; opens us for love and grace, erasing doubts about the divine path.

8: The symbol of power and infinity; establishes recurring patterns and illuminates karma; can be used to erase old and entrenched patterns or syndromes.

9: Represents change and harmony; eliminates the old and opens us to a new cycle; can erase evil.

10: Signifies building and starting over. The number of physical matter, it can create heaven on earth.

11: Represents inspiration; releases personal mythology; opens us to divine powers; erases self-esteem issues.

12: Signifies mastery over human drama; accesses own divine self, but still encompasses humanity; excellent for forgiveness.

22: For success in anything you do.

33: For teaching and accepting our own wisdom; invokes bravery and discipline.

Here are a few suggestions for using the numbers in your energy fields to transform your energy syndromes.

- Use a 1 for victim syndromes (Vampire, Mule, Healer's) that cause you to put others first or take on their energy.
- Employ a 2 if you want to partner with someone, but not give away your power, such as when you're afflicted with the Healer's or Vampire Syndrome.
- Try a 3 if you're dealing with the No-Boundary or Environ Syndromes and are constantly in chaos.
- Use a 4 if you are too often pulled on by others and need to ground yourself. This number benefits all the syndromes.
- Utilize a 5 if you are overworked, such as in the Mule Syndrome,

and need to perceive different directions. A 5 is also good for breaking the repetitive cycles of Paper Doll Syndrome.

- Call on a 6 if you're afflicted by evil, such as through the Psychic-Sensitive Syndrome, or to choose higher service instead of the chaos of the No-Boundary Syndrome. A 6 is also good for helping those with Paper Doll Syndrome face and release the unconscious benefit of a repetitive pattern and find a more joyful way to respond to life.
- Try a 7 for any syndrome because it will invoke divine assistance.
- Employ an 8 to break or erase cycles caused by the Paper Doll Syndrome.
- Use a 9 with any other number to state you are done with a syndrome.
- Insert a 10 to boost your new intention.
- Formulate an 11 to access spiritual guidance and transform the storyline that established the syndrome.
- When working on your spiritual boundaries, try a 12 to support forgiveness.
- Add a 22 to a boundary to help achieve success.
- Use a 33, especially for the No-Boundary and Psychic-Sensitive Syndromes, to open to our own wisdom.

Energizing Your Boundaries with Stones and Metals

Stones, including precious and semiprecious gemstones, carry vibration and can be programmed, using intention, to hold and reflect specific needs, goals, and desires. Their vibrations interact with our body because many of our organic systems are made of cells that form crystal lattices, including our bones[6] and parts of our connective tissue and neurology, which we'll discuss in chapter 5. This means that energy held within or sent through a crystal transmits directly into our bodily cells, especially those that are crystalline in shape. We are perfect "senders and receivers" for each other. We can, therefore, use stones to carry our intention and transfer this intention into our body to support our objectives, including cleansing, healing, and sustaining our boundaries.

Setting an intention into stone is a powerful method for change because stones can "remember" your intention longer than your body can. The crystal structures within stones are more stable than those in our body;[7] therefore, they can serve as templates, reprogramming our intentions into our bodies when we slip up. You can program or pray a request into the stone and rely on that stone to act like a coach to keep you on track.

I've even used the power of stones to regrow physical tissue. Years ago, I was physically attacked, and my back was a mess. I used various crystals, one for each chakra, to carry healing into the related parts of my spine. I actually prayed into the stones and then set them in water, which I then drank. My back healed completely, with no physical care, within seven days.

What makes stones this powerful? Energy. Science is proving that everything in this world vibrates and contains information. Different stones are organically able to hold, carry, and transfer different types of information. Some of the most enticing research on this subject was officiated by IBM researcher Marcel Vogel, who was fascinated by the power of crystals after discovering a subtle energetic connection between beings, including people and plants. For instance, he was able to demonstrate that a shift in his breath and thoughts created a response in plants that were eight feet, eight hundred feet, and eight thousand miles away. Until his death in 1991, Vogel worked to discover the healing and practical properties of crystals, which he saw as elements that responded to, stored, and generated subtle energies that could provide healing and other practical applications. Of his many discoveries, he found that he could spin water around a tuned crystal and change the characteristics of water, converting the water into an information-storage system.[8] Our bodies are 70 percent water; different crystals can literally reprogram the information in our fluids and, by extension, our bodies. Vogel also discovered that crystals grew from light that first formed into geometric shapes, which then served as the template for the emerging crystals. But the crystals grew differently when interacting with humans and human thoughts; the crystal formation reflected the data they were exposed to.

Vogel demonstrated that crystals are quite complicated. They respond to "carrier waves" or, you could say, sensory and subtle thoughts, and amplify them according to the cut, size, color, and type of crystals. In his opinion, however, the ultimate carrier wave was love: programmed into a stone with intention, love creates the most beneficial effects during our interaction with a stone.[9]

Because stones convey energy so powerfully, I've included suggestions for using different stones throughout chapters 5 to 9. Amethyst, for instance, repels negativity and amplifies our personal vision. It is highly useful for deflecting would-be vampires or psychic attacks and keeping us on path. Pink quartz conveys love and lifts us to the highest level of thought and deed. I've skipped the techniques usually taught in working with stones, such as how to clear, cleanse, and choose a stone, because I think we've only to select, carry, and intentionalize our stones with love to have them serve all concerned. Using the Spirit-to-Spirit format and the intention exercise already offered will ensure you use these important objects properly.

Metals also convey energy. In Ayurveda, an East Indian science that is thousands of years old, all metals can be used to heal, strengthen, and protect. Copper, for instance, reduces fat (as in the tire around the waist); gold boosts our intelligence; silver reduces inflammation; and iron improves circulation. These metals are carefully purified and produced so they don't damage our bodies and are usually worn, not ingested.[10]

For our energetic boundaries, it's enough to understand the core benefits of gold and silver, the two most prevalent and basic metals. Gold attracts and absorbs; silver deflects, but also transfers energy into us in a usable and safe form. It's enough to simply wear these metals or colors. In the following chapters, I provide advice about which of the two metals to wear.

Connecting to the Universal Field: A Technique for All Concerns

No matter your energetic issue, here's a concept that can open you to almost instant support and healing: *you are surrounded by a living and unconditionally loving Universal Field.*

Scientists have spent hundreds of years searching for a connection between natural law, which is uniform, and quantum physics, which is less than orderly. (Albert Einstein's unified field theory postulates that the two are indeed connected.) Subtle or psychic energy, which is what this book is largely concerned with, is better explained by quantum physics, but we live our normal lives in the natural world. Our energy centers, channels, and fields interconnect these two different types of being. At the highest possible level, these seemingly different worlds already interact, and under divine decree, we are to benefit from both realms. By linking with that highest level, the Universal Field, where the physical and quantum interact, we can cut through the problems creating chaos in our energetic fields, as well as other problems affecting us, and open to immediate assistance.

One of the reasons it's so hard to make real changes is that energetic fields beyond ours affect us. Call your own energetic fields your personal fields. Around these are family fields, or miasmic fields, and then mor- phogenetic fields, which connect you to the rest of the human family. Around these are countless other fields, including cultural, nature-based, and even spiritual fields, such as fields holding the entire history of the earth and the heavens. We can't even number the fields generated by other individuals and beings—visible and invisible—with which we might interact. How do we clear through this myriad of complexity and just get *help*—as in, divine help?

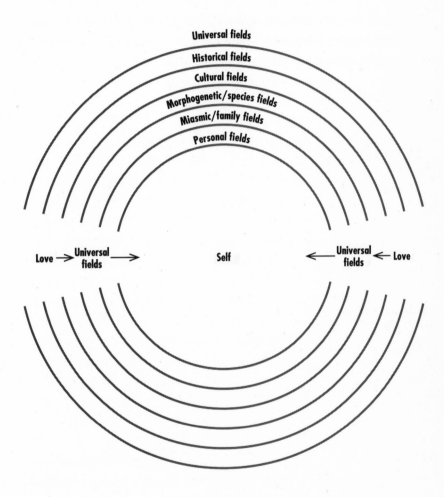

Figure D. *The Universal Field contains love and grace generated from the Divine. This divine power can cut through all energetic fields affecting us, and it can deliver love and healing.*

Surrounding and interlaced within all these fields is the Universal Field, which I believe is the energetic field of the Divine, the Creator, Christ, the Holy Spirit, the Great Mother, Allah—whatever you call the highest power of all. Just by asking, such as when we use the Spirit-to-Spirit meditation or set an intention, we can open to divine power and bolster our own healing powers. Other tools, including the healing streams of grace discussed in chapter 3, also provide a direct connection to the Universal Field and divine assistance. Opening to the Creator's love is the best way to protect ourselves and access the energies that can nourish us, body, mind, and spirit.

Healing Our Bodies by Healing Our Boundaries

Eventually you will come to understand that love heals everything, and love is all there is.

GARY ZUKAV

This walk called life teaches us how to live with pain, suffering, injury, and trauma, but also how to create wholeness within the states that leave us broken. This is the meaning of healing: the recognition of wholeness no matter what is occurring in our body.

The job of our energetic boundaries is to support our body, mind, and soul in being as whole in the material world as they are spiritually. Unfortunately, many of the energies that cause illness, tension, trauma, mental imbalance, and other distresses enter through our energetic boundaries.

What can we do for our physical, emotional, relational, and spiritual boundaries to ensure ourselves an optimum level of health and happiness? In this chapter, I share some of the scientific research that shows how bolstering our energetic boundaries can create wellness. I also share the various ways we can allay the seven syndromes that drain and strain our health.

The Science of Our Energetic Boundaries and Health

Our energetic boundaries are the first line of defense in regard to our health. If working correctly, they'll deflect or transmute energies that can make us sick. They'll also release and cleanse us of physical and psychic toxins, assuring us a healthier immune system and better overall health. But, as explained by well-respected researcher James Oschman, PhD, once our energetic field starts to sputter and work at a less-than-optimum level, our bodily system becomes overtaxed and has to assume the field's job. This depletes our body, leading to cancer, diabetes, allergies, chronic fatigue syndrome, sleep issues, migraines, cardiovascular problems, infections, adrenal stress, epilepsy, weight issues, and asthma, in addition to mental, behavioral, and emotional challenges, such as aggressiveness, anxiety, criminal activity, depression, memory issues, and accidents.[1]

Oschman explains that these pulsing, oscillating sets of electromagnetic and etheric fields operate like skin, protecting us from energetic phenomena, including external EMF fields, such as fluorescent lighting, radiation, sunspots, and other dangerous rays. They help us communicate our intentions to the world and assimilate the information we're receiving. Through our various fields, we interrelate with the people around us, and how we relate to people is a key predictor of good health. Our personal fields also connect with the magnetic field of the earth, which in turn, balances and soothes our internal systems. When our fields are damaged, we are simply unable to assimilate or transmute negative energies.[2]

As you might imagine, working with these fields can make an incredible difference in our ability to heal from disease. We can even diagnose disease by examining our energy fields. One particular investigator, Leonard Konikiewics from the Polyclinic Medical Centre in Pennsylvania, used Kirlian photography to identify 16 out of 18 patients with cystic fibrosis from a sample of 140. He was also able to pick out 37 out of the 48 carriers of the gene.[3] Another well-known researcher, Dr. Thelma Moss, used Kirlian photography to accurately determine which of 200 rats were cancerous or not based on the energy emanating from their tails. Stomach cells revealed the signs of malignancy as fine white or gray granular shadows, whereas healthy tissue was more clear. Able to discern the diseased from the nondiseased rats, Moss performed a task that challenges today's medical diagnosticians. When the same Kirlian process was used on 6,000 Romanian soldiers, researchers found forty-seven tumors, compared to forty-one tumors discovered by normal methods.[4] Electronography, another process even more sophisticated than Kirlian photography, has been used to differentiate healthy from nonhealthy tissue among more than 6,000 people in studies in Bucharest, performed by Romanian scientists at the Labor Protection and Hygiene Centre.[5]

Dr. David Sheinkin and his colleagues at Rockland State Hospital in New York have shown that this exciting ability to diagnose a disease state through our energy fields isn't limited to a certain type of disease. Sheinkin has studied patients with respiratory, gastrointestinal, and mental illnesses, and determined that the field is different with different diseases. Not only can we diagnosis illnesses, but we might also be able to predict and prevent them upon figuring out which energetic patterns describe which disease.[6]

Even relationships can be analyzed through energetic means. Using Kirlian photography, investigators have shown that the fields of close friends are brighter and more connected than those of strangers. The fields of people thinking loving thoughts or kissing are also bright and interconnected, while those thinking unpleasant thoughts are separate. And when we are friendly, people notice, because our coronas are bigger than those of strict people, who have narrow fields.[7]

Our fields are truly our connection with the world, but as Oschman said, what can keep us well can also make us sick. Just as we can catch the flu from another person, so can we catch health problems through our energetic fields, because our energetic boundaries are part of a giant crystal network incorporating our connective tissue and our nervous and cardiovascular systems—a fibrous web spreading through our bodies.

Physician Robin Kelly notes that our energy channels, or meridians, lie within our connective tissue. (Many researchers testify to this fact.) This tissue conducts electricity through collagen molecules arranged in a triple helical pattern. These collagen molecules conduct electricity through water molecules that lie on their cellular surfaces; the water allows them to conduct electricity the same way that crystals do, and the collagen molecules create a sort of cytoskeleton in our muscle, bones, and organs. This connective tissue acts like a receiver and sender of subtle energy, the invisible matter that comes in through and emanates from our energetic boundaries.[8]

Our heart is the largest generator and receiver of this subtle energy, passing the energy through our cardiovascular system and into two different nervous systems: (1) our primary nervous system, which includes our spine and brain, and (2) a secondary nervous system, so named by researcher Dr. Björn Nordenström and consisting of our connective tissue and our meridians. Each heart pulse sends two and a half watts of electricity through our connective tissues via our blood, the cells of which swirl like vortexes in the shape of a torus, a somewhat spherical doughnut. Even one ion, or charged particle, thrown in this mix generates a powerful magnetic field.

Technically, the shapes of our electrical fields and magnetic fields are different. Our magnetic fields look more like the torus, mirroring our twirling blood cells. A torus is a magical figure. It looks like a doughnut, but the only part of it that exists is the outside surface. Instead of a hole in the middle, there is a vacuum. This void begs a question of quantum physicists: are we dealing with a shape that entices subatomic particles or waves out of other dimensions? The torus-shaped field emerging from the heart is so intense that it stretches to the rim of the universe.

If you cut a doughnut, you end up with two or more pieces. If you cut a torus, you still have only one piece. This fluidity establishes a uniform magnetic field generated by a single pulse of the heart, even though the slightest shift internally alters the spin of our blood vessels and, therefore, our heart field.

Our heart's magnetic field is stronger than the magnetic field generated by any other part of us. Not only does it extend continually through space, but it also forms a torus shape around us.[9] Once the magnetic field merges with our electrical field, which is produced by the electrical energy pulsing from our cells in a wavelike fashion, the combined field, called the electromagnetic field, stretches beyond us (as does the magnetic field alone). The electromagnetic field also forms a sort of womb, which constantly bathes us with our own heart energy.

The first and most important heart energy we were ever exposed to was our mother's. When pregnant with us, she generated an electromagnetic field that was between ten and a hundred times stronger than any emanating from the outside world.[10] This protective field could be considered our first energetic boundary, one that increases in power and strength if fed by love and decreases in less loving circumstances. When amplified, this field can guard us from external EMF fields, such as from power lines or radiation, others' negativity, and other dark influences. I propose that some of our health problems, as well as problems in other life areas, originate from receiving inadequate protection in utero, such as might occur if our mom didn't want us, wasn't loved by others, or didn't love herself.

As discussed, our magnetic fields are toruslike, while our electrical fields can be measured as pulses that vary in length, breadth, and intensity. At some point, however, we have to stop differentiating between our heart's magnetic and electrical fields, for they combine and change with each heartbeat. Extending far beyond our physical body, this EMF field communicates our own energetic information to the world and receives energetic information from people, places, objects—everything—drawing it back into our bodies.[11]

The information our fields pick up can instruct our genes, determine cell differentiation, and shift our health, because that information is sensitive to our DNA. At every level, our energetic fields act like radio waves, allowing us to touch others' EMF fields and exchange energy. This means that our energy boundaries are models of perception and communication and vehicles for determining and creating our health. In fact, the healthier our heart rhythm is, the healthier our body is. Studies have shown that a coherent or harmonious heart, which is produced when we center on positive emotion and spiritual truths, can prevent infection, improve arrhythmia, and help heal mitral-valve prolapse, congestive heart failure, asthma, diabetes, fatigue, autoimmune disorders, anxiety, depression, AIDS, and post-traumatic stress disorder (PTSD).[12] The most potent EMF generator, a loving heart, has the capacity to entrain or coordinate all bodily functions and organs, as well as our emotional, mental, and spiritual well-being, creating optimum physical health.[13] It ensures a heartbeat-to-heartbeat sharing of healing energy within ourselves and between us and others. It also establishes a protocol for all our energetic boundaries, instructing them to allow in only what supports our overall well-being and to keep out everything that could hurt us.

Healing Through Your Physical Boundaries: Your Red Field

Issues with the physical energetic field are usually caused by violations of touch—whether sexual, physical, or implied—or by witnessing such violations. Any significant trauma to the body or neglect of our basic needs can also rigidify, rip, or weaken our physical energetic boundary, which leads to any of the seven syndromes and any number of health conditions. Touch isn't always physical. A mean, cutting word or slew of insults qualifies as a physical violation because their energetic vibration can penetrate our physical boundary and injure our tissue.

As an example, I was conscious in my mother's womb before birth, and I can still remember the angry words exchanged between my mother and father. The sound waves from their "discussions" would spiral into my body and scorch my little self. I could both psychically perceive and physically feel these sounds. Everywhere those angry words hit me in utero, I've since had physical problems, including infections, allergies, and a heart arrhythmia. The arrhythmia was linked to alcohol. Until I was in my forties, I was plagued by an arrhythmia every night between 10 p.m. and midnight. I couldn't figure out the cause until I called my mother and a sibling and discovered that before I was born, my parents had drunk every night between these hours (and my relatives, including my mother, continue to drink during these hours). Once I uncovered my storyline, I was able to release the cord between my loved ones and myself and repair my physical (and emotional and relational) fields. The arrhythmia dissipated. In the end, I discovered that I was afflicted with the Healer's Syndrome. I was absorbing my parents' toxic energy and sending love to them in response, losing ground in my own body through this process.

If we're really struggling with a physical disorder, it's important to discover the root cause. Using the exercise "Uncovering Your Storyline" in chapter 4, you can search for the situation, person, word, phrase, or trauma that was the original violation and figure out which syndrome is affecting you. You might also want to probe for circumstances in which you should have been lovingly touched, held, or nurtured, but were not. Neglect also constitutes a violation. Once you find the source violation, it is important to forgive yourself for "allowing" the energetic injury to occur and recur. Under stress, we unconsciously do anything necessary to survive. The initial strategy seldom works long term, but we hold onto the pattern because it seemed to help, at least once. Forgiving ourselves for reacting in a way that hurts us, or perhaps others, isn't about accepting blame. It's about understanding our motive for establishing an energetic pattern. Once we forgive ourselves, the pattern dissipates. Then, when we're ready to also forgive the others involved, our job is done. The pattern usually disappears or can be treated.

To forgive others doesn't mean approving abuse. Instead, it means giving them back their energy, so they can deal with it and we no longer have to. There's a gift in every situation, every energy, good and bad. It's not for us to hold onto another's energy, even if it is dark and negative, for then that person can't open the gift contained within it.

I always return others' energies to their higher selves or pass it to the Divine to hand back, instead of directly sending it back to the others. I learned this lesson the hard way. I once had a client who had been suicidal for decades. We determined that her father's death wish had entered into her own system through her physical energetic field. We returned this wish to her father energetically, and he committed suicide the next day.

As a healer, I now send energy only through higher channels, so it will produce loving, rather than acute, effects. I ask the Divine to link each person involved to his or her own *healing stream of grace* (as introduced on page 65). Healing streams of grace surround and emanate from everyone. They are, essentially, energetic strands of love. The very fact that these exist means that we don't have to earn this grace/love, but only to allow it. Healing your energy boundaries requires only that you connect yourself to the healing stream intended for you; healing others or keeping them from penetrating your boundaries invites them to access their own healing streams of grace. I then ask the Divine to lift the negative or intrusive energy from my client and return it to the other's higher self. This process works for illnesses, death wishes, curses, cords, entity release, and all other concerns. Finally, I ask that my client receive the healing needed for both his or her body and physical energetic boundary.

Following are other tools that support health and healing through the physical energetic boundary.

Because our body responds to matter, I suggest programming your food and drink with intention. You can use the exercises for setting intention (in chapter 4) to perform this process. To rebuild your physical boundaries, bless your protein and mineral sources. The chakras related to the physical energetic boundary are highly physical and strengthening in nature; in terms of glands, you're dealing with your adrenals and bones. These systems require a lot of healthy protein and mineralization. If possible, eat only grass-fed, free-range animal meat, for these animals were more likely to have willingly, if unconsciously, given their lives in service. If you eat meat butchered and processed at commercial slaughterhouses and meat-packing plants, you'll pick up on the animals' fear and further injure your boundaries.

Liquid minerals and vitamins are easier to program with your intention than powdered or solid. Water, as discussed in our science lesson at the beginning of the chapter, conducts electricity. Minerals are ions and, as such, bolster your EMF field. Programming your minerals with an intention can boost your physical boundaries even more.

When assessing your physical energetic field intuitively, examine it for brown and red tones, as these are the colors that relate to the corresponding chakras. Check for blotchy or intrusive colors, missing spots, holes, gaps, or areas that are too thick or distended. Look, too, for cords and other energetic attachments. Then begin to repair your field on the screen in your mind, adding colors or taking away colors as needed.

Countless gemstones and metals can be programmed to improve your physical health and well-being. A favorite is the red ruby, considered a sacred stone for healing. The red color supports your first chakra, which generates the auric field in and just around your body. This first auric layer is one of two that comprises what I'm calling the physical energetic boundary. The tenth auric layer, which relates to the tenth chakra, is the other. Refer to the chart provided on page 104, in the section "Centerfield: The Chakras and Your Energetic Boundaries," to figure out which chakras and their related auric fields you are working on. You can then select metals and gemstones accordingly.

Some gemstones or metals that can be programmed with a healing intention for a chakra-diagnosed health concern include:

- First: Ruby
- Second: Coral
- Third: Citrine
- Fourth: Emerald
- Fifth: Sapphire
- Sixth: Amethyst
- Seventh: Diamond
- Eighth: Silver
- Ninth: Gold
- Tenth: Agate
- Eleventh: Rose quartz
- Twelfth: Personal to you

Using shapes, sounds, and numbers can significantly alter the vibration of your blood cells, which, as you recall, spin in toruslike fashion, generating our magnetic EMF fields. Change the physical intensity, direction, and momentum of the spin of your blood cells, and you alter the function of your physical energetic field. The most fundamental tones to use are the Hindu *Lam* and the octave note C. The primary number is a 1, although if you want to create change, try a 10. For shapes, I find it really helpful to use a spiral, which mimics the toruslike movement of our blood cells and magnetic fields.

Meditate upon the particular illness or condition that you're experiencing. Think back to your storyline and ask the Divine to help you perceive the energy (or syndrome) causing this problem. Now picture the negative or intrusive energy being lovingly set in a red, counterclockwise spiral and ask the Divine to send it out of your body and energetic field. Next, ask the Divine to bring beneficial energy into your field and body through a clockwise, gold spiral. Through this process, you release physical toxins and energies that aren't your own, and you invite in the higher harmonic of gold.

Miasms and Vivaxis cords are energetic issues pertaining to the physical energetic field, but not the other boundaries. Miasms are energetic patterns that interlace within our physical energy field. They relate to the tenth chakra, but are really programmed into the epigenetic chemicals that surround our genes and hold our ancestral memories, emotions, and experiences. A miasm is a disease pattern. We are born with certain patterns woven into our epigenetic soup and our physical energetic field (specifically into the part of it called a morphogenetic field, a certain type of energy field that links us to other people). This means our cells and our physical energetic boundary carry predispositions to both certain illnesses, physical or mental, and to certain traumatic events, such as accidents or abuse.

A Vivaxis is an umbilical-like cord that enters near our navel and attaches to the land we were born on or near. Through a Vivaxis, we send energy to and receive energy from this geographic site. This exchange can be life sustaining, unless the actual land has been poisoned. My Dutch-Canadian client, whose case I described in the Environ Syndrome section of chapter 3, is an example of someone sickened by a Vivaxis between her physical energetic boundary and the toxic farmstead where she was born.

We can spot miasms or inappropriate Vivaxis connections by intuitively reading our physical energetic boundary. A miasm will look like a net of interlocking and pulsing threads. We will see the same mesh around our genes in the epigenetic fluid, if we examine these spots as well. The other way to figure out if you have a miasm is by exploring your family tree. What disease patterns emerge? If there is a recurring theme—or worse, if you are affected by a family pattern—you are most likely dealing with a miasm. A miasm can set you up for any of the seven syndromes and itself is a vampiristic energy, feeding the ancestor (or spirit of the ancestor) who first established the pattern.

A Vivaxis will look like a cord, which appears to me like a garden hose, but much bigger. It will plug into the belly area and, like a tree trunk, will extend roots into your body. You can tell if it's poisoning you based on the coloration of the energy moving through these roots and into your body. If the energy is black, moldy brown, or a dirty red, you need to remove the Vivaxis, because the land is sending you negative energy. If your own energy is being sucked out as well, you are involved in a strange sort of Healer's Syndrome, serving the environment instead of a person or being.

Using a variation of the exercise "Uncovering Your Storyline," you can heal both energetic anomalies. In these cases, you are uncovering someone else's storyline instead of your own. For a miasm, ask the Divine to show you what happened to the ancestor that initiated the miasm. Usually there is a tragic event, such as a death, famine, loveless marriage, illness, or catastrophe, that created the pattern of illness. In the case of a Vivaxis, ask the land to tell you what happened to it and why it's seeking your help.

In both cases, ask the Divine to heal the original problem. Send healing to your ancestor, even if she or he has been deceased for centuries. If the pattern is still recurring, your ancestor's soul isn't at peace. Heal the ancestor and then accept the same healing for everyone in your bloodline, including yourself and your children. Insert a healing stream of grace where correction is needed in your genes, epigenetic chemicals, and physical energy field. For a Vivaxis, ask the Divine to heal the land by establishing a healing stream of grace for it. Ask for another healing stream of grace to replace the Vivaxis entering your system, inviting that love to fully cleanse and repair your body, chakras, and physical field. You can also transplant your Vivaxis to a new place, such as a favorite locale, your current home, or even in the heavens.

Healing Through Your Emotional Boundaries: Your Orange Field

Study after study shows that emotions can make us sick.

Any time we remain locked in a negative emotional pattern, we create the conditions for physical and mental illness. Chronically stuck feelings, especially those we don't deal with, damage our neuropeptides, the cells that promote communication between all parts of our body. We then become disconnected from ourselves, and that disconnection creates alienation and disease.

Excessive anger, for instance, when not expressed in harmless ways, leads to heart conditions, drug and alcohol addiction, headaches, domestic violence, and depression.[14] Incessant fear pumps cortisol and other hormones into the body, which leads to cellular breakdown and more stress. Unhealed sadness and grief is the formula for deep depression, and shame and guilt often underlie addictions.[15] And self-defeating beliefs, the other half of the emotional equation, set us up for stress and bad decisions.

There are four main ways of dealing with stress: fighting, fleeing, freezing, or feeling. Only the last leads to growth and transformation, but it's hard to get to your feelings and related beliefs if you're afflicted with any of the seven syndromes, especially those that cause you to absorb others' feelings. So the first step in healing the emotional field is to separate your own emotions from those of others. The second step is to use various energetic tools to restore your emotional boundaries. The third and ongoing step is to mature your feelings and beliefs.

How do you separate your emotions from those of others and release emotions that aren't your own? First peruse your emotional field. You want to perceive a healthy, sunny orange energy glow (because orange and yellow are the colors of your second and third chakras). Anything else, and you're most likely losing energy, taking on others' energy, missing necessary boundaries, and/or being invaded by outside forces.

When working with the emotional field, I usually track damage or distortions back to the chakras, especially if I'm perceiving off or missing colors. If orange is missing altogether, you might be repressing your own feelings. If your field is missing orange and has too much yellow, you might be dealing with autism-spectrum disorders or attachment disorders. Attention-deficit/hyperactivity disorder (ADHD) often involves a burned-out third chakra and an emotional boundary with too much yellow, which means you are absorbing too much information from outside of yourself. If there's also too little orange, you have too many thoughts and not enough feelings. For both situations, refer to chapter 9 and the discussion on crystal souls.

When checking your emotional field, also look specifically for damage contributing to syndromes. Gaping holes indicate the possibility of Vampire, Mule, or Healer's Syndromes. Cords and attachments can lead to Psychic-Sensitive and No-Boundary Syndromes. An overload of environmental information indicates Environ Syndrome. Repetitive symbols, images, or patterns are psychic signs of Paper Doll Syndrome. Determining what's going on will help you rebuild your emotional field.

Ask the Divine to replace any energies that aren't your own—whether these energies are emotional only, mental only, or a partnership of the two—with a healing stream of grace. (The Spirit-to-Spirit technique given in chapter 4 is a good way to separate and release others' emotional energies.) Request also that your own feelings and beliefs, those lodged in and pertinent to your spiritual self, become animate and accessible.

You might need a few days, weeks, or even months to integrate the changes. Sometimes we allow others' feelings to overshadow our own because we don't want to feel the pain of our feelings. (Not having to feel and deal with our own feelings is sometimes the payoff for establishing the energetic pattern of a syndrome.) If this process of change becomes intense, I recommend working with a therapist, especially one that uses energetic tools, such as EMDR (eye movement desensitization and reprogramming), regression, light-based or color therapy, sound therapy, or the acupuncture points to enable healing. Medical qi gong, an artful practice of moving the life energy through our body, is also extremely useful, as is receiving therapeutic bodywork, such as massage.

Now it's time to separate your feelings from your beliefs and mature them both. To mature our feelings and beliefs is to respect and follow the message inherent in them, so that they can lead us to joy. (See "The Messages Within Our Feelings and Beliefs.")

Psychically examine your emotional field for a visual representation of your feelings. Current or healthy anger is usually seen as red; sadness is blue; fear is yellow; disgust, the healthy version that suggests something or someone doesn't suit us, is a brilliant gray. Joy is bright orange or any version of a primary color that is clear and bright.

Any off color will indicate an emotional issue. Color distortions occur when we judge a feeling as bad, if someone else has done the same, or if we're holding another's energy. Old anger or someone else's anger will be dirty red, brown, or black. Black often indicates a form of depression. The closer we are to ebony, the more rage we have; rage is a combination of deep hurt, pain, and anger. Ignored or others' sadness appears as dark, moody blue. If we're losing our energy to someone else, the leaking area might be light blue.

Long-standing fear will appear as an erratic, frenzied yellow oscillation. The yellow will be brownish if it indicates repressed fear or if the fear belongs to someone else, and the yellow will be pale if the fear has been externalized. The more off-color the yellow is, the more anxiety that is present.

Unhealthy disgust, or shame, blame, or guilt, will be an offensive gray. Such spots will also look moldy and probably connect through a cord to the person who first hurt and shamed us.

Using color healing, we can delete the negative colors and fill in our energetic field (and chakras) with healthy ones. I also suggest chanting the Hindu tones *Vam* and *Ram* and the octave tones D and E to boost our emotional healing. These can be directed at the second and third chakras, respectively. We can also psychically insert any version of the numbers 2 and 3 into our energy field.

In addition to evaluating the colors of our emotional boundary, use your psychic vision to look for shapes stuck in your field. A warped or entrenched square indicates depression or repressed emotions. A broken circle tells you the causal issue originated in a relationship, and a deformed triangle suggests anxiety. An X indicates an energy marker or perhaps the location of a cord or curse. The spiritual section of this chapter discusses how to deal with these types of interference. In general, fixing the misshapen symbol boosts your emotional field and helps you become clearer about the true nature of your feelings and thoughts.

Good gemstones to program with an emotional healing intention include ocean jasper, which releases others' emotions from your field, and lepidocrocite, which promotes emotional healing.

All of these strategies support the real purpose of emotions and beliefs: to guide us into joy. Once you hit upon a strong feeling, isolate it. Ask the Divine to help you figure out the message behind the feeling. Ask also what you should do, think, or believe to transform it into joy. Do the same for your thoughts. Especially when you're stuck, ask the Divine to pinpoint the belief that is undoing your happiness. Now transform it into a more sustaining belief, a real truth. A thought like "I don't deserve to be well" could become "I open to the healing that the Divine holds for me."

|||||||||||||||||||||||||||||||||||||||||||||||||||||||||||||||||||||||||

The Messages Within Our Feelings and Beliefs

There are five major feeling constellations or groupings. All other feelings fall under these categories, and each of these five hands us a specific message that, if respected, can lead to joy.

- **Sadness** tells us we are out of touch with love. If we follow our sadness, we will rediscover the joy of having loved and be able to love again. Joy flourishes where there is love.
- **Anger** signals a boundary violation. Either someone (or something) has violated our boundaries, or we have done that to someone else. We need to set boundaries for ourselves and, if necessary, protect ourselves from the other person. Following through on our anger creates structure and, therefore, the joy of safety. Joy can only expand in safety.
- **Fear** tells us that we or someone or something else is in danger. We need to move forward, backward, or to one side or the other. Fear prompts us to take action that provides us with enough space to decide what will bring joy.
- **Disgust** suggests that someone or an act, behavior, or substance is bad for us. Getting rid of or abstaining from the toxin cleanses us. It transforms shame and guilt and allows us to fly forward and seek the people and situations that bring us joy.
- **Joy** says, "I want more of the same." Joy begets more joy!

Beliefs are the perceptions that underlie our decisions. Like feelings, any belief can lead to joyous and productive emotions, but only if we are willing to reframe destructive beliefs so they support unity and oneness rather than separation and discord.

There are six categories of misperceptions that lead us astray and damage our emotional borders. These involve issues of (1) unworthiness, (2) unlovability, (3) undeservedness, (4) lack of value, (5) being bad or evil, and (6) powerlessness. Energetically, these undeveloped beliefs lock into our brains and run our neurological chemistry, creating havoc in our emotional energetic boundary. They attract people and situations that reinforce the immature belief rather than inviting growth and change. Having one of these beliefs imprinted on our emotional boundary is like wearing a sign that broadcasts a lie about ourselves.

To change a destructive belief, we must first isolate it. Once we've figured out the misperception, it's important to refrain from shaming ourselves. We are dealing with an incomplete or immature belief, not a bad one. Teenagers aren't unsuccessful adults; they are merely older children who haven't yet arrived at an adult state. Just as it's our job to teach a teenager how to think more lucidly, so it is our job to transform an immature belief into a more mature version of itself. This way, instead of fighting the belief, we cultivate it, so it becomes useful, not harmful.

The six immature beliefs can each be reframed as follows:

- **Unworthiness.** If you believe that you are unworthy, acknowledge that, at this time, it's simply hard to perceive your innate worthiness. Try saying something like this to yourself: "My worthiness is becoming apparent to me and others."

- **Unlovability.** When you feel unlovable, recognize that right now you aren't able to feel or sense love. Tell yourself, "I am open to feeling and sensing love."

- **Undeservedness.** When you're thinking yourself as undeserving, remind yourself about the nature of grace, a gift that never has to be earned. Say something like this to yourself: "I accept grace from any loving source."

- **Lack of value.** When you perceive that you aren't valuing yourself or someone else, or that someone isn't valuing you, say this to yourself: "My value is becoming clear to everyone who needs to see it, including me."
- **Being bad or evil.** When you believe you are bad or that someone else is bad or evil, admit that you are occupied with shame. Shame tells us that there is something wrong with us rather than that there is simply something wrong.

Shame is a form of control. When someone hurts us, especially when we are young, we have two choices. Either we must believe that the other party was injured and didn't know how to love, or we must believe that the abuse was our fault. The first option leaves us feeling helpless and despairing. We would rather feel bad and defective than overwhelmed and unloved. The second option is erroneous, but it enables us to feel like we still have control over the situation. If we change, the situation might change. To avoid either view, tell yourself this instead: "I can love myself for who I am and love others for who they are right now."

- **Powerlessness.** The above scenario describes what leads to powerlessness, the sense of helplessness over how others perceive or treat us. At many times in our lives we actually are powerless. Does that make us guilty of what others choose to do? No. To argue this would be to deceive ourselves and increase our inner terror and shame. The key is to assert the following: "I accept that which I have power over and release what I do not."

||||||||||||||||||||||||||||||||||||||||||||||||||||||||||||||||

Healing Through Your Relational Boundaries: Your Green Field

Healing your relational field is the most powerful way to create health and wellness because your heart, the controlling center of this field, also manages the rest of your body. As discussed at the beginning of the chapter, it also generates the most expansive and interactive of your electromagnetic fields.

While relationships are the source of most of our boundary injuries, they are also the key to healing. I believe that people are good at their core. As humankind, with an emphasis on "kind," we long to be loved and to love. Love heals and creates wellness. A Yale study conducted by cardiologist Dean Ornish showed that men and women who felt loved and supported had fewer blockages in their heart arteries. In fact, the men in the 10,000-man study who felt like their wives didn't love them had twice the incidence of angina.[16]

Love is also contagious, as shown in a fascinating study conducted by the Soviets. Relayed by physicist William Tiller in his book *Science and Human Transformation,* the study revealed that two hearts can relate to each other through the relational field, even when separated. The Soviets removed two animal hearts from their respective bodies, put them in separate chambers, and maintained the hearts in stable conditions. The hearts were then placed as the focus of an elliptical mirror so that any subtle radiation leaving one heart would be received by the other and vice versa. In the beginning, the two hearts beat in different rhythms, but as time went on, their heartbeats synchronized.

Tiller believes we humans create these connections through our heart, specifically our heart chakras and related energetic field. The greater the signal power of a large band of frequencies (or bandwidth), the more people we reach, near and far. The tinier the power signal and more narrow the bandwidth, the fewer the people we can connect with, and then, only close up. Guess what creates a big signal and huge bandwidth? The most loving linkages? Love. Judgmental attitudes and negativity, points out Tiller, reduce our heart's signals and close down our energetic field. It also makes it harder to feel any love being sent to us.[17] Can you imagine what might happen if we actually intended to send or receive love through our relational field?

If healing is available through our relational field, why do so many of us experience illness? The reason is that most of us have been injured, usually during childhood, and our wounded inner children hold onto relational boundaries that seem protective, but aren't. The child within thinks he or she will survive only by sticking with known patterns, by giving away energy, by taking on others' energies, or by linking with negative spirits. She or he is convinced that safety lies in erasing boundaries, being codependent, or becoming too unified with the environment. To really heal from health challenges, including mental and emotional illnesses and addictions, we need to provide for our inner child. Once he or she is restored and rejuvenated, our relational field will automatically begin to refresh and renew. At that point, we can conduct a variety of energetic techniques to boost our relational field. Some of these techniques can also help us uncover and assist the wounded child.

You might find some of the techniques in chapter 9 helpful. They were designed to assist parents with their actual children, but they can also help adults with their inner children. Therapy and twelve-step programs are also vital keys. To work energetically, I suggest you concentrate on the syndrome providing you the most trouble and do the exercise "Uncovering Your Storyline" in chapter 4. This exercise will help you figure out the reason your inner child is stuck in a deformed relational field. Once you connect with the injured child, proceed with love and care. A therapist can educate you about reparenting this little one, but for the purpose of physical healing, here are some energetic techniques that will help.

First, redesign your relational field. Psychically add green to it if you are dealing with a physical illness or trauma; add pink if your core issues are relational in nature, such as social phobias or abuse issues. Add gold if the most striking symptoms are chronic, repetitive, or addictive in nature; if your issues are spiritual (linked with entities or attachments); or if you are lacking in boundaries altogether. You can also combine these colors.

Now ask the Divine to link your inner child with a healing stream of grace and to then plug the same stream of grace into your relational field. Request that the Divine fill this field (and surround the child) with the appropriate hue, intensity, and amount of the heart colors just described. Know that this incoming energy will push out all undesirable energies. Allow this healing stream and the incoming energy to continue flowing as long as necessary.

If your problems are physical, you can also intuitively picture a square around the entirety of the field; this shape will keep you safe until you heal. If your challenges are relational in nature, use a circle, and if they're mental, try a triangle.

Any green gemstone is useful for healing physical issues through your relational boundary. Green jade provides strength and protection and is great for pairing with a square. Malachite and rose quartz assist with physical healing and relational concerns, and they partner well with a circle. You can either purchase a jewelry piece with the stone shaped like a circle or attach a circular shape to your jewelry, such as a charm on a charm bracelet. Emerald and green tourmaline can cleanse energy on every boundary and embolden our inner spirit to release others' energies, including energies from entities and psychic attachments.

The heart is especially available to the Hindu sound *Yam* and the immortal *Om*. The octave note F delivers healing, and the number 4 provides security. If your energetic issues are communication based—for instance, you were originally injured by verbal threats, criticism, or spiritual interference—you can utilize the fifth chakra's tone of *Ham* and the G note, in addition to the number 5. Communication issues also respond to programmed chrysocola, lapis, and blue opal.

Figure E. *The heart-chakra symbol empowers our healing abilities and relational energy fields because it incorporates several important symbols: the twelve-petal lotus, the circle, and the triangle (two, superimposed on one another). The innermost symbol represents the mantra or sound Yam.*

The twelve-petal lotus is another powerful tool for healing physical conditions through the relational boundary. In the Hindu tradition, the symbol for the heart chakra is two superimposed triangles set within a circle, both surrounded by lotus petals. One triangle is right side up; the other points down. These differing directions symbolize a choice: we can either rise to feelings of unconditional love and devotion or fall into despair and negativity. The twelve petals of the lotus represent the higher virtues, those that can lift us up: love, understanding, peace, harmony, empathy, blessing, clarity, unity, compassion, kindness, purity, and forgiveness. The circle reflects unity and perfection.

To meditate on this lotus, breathe deeply. Then, with each breath, concentrate on one of the twelve virtues and on the uplifting energy of love. Breathing into each virtue, or lotus petal, entrains your heart to positive emotions and healing. I recommend that every day you picture your inner child within this lotus, blanketed by your relational field. Now envision the twelve virtues as streams of energy, shining into and through your relational field around your inner child, holding and protecting him or her.

Laughter and inner smiles also support healing your heart and relational field. And they're especially fun energetic tools to work with.

Laughter boosts your immune system and reduces stress by lowering levels of the stress hormones epinephrine, cortisol, dopamine, and adrenaline, as well as human growth hormone. It also increases your levels of healthy hormones, such as endorphins and neurotransmitters. When you laugh, your body produces healthy antibodies and T-cells.[18]

Combine laughter with inner child work by telling your inner child a joke. Let the humor flow through your body and energy field, and see how quickly your health shifts.

If you're not in a position to break out in a huge belly laugh, consider an inner smile, a Taoist technique for opening to love and the high-grade energy of joy. The respected Buddhist monk Thich Nhat Hanh teaches us how to achieve an inner smile. First, sit with your spine straight, but not rigid. Relax your body and breathe in, bringing your focus to a specific part of your body. (You can select an area that is stressed.) Now breathe out and smile to that part of the body. You can simply imagine the smile being held inside of you, or you can let your face smile at the same time. There are about 300 muscles on your face, and when we're worried, these harden. But when we breathe while smiling, the tension immediately dissipates and increases our joy.[19] French physiologist Israel Waynbaum demonstrated that a deep inner smile triggers specific brain neurotransmitters, such as endorphins and immune-boosting T-cells. It also lowers the stress hormones cortisol, adrenaline, and noradrenaline and produces hormones that stabilize blood pressure, relax muscles, improve respiration, reduce pain, accelerate healing and stabilize mood.[20]

Healing Through Your Spiritual Field: Your White Boundaries

"I'm sick in my body because I'm sick in my soul," my client said.

For several years, Joanne had experienced an array of issues, including chronic fatigue syndrome, depression, borderline personality disorder, anxiety, and a general feeling of malaise. She felt isolated and alone, even though she loved her husband, two children, and job. She simply didn't feel good about herself or her life. Her only excitement came from being chased by dark angels during nightly dreams.

Joanne's mood and mental-health disorders didn't clear up until she worked on her undernourished spiritual boundaries.

Although our presenting symptoms might be health related, we'll know when we need to work on our spiritual boundaries instead of our other fields. We'll sense that our health problems stem from events, entities, or energies that are more supernatural than natural. Deep down, we'll understand that underlying the outward problems are questions about our purpose, value, worth, relationship with the Divine, and sense of goodness, as well as our own soul issues. Our soul is that part of us that travels through time, accumulating both gifts and injuries. Every soul is affected by an original soul wound, a trauma that caused us to formulate a spiritual misperception. This soul wound often underlies our childhood issues.

If I believe a client is dealing with spiritual issues, I usually start by seeking the original soul wound. I then support the process by performing spiritual-boundary work. Any illness or condition can result from a spiritual-boundary violation, but the most common are mental illnesses, such as borderline personality disorder, paranoia, and bipolar disorder; learning issues; sleep issues; depression; and anxiety. Spiritual healing almost always involves dealing with cords, entities, attachments, and other spiritual intrusions. Thus, the Psychic-Sensitive Syndrome is almost always a part of a spiritual malaise.

For instance, I believe that bipolar disorders often start with a split in the soul. Characterized by intense mood swings, the bipolar person usually holds a spiritual misperception such as, "God won't love me if I do something wrong." Unable to always be and do right, the soul splinters into two parts, as does the brain. On one side of the mind is the self who can do no wrong—the perfect, happy, charismatic "good self." On the other side is the "bad self," the mean, cruel, and crazy self we can't help but become every so often. Because of the spiritual misperception, the bipolar person has to reject the bad self, who consequently is never healed.

Often fueling the dark spiritual belief is a bevy of spiritual entities. They actively want to recruit our bad side, because they don't want our good side to achieve its spiritual purpose. But lacking the power repressed in our dark side, the light side can't get anything done.

My assessment of a spiritually caused borderline personality disorder is similar to that of a bipolar disorder, except that the patient is hijacked by one of his or her own inner children rather than an entity (although entities might be present as well). Schizophrenic conditions are often caused by a disbelief in divine protection and love. The resulting terror can cause the person's soul to literally climb out of the body; a true schizophrenic break occurs when the soul punches through the roof of the head (the seventh chakra) and is dangling in the spiritual field.

Dealing with any physical or mental condition of this ilk requires medical assistance, therapy, and nutritional support. These activities alone, however, won't dent the problem if we are really dealing with a spiritual issue—and, therefore, a spiritual-boundary issue. To really heal, we must uncover our original soul wound; challenge and change our spiritual misperceptions; release any negative attachments, such as those connecting us to entities or evil beings; and repair our spiritual energetic boundaries. Following are meditative processes that can help you accomplish all of these goals. I encourage you to also seek professional help for these types of issues.

Healing a Soul Wound. To heal a soul wound, you must first find it. I suggest using the "Uncovering Your Storyline" exercise and allowing yourself to drift as far back in time as you can. While your soul might have become injured in this lifetime, chances are it earned its first scars in a past life or upon separating from your spirit. Let yourself reexperience the original wounding and then ask the Divine to heal you from it, providing you with help and boundary support until you become fully whole again.

Know also that you might find different parts of your soul scattered in different times, spaces, and lifetimes, and even lingering in between lifetimes. Ask the Divine to gather all parts of your soul and sew them together with love, cleansing, healing, and integrating them through this process. Many mental health disorders are actually outgrowths of a fragmented soul and begin to heal once we're made whole again.

Releasing Cords and Other Attachments. Review the information on cords and energetic attachments in chapter 3. Then examine your spiritual energy field to determine which type is affecting you. You might also want to trace the attachment into your body and find out which chakra it's hooked into. Locating this charka-attachment point will tell you more about why the cord is there and who attached to you.

Besides cords, look for any energy markers, which appear like a big X. This X is often written on your spiritual field, facing outward. It tells people how to treat you and isn't usually a good thing.

To release a cord, energy binding, or marker, close your eyes and visualize your spiritual field. Ask the Divine to show you the entry point of the attachment and show you how the attachment affects you. Check to see who or what outside of yourself the cord is attached to and where inside of your body the cord is hooked.

Now ask the Divine to substitute a healing stream of grace—or several, if necessary—for this energy attachment. As it is put into place, ask what you need to better understand about the nature of love in order to allow the attachment to fully release. Then bless yourself and all others that were involved, and ask the Divine to continue to provide you protection while healing all of your energetic boundaries.

You can support your spiritual-field repair with prayer, meditation, or contemplation. *Prayer* sends messages to the Divine; *meditation* quiets the self so it can receive a response. *Contemplation* is like having tea with God; we can sit and stare into the Divine's eyes forever, basking in this eternal presence, and simply enjoy our own nature.

Chanting the Hindu *Om* or the octave notes A or B supports spiritual-boundary repair. Various stones can also be useful. The diamond is always the soul's best friend, clarifying and clearing. Moldavite invites spiritual transformation, and black opal assists with releasing psychic intruders. Celestite accesses higher dimensions for healing, and amber grounds you after a soul clearing.

Finally, I recommend spending time opening your spiritual gifts. My book *The Intuition Guidebook* can help you identify and work with your unique gifts.

Chapter 6

Boundaries for Work Success

*Your work is to discover your world and then
with all your heart give yourself to it.*

THE BUDDHA

We are here on purpose. As spiritual beings, we are part of the global family creating a community of love. Toward this end, each of us is invested with unique gifts necessary to make this world a better place. Work is the process of unfolding these gifts in the world, which includes your circles of friends, family, the marketplace, and the greater community.

When we work, we contribute. It doesn't matter if we work for ourselves or someone else, at home or in an office, store, restaurant, health-care facility, or stand-alone company. It doesn't matter whether we get paid for our efforts or not. If we're using our gifts to develop more love in this world, we are working. If someone or something is blocking our gifts or our ability to use them in this world, we'll be frustrated, angry, depressed, anxious, and maybe even ill.

The least recognized, and consequently, least understood and discussed, cause of work problems is poor energetic boundaries. What if we thought of workplace stress and conflicts, and even under- or unemployment, as energetic issues? And what if we perceived that the most critical work-stress symptoms, from acute illness to chronic exhaustion to interpersonal conflict, are at least partially energetic in nature? If we realized that energy is causing at least some of the problems, then we know that energy can change some of the problems. *Since energy is unlimited, you have unlimited energy at your disposal.*

If we find ourselves chronically or acutely struggling with work concerns, we are probably afflicted with distorted physical, emotional, relational, or spiritual boundaries, which create any of the energetic syndromes. Clear up your boundary problems, and you begin to clear up your work issues. Then your heart can open again, and success—however you define it—will be yours.

Sewing Up the Seams: Tips for Good Physical Energetic Boundaries at Work

Work is a way to achieve our spiritual mission, but for most of us, it is also the primary way we meet most of our concrete life needs, which involve our bodies and materiality. Stress at work often activates our survival issues, which are governed by our physical energetic boundaries. In other words, work issues often cut to the core of our physical self and boundaries. We must, therefore, employ concrete activities to clear and sustain our physical energy boundaries. That's why, for work issues, I'm offering more ideas for strengthening and repairing your physical boundaries than any other boundaries.

The place to start is figuring out what you want your work life to be like. Don't concentrate on when you want to retire or the title of your job. What's important is how you want to *feel* at work—about yourself, the people you're serving, and the contribution you're making.

We want work to be an expression of our immortal gifts and true essence. As big a statement as that sounds, I think nearly everyone would agree with it. We want to bring all of ourselves to work. Whether you sit in a cubicle counting numbers or make children go "ah" while you look at their tonsils or paint murals on the sides of buildings, you need your efforts to contribute toward a higher end.

We also want to work in line with our ethical standards. You don't want to be forced to drink at a conference if you don't drink alcohol or flirt with the boss just to get a raise. We long to be our higher, not lower, selves in the workplace.

Nor do we want to be abused in order to obtain or keep a job. Work abuse comes in many forms: harassment, overwork, underutilization, criticism, negativity, ridicule, poor working conditions, and inadequate pay. Unfortunately, such negative factors are the norm, rather than the exception, these days.

We can't change our work situation unless first we set an intention or a goal. To arrive at this intention, let your imagination soar and your heart sing. How do you really want to feel at work? Creative? Inspired? Important? Respected? Respectful? Sustained? Joyful? Rewarded?

Who do you want to primarily help? Children? Adults' inner children? Artists? The ill, depressed, or anxious? People striving toward their goals? Animals? Nature?

What is your unique contribution? Do you empathize, help people manifest or create, add truth, communicate, provide spiritual direction or healing, organize, strategize, lead, command, or follow?

Once you can answer a few of these questions, lock your desire into an actual intention, using the five steps for setting an intention (see page 86). You will want to program this intention into physical activities or substances for repairing and establishing your physical boundaries.

One of the most important ways to shift your physical energy boundaries is to alter the molecular structure of your body's fluids. Coffee and tea are considered medicinal in many cultures. Both absorb and flush negativity out of our bodies, but they can also carry others' negativity into our bodies. Blessing our beverages, especially water, invites them to clear out foreign energies, a really important activity for those who pick up others' energies. I go a step further and program my tea or water with an intention that reflects what I want to achieve on a certain day. For instance, one day I programmed my tea for luck. I later figured out two clients had mixed up their appointment times, but because they had simply reversed, it all worked out. To bless or program your beverage, follow the steps for using intention to bless an object, given in chapter 4.

Food is an imperative healing tool for our physical energy boundaries. Not only does it nourish us, but the energies of different foods also affect the electrical properties of our cells, which in turn, shift our physical energetic boundaries. Most of us know what it means to eat right, but do we know how to eat to repair our physical borders?

A simple tip: the most effective food source for fortifying physical boundaries is protein. Grass-fed red meat that is antibiotic and hormone free almost instantly strengthens weak physical boundaries. If you are vegan or vegetarian, eat legumes or nuts; these instantly ground and anchor you, and help you think straight when your energy is being distorted. Red- and brown-colored foods and earth-based vegetables also encourage strong physical boundaries. I also recommend supplementing your diet with extra minerals. Magnesium especially relieves us of tension, leaving us calm enough to figure out how to approach our boundary problems.

Any and all movement encourages the release of others' energy and instantly rebuilds weak physical boundaries. During a challenging work event, wear loose clothing and make sure you can get up and go to the bathroom or find some other excuse to leave the room from time to time. If you can't get away, jiggle your legs or feet, or take off your shoes and imagine them sinking into earth or sand. Then breathe. Breathe through one nostril at a time, holding the other closed, to eliminate toxins and connect your physical energetic field with your other fields. Or just breathe deeply, releasing others' energies on the exhale and bringing in new energy on the inhale.

During your nonwork time, consider doing energetic-based exercises, such as qi gong, yoga, Pilates, tai chi, or karate. When performing these activities, focus on your intention. Running, walking, or biking before or after work or during lunch break are excellent ways to release others' energies and rev up your own.

Your skin is actually part of your physical energy boundary. If you can't exercise on a difficult day, rub your skin, itch your face, or go after those spots where you feel the vacuum-cleaner-hose-like energy attachments sucking out your energy. Touching your skin with intention activates your physical borders. Using your hands to surreptitiously snip off those invisible attachments will actually remove them, leaving you free and relaxed.

Your clothing and environment are also extensions of your physical boundaries. Not only does clothing affect how others see and, therefore, treat you, but also various textures and colors determine the shape and frequency of your physical boundary.

- *Wear red* if you want to kick other people's energies out of your energy field.
- *Wear earth tones,* including russet, citrine, olive, goldenrod, or brown if you want to fill in boundary holes, repel negative environmental energies, and feel more grounded in your own unique energy.
- *Wear gray or black* if you want to hide yourself, thus avoiding those who want to dump their energies onto you or slide their work onto you.
- *Try purple.* In feng shui, purple is a sign of workplace success. Small touches of it on or around you will encourage your field to open only to growth and to eliminate or reject negative influences.
- *For interviews, consider soft touches of pink, yellow, or blue.* These colors open your physical energetic field. Pink guarantees that you will fit in and get along with coworkers. Yellow reflects intelligence,

and blue soothes jagged edges of your physical energetic field, leaving you seamless and calm.

Thick weaves will catch nasty energies, while slick fabrics will act like a mirror, deflecting others' bad wishes and illnesses. Smooth fabrics will even out your physical energetic boundaries. Flannel, especially pink flannel, shifts harmful EMF fields, reducing carpal-tunnel symptoms and the effects of other environmental energies.

Your jewelry or accessories can also make a huge difference in your physical borders. Metals, stones, or gems can be programmed to support your intention. Different metals fulfill different purposes; wear them alone, or combine them with gemstones that also meet your higher needs. Natural chunks of these elements can also be hidden at your desk, buried in your purse, or carried in your pocket.

The basic metals are gold, silver, and copper. Gold attracts. Program gold to attract opportunities, such as those that might break you out of a paper-doll pattern. Are you unemployed or underemployed? Program gold with an intention for success or maybe a job offer. Use gold sparingly and never without programming it with intention; otherwise, it will attract unwanted energies. Silver deflects others' energy, including their illnesses or poverty issues, but also opens you to receiving guidance. Copper cleanses others' energies from your body.

For really dark and stark work issues, I recommend using obsidian or hematite. These stones absorb others' negative influences and stop people from injuring you. Amethyst deflects negativity and is very important to use if you believe you are under attack from extremely negative, malignant, or evil people or spirits. Jade alleviates environmental toxins. Pink quartz creates a more loving atmosphere; it is highly helpful for healers who don't want to fight power with power, but instead share love and compassion. Rubies (especially worn as earrings for women or cufflinks for men) keep away energy vampires, cleanse the blood, and regulate hormones, including adrenal stress hormones. Garnets attract financial abundance. I recommend wearing or placing any of these stones in the work environment.

Plants can reinforce your physical energetic boundaries, because they add loving support. Avoid those with sharp-edged leaves, which will prick your energetic boundaries. Smooth, circular leaves plump up your physical borders. Fresh or living flowers will open your physical energy field and encourage a positive attitude, and their smell (especially that of roses and orange blossoms) will cleanse your field and open you up to opportunities.

If possible, get a fountain for your workspace. Running water cleanses your energetic fields. Throw in a few pieces of wood to buoy yourself against others' manipulation.

Lighting your work area with full-spectrum light will open your field and cleanse you of others' physical energies. If you can, purchase a pink full-spectrum bulb. The red energy in the bulb guarantees physical protection, and the white opens you to support for your spiritual mission.

Nature sounds, especially the sound of the ocean, will also cleanse your physical borders and open even the most rigid of fields.

Can you hum at work? A little? Sweet sounds deflect negative environmental toxins and align our spirit with our body. I've even had a client use the mantra *Om* when her office's copy machine jammed; the machine would unjam for everyone but her! Consider using the tone C when possible, because it heals our physical energetic boundaries specifically.

If you really desire workplace change, such as a promotion or a job, you have to clear your physical energetic field of everyone or everything in the way. Start by decluttering, throwing away everything at home or at work that no longer describes who you are. Toss that old paperwork and applications for jobs you didn't get. Ready to move forward? To attract workplace prosperity? Put red or purple objects in the southeast corner of your workspace.

I heartily recommend using shapes, symbols, and numbers. I once had a client envision himself within a pink pyramid during a weekly meeting in which the other attendees frequently attacked his ideas. Pink is the color of love, and a triangle symbolizes creativity. The base of a pyramid is a square, which reflects stability. As the pink pyramid shifted his physical field, his coworkers began perceiving him as highly approachable and creative, and they listened to his money-saving ideas. Now perceived as trustworthy, my client was eventually given a promotion.

We can use intention to ask our physical energy boundaries to change. Visualization is a terrific tool. By simply picturing our field morphing into and then holding the new shape or color, we can shift it. For workplace physical stressors, I advise adding pink to our physical energetic boundary to transmute negativity for positive outcomes; gold to command change and immediately stop an energetic, personal, or professional attack; green to stop a repetitive pattern and initiate a new track; and silver to deflect others' issues and energies back to them.

Shape-shifting your physical boundaries into a circle keeps others' illnesses, work, and malignancies out of your energetic fields and encourages connection. Shaping them into a square provides immediate protection and repels vampirism and psychic attacks of any sort; establishing new boundaries in a square is especially beneficial if you are a no-boundary or psychically sensitive person. Using a triangle invites a new response or outcome. Invoke more power from these shapes by wearing jewelry with the noted shape and color, or even drawing the desired symbol on a part of your body.

A clockwise spiral draws in desirable energy, filling in boundary holes and attracting life-enhancing support. Use intention to bring healing and higher-order energy spiraling into your physical energy field, visualizing them coming straight into your field and then into your hip area. A counterclockwise spiral carries others' energy out of you, thus clearing both your field and your body. Imagine any negative energy spiraling out of your hips, through your field, and then to the higher heavens.

Numbers, too, hold significance. I encourage clients to mentally repeat the appropriate number, envision it written on their physical energetic field, or actually inscribe it on their skin. For workplace protection, use a 1, which underscores your own identity and needs as the most important. To create new opportunities, turn to a 10, which provides protection against others' interference, but opens you to possibilities.

I find that the more broken or ripped one's physical borders, the greater his or her sensitivity to the environment. The discipline called BioGeometry, based on ancient Egyptian principles, shows us how to use shapes and symbols to create energy fields around us and in our physical space. Various BioGeometry pendants and electromagnetic devices can shift the physical fields of your body, home, and other geographic areas, as well as heal diseases. Products and more information are available through Biogeometry and Vesica Institute sources.[1]

If you can't afford fancy products, know that using any symbol important to you will repel negative energy and provide energetic protection. I once encouraged a client to wear a Christian cross necklace on her back, instead of her front side, to protect herself from her backstabbing boss. Almost immediately, she felt better.

Don't forget also that simple human touch—and not-so-simple touch—has healing properties. Hands-on healing methods, massage, chiropractic care, and osteopathic treatments release others' energy from your boundaries and shift your body's electrical system, which in turn, nourishes your magnetic shields. I also recommend taking Epsom-salt or tea baths to release the toxins from your physical field. For tea baths, brew four to five bags of black tea in a saucepan on the stove. When the water is really dark, pour it into an already-filled bathtub. The medicinal properties of the tea will pull others' energies out of your physical borders and restore you to sanity.

Sensing Your Way to Sensational Emotional Work Boundaries

I once had ten clients follow each other, one-by-one, into my office in agony, seeking refuge from their boss. He sounded like one of the most emotionally abusive men I'd ever come across. Each employee reported that this CEO, one of the most famous independent business owners in America, was so mean that his employees were all struggling to avoid nervous breakdowns. Each reported sleep difficulties, and one woman had just been diagnosed with an ulcer because she worried constantly. Most of them confessed that they were avoiding social situations because their self-esteem had fallen to an all-time low, and many could care less about how they dressed or appeared. Those in relationships had almost stopped having sex with their partners, and each was a bundle of pure nerves. The boss had only to call in from out of town, and everyone in the office would stop breathing. He would walk in the room, and most employees would start shaking uncontrollably.

At one time, each employee had been the CEO's favorite. He would then find something small to correct. That single problem would bear twins, then triplets, before cascading into a litany of complaints. Pretty soon, that particular employee was on probation. Everyone was looking for a new job. One new human-resources director, seeing the stress the employees were going through, quit after one day.

These employees might have started their jobs with erratic emotional energetic boundaries, and whatever weaknesses were present were soon blasted open. There was nothing I could do to make the overall situation better, but I recommended certain actions for each employee—actions that would bolster his or her emotional boundaries and help them find new employment, pronto. For each, I encouraged a number of boundary-cleansing methods and ways to fill their emotional cracks. Each person used many of the tools listed in the next part of this section and reported great success. One woman had used the techniques for only a day before she applied for and was hired for another job.

What I learned from this experience was that you can't control others' emotions. Nor can you heal or fix emotions that aren't your own. They stay stuck in or around you and are impossible to dissolve. And stuck emotions, especially others' intrusive emotions, can form blocks to our work success.

On the other hand, by fully embracing your own emotions and their messages, you can prosper no matter what. Feelings and beliefs really are forms of beauty and grace, as long as we are willing to embrace their latent gifts.

By far, the most important activities for healing your emotional energy boundaries are *separating others' feelings and thoughts from your own and then cracking the code of your own emotions.*

There are many ways to separate others' emotions from your own, and once you've done so, you can begin to energetically repair your emotional boundary.

I recommend starting with the Spirit-to-Spirit technique given in chapter 4. Spend some quiet time in meditation and think about your workplace. Now connect your own spirit with that of a spiritual guide. Ask the Divine to help you separate the wheat from the chaff, your own emotions from those of others. Ask it to show you how your emotional field looks right now. Where are the stretch marks, folds, and holes? Where are the areas that are armored, nailed shut, unwieldy? You might see distorted shapes or blotchy areas, or energetic cords that look like garden hoses; the latter connote links between you and others through which energy is bled, dumped, or exchanged. On the opposite end of these cords, you might discover people you know, images of the deceased, or the gray shadows of unfamiliar spirits.

Now ask the Divine to show you how many emotions from these outside sources are stealing energy from or dumping energy into your emotional field. Ask about the effects of any related syndrome. How is that syndrome affecting your work? Your career success? Your ability to motivate, make a difference, or be yourself at work? As you watch and perhaps sense the impact of this process, decide if you are willing to change the pattern of the syndrome.

If you are, simply request that the Divine change it for you. Observe, experience, and delight in the alterations. Then establish an intention for permanently healing and enjoying your emotional energy boundaries, and reduce that intention to a sentence or two. A helpful emotional boundary intention for the workplace might be, "I am employing my emotions to soar up the ladder of success," or, "All my emotions and only my emotions are fueling my contribution to the world as a sole proprietor."

You can maintain this shift through many of the means discussed in the section on physical energetic boundaries for work, substituting the emotionally based intention for the physically based one.

Now commit to noticing, supporting, and following your own feelings and beliefs. Every time you feel a feeling that is your own when you are at work or thinking about work, stop and label it. Consider the five constellations (see chapter 4, "The Messages Within Our Feelings and Beliefs") and determine which category your feeling falls into: anger, fear, sadness, disgust, or joy. Then ask what you must know or feel about this feeling to lead to joy at work.

Do the same when you sense twisted thoughts or worries. Isolate the belief, deciding which of the six fundamental misperceptions it reflects. Then mature that belief. What is a healthier and higher way to perceive yourself or this situation?

If, as is the case with vampire victims and those with the Healer's Syndrome, you can't even sense your own feelings or thoughts, return to the first exercise of picturing, clearing, and sustaining your emotional field. Concentrate on your inhalation and draw your own feelings and thoughts back into you. They are yours to use to energize your success, not to only bolster others' goals!

Want to use physical techniques to continue providing yourself with emotional protection? Bless your food and beverages with your emotional intention. Abstain from foods and beverages that seem to fill in emotional holes, but actually don't. I'm referring to high-octane substances, the stuff we indulge in when we're stressed at work, like chemically produced coffees, soda pop, and white-flour bakery items. These substances close down your internal emotional centers, which, in turn, distorts your emotional field. Instead, go for healthy beverages and foods, such as those loaded with vitamins A, C, and B. Also make sure you get enough omega-3 fatty acids. If you feel "gotten" at work, make sure you go for healthy, not unhealthy, foods, or your boundaries will completely crash.

Good activities for cultivating a healthy emotional field include smooth and expressive exercises, such as swimming or dance, or creative outlets, such as drawing or music. Can you take a swimming break at lunch? Dance in the park when no one is watching? Sketch and draw during a meeting to relieve your emotional stress?

Remember also to breathe. I recommend that you intuitively picture your emotional field as a bright, sunny yellow-orange bubble. Let each exhalation push others' toxins out through this bubble and each inhalation fill you with warm thoughts and joy.

If you know you'll be with a work contact who compromises your emotional health, amp up the color of your clothing. Wear any color, but the brighter the better. If you work in an environment that requires more sedate colors, make sure you plant a few bright colors somewhere on your person: on a tie, a dangling bracelet, swinging earrings. Bright colors will repel negative emotional energies. Avoid pastels, as they will attract others' emotions or cause yours to bleed off.

For the emotionally sensitive seeking work success, it's imperative to have an *objet d'art* in your environment, such as a sculpture, painting, or even a child's finger painting. You can also wear your art, such as a great piece of jewelry or pair of shoes. Also consider how much more powerful your work intentions will be if you tack up a poster showing you at the top of the world or if you work at a desk that only "rich people" could own.

Almost all emotionally sensitive people are environmentally sensitive, which is another reason it's important to carefully consider, and perhaps fear, the objects in your work environment. As silly as it may sound, don't touch objects that aren't your own or sit at the desk of someone you don't admire. Their energy will nab you. Avoid the computers, pens, or work objects, even coffee cups, owned by the people who abuse your emotional boundaries. If you feel like you've picked up others' emotional energies through touch, wash your hands under warm water and imagine a waterfall clearing your entire emotional energy field. I actually do this in between each client session in order to release my clients' emotional energies, which are often stirred while we're working together. I even blow a blessing energy over my phone receiver before and after client phone sessions, to release the client's energy.

Clearing your emotional field is as easy as setting and holding intention, but it can be helpful to use stones and gemstones to hold your higher work ideals. Think elements. Red stones, including carnelian, garnet, and ruby, will stimulate your passion, fire, and anger, so use these only if you intend to transform anger into joy. Orange and brown stones, including agates, can improve our work function. I like agates for good luck; they also balance physical and emotional well-being, inviting positive change by helping us center in our own emotions. Various types of agate will perform various duties. The blue lace agate heals emotional wounds, while the fire agate takes the edge off our difficulties. Amber aligns our thoughts and emotions and releases depression and anxiety, while pink calcite bonds our feelings and thoughts and encourages loving outcomes.

Also consider using shells. For instance, abalone releases negative emotions, stimulates higher thoughts, and encourages love and peace. Put a shell in your office, and you'll be transported to a balmy beach—really!

If you absorb others' energies, don't wear gold unless you have programmed it for work success. Otherwise, you'll leave meetings feeling junked-up, heavy, and irritable, signs of having picked up others' emotional energies. White gold, however, can encourage success and deflect others' energies.

Employ circles, squares, or triangles to connect or disconnect from others' emotions. If you feel overtly affected by someone at work or are stuck in a repetitive pattern, intuitively picture a circle around your emotional energy body and then break apart the circles connecting you to others. If you overwork, upon accepting (or overthinking about) a work project, literally or intuitively put it in a box, a form of a square. That way, you won't feel emotionally prompted to act like a mule. In fact, if you have any overindulgent boundary issues, including psychic sensitivities or no boundaries whatsoever, walk around with a box shape in your field. And if you constantly lose your emotional energy to others, insert yourself into an intuitive triangle. Envision a spiritual guide at one side of the base, you at the other, and the Divine atop. You'll be able to create, and no one else will steal your ideas or plug into your energetic boundaries.

Are you into numbers? Play with digits 2 and 3. A 2 connotes ideal partnership and respect between two people, while a 3 services creative endeavors. With a psychic magic marker, draw a 2 on your emotional energy field if you want to get along with someone and a 3 if you want to create a lovely opportunity, such as a job offer or promotion.

Getting to Your Relational Boundaries at Work

If you suspect that weak relational boundaries are undermining your career, the best place to start is by tracking your storyline. You can use the "Uncovering Your Storyline" exercise provided in chapter 4 on page 91. What's important to figure out is why you are more concerned for others at work than you are for yourself.

Here's a tip: the problem usually originates in early childhood and repeats a relationship arrangement established between you and one or both of your parents. The unconscious agreement creating the pattern comes from believing that it's your work to take care of a parent. When you're at work as an adult, the job continues. You can't get to your job duties until you've fixed everyone else.

We can also experience problems if we model our relational boundaries after those of our parents. For example, Justice was a film writer in Hollywood who could go only so far with her scripts. They'd end up on the desk of major producers only to be rejected at the last minute. What was her personal storyline? Her father was a cult leader hiding from the law. Her relational boundaries said that her work, like that of her father, had to be kept secret, to the point of becoming invisible. As soon as we shifted her boundaries to suit her own needs instead of his, she signed a contract for one of her scripts.

Once you uncover your storyline, I encourage you to take these two steps: First, walk through the original drama, but give it a new ending. Change the story, and you change your energetic system—and your neurology. Second, rewrite the characters. In your life play, replace the needy mom with a giving, kind one. Instead of an alcoholic, absent dad, give yourself a super-supportive one. Your workplace dramas will shift as your internal script does.

Having rewritten your story, you can formulate an intention for attracting and maintaining supportive work relationships. After all, success really does depend on being open to serving others and receiving help in return. Design an intention with your long-term heart's desires, not just the next step, in mind.

Because relational boundaries are heart-based, I encourage you to practice the art of intentional breathing as often as you can at work. Breathe in, concentrating on your intention. Do the same when breathing out. If you're stressed or have fallen into a syndrome, hold your breath at the high point of your inhalation and the low point of your exhalations, restating your intention in each pause. This will reprogram your energetic field and thus shift the way you are connecting with others.

I encourage anyone experiencing relational issues at work to bring two mirrors to their workplace. Face one away from you; this will deflect others' energies. Keep the other one at hand to use for this exercise: When you sense the symptoms of a syndrome coming on—usually triggered by looking at, sitting near, interacting with, or even thinking about a particular person—look into your second mirror, but picture the troublesome person in the mirror instead of yourself. Which of that person's traits is causing you to react? What quality or need is the person reflecting back to you? Why are you responding negatively to it?

As you mull over this trait, think about its positive qualities—the innate beauty, gift, or ability that lies underneath the negative appearance. Most likely, this person is merely misusing this attribute, but it also may be that you haven't claimed the true goodness of this trait within yourself.

If you are willing to do so, allow the image in the mirror to transform into your own. See the new you, who now has the formerly missing or unclaimed characteristic. Now picture and sense yourself using it. Finally, thank the person who revealed it to you and promise that you will employ the quality in an ethical and healthy way, no matter how the other person chooses to embrace and express this trait. Then you can release this person to his or her higher path.

You can take this process a step further even without a mirror. Whenever you sense yourself slipping into a relational syndrome at work, immediately ask to see, in your mind's eye, what you have the opportunity to shift, embrace, or change. Then intend this change for yourself.

Want a few more practical tips? You can borrow techniques from our discussions about physical and emotional boundaries earlier in this chapter, with a few changes.

The best diet for the relational sensitive is what's called the heart-based, or Mediterranean, diet—lots of seafood, tomatoes, greens, and whole grains. Bless your food, and it will bless you. Green tea is much better for you than black, and coffee might be a challenge.

If you want to employ stones or gems, go for anything pink or green. Pink is the color of love. It establishes strength in your relational border and invites others' higher spiritual responses. Green clears the heart and focuses our intention, so our hopes assist others and us.

Emeralds especially are useful in business, because they establish healthy relational boundaries. In India, emeralds are related to the planet Mercury, which energetically affects business, communication, and workplace success through relationships. Coral instills courage and bolsters career success, as well as boosting our social status and wealth. Hessonite garnet, a specific type of garnet, brings out your best to others, showcasing your attractive nature, which is a boon if you need to impress a supervisor, client, or potential employer. Adding a splash of personal magnetism is critical in today's competitive environment; turquoise will help you communicate higher truths and help you find the right words when you don't know what to say.

If you like symbols, imagine a circle joining you and someone you want to connect with—say a potential employer, vendor, or client. To form creative relationships, imagine triangles connecting you to the other person. Box yourself into a square if you are being plagued or vampired.

Imagining the number 4 drawn on your relational field will encourage balance in a work relationship and protection for you. Do *not* use a number 8, or you'll find yourself playing out childhood patterns within your work relationships. But if you believe you are stuck in a repetitive paper-doll pattern, picture the 8 on your relational field and break it into two parts: a 0 and a 0. This will nullify the old pattern.

One of the keys to releasing relational patterns is to let go of cords and other energetic contracts. This imperative process for relational or spiritual boundary clearing is covered in the next section on spiritual-boundary healing for work.

Spiritual Boundaries for Your Spiritual Work

Most of us have been raised to believe that spiritual matters belong in our place of worship or maybe locked deep within our heart and soul. But work *is* a spiritual matter: it's the way our spirit infuses love into all things material.

I personally believe that the most vital two boundaries to heal and maintain in regard to work are the physical and the spiritual. Work is our source of physical resources, but it is also a means of expressing our truest selves. The fear and shame that often swirl around workplaces can be overwhelming, opening our spiritual boundaries to invasions and attacks from both visible and invisible sources. In general, you'll know there are spiritual forces operating against you at work if you experience any of the following:

- **Disillusionment:** This is the sense that you don't count. The world is dangerous and bad. Why value yourself? Why live out your values? Why even think you have something to offer?
- **Evil:** You sense, maybe even smell, a dark force coming from someone at the office or lingering at the workplace. When you think of work, it seems as if a spell comes over you. You certainly couldn't explain this malignant presence to a human-resources director, but it's there.
- **Spookiness.** It seems as if there are real entities or energies intruding on your work success or linked to your workplace. You might also sense the presence of a ghost around a certain person.
- **Interference.** Something, you don't know what, keeps interfering with your thoughts, potential success, job, employment, or performance. It's not something you can prove, but you know it's real.
- **Purposelessness.** All the spiritual literature you read insists that you are gifted, loved by the Divine, and on this planet for a purpose. But you can't figure out what your purpose is. Maybe that means everyone but you has a purpose and is important.

- **Addictions and bad behaviors.** Every time you get close to success, you seem overwhelmed by an inexplicable compulsion to do something wrong. You've tried everything you can to get this pattern to cease and desist, but it pervades. There are forces you can't explain egging you on.
- **Misfortune and mishaps.** You're almost there—and out of the blue, tragedy strikes. If it happened only once, you wouldn't question what's going on. But why are you blocked by some unseen force *every time* you're almost there? You're working on your physical boundaries, but you sense a hidden source of tribulation that can't be explained as natural.

Almost every spiritual tradition testifies to the presence of what I call *interference,* or intrusive supernatural forces. These forces usually originate from the unseen universe and creep in through the cracks between the worlds. They could be called negative entities or forces, fallen angels, demons, ghosts, spooks, ancestral hauntings, or jinn. Whatever you call them, in relation to work, they don't want you fulfilling your spiritual purpose, because your doing so would create more love and light in this world. Basically, these entities are scared of the light, so they encourage and feed on darkness.

Not everything that goes bump in the middle of the night, or atop your desk, is supernatural. Parts of people can separate from their bodies or conscious selves and operate exactly as spooks do. Perhaps some aspect of a supervisor, coworker, patient, or client, or maybe a ghost attached to one of these people, is seeking to steal your energy or block your success to dim the light in your workplace.

These forces, whether from the living or the dead, connect to us through energetic cords, the bindings or energy contracts described in chapter 3. These cords can stretch between two people or between entire groups. They can draw out our own energy and/or dump others' energies into us. They can expose us to others' thoughts or feelings, issues or needs, addictions or illnesses. Sometimes called curses or spells in various cultures, they very much limit our success in every way, especially at work.

What can you do if you think you are experiencing unseen interference in your work life? Two simple techniques work every time: prayer and healing our spiritual boundaries.

You don't have to be a religious person to pray. Prayer is sending a message to the Divine. Personally, I don't care if your name for the Divine is God, Allah, Christ, Mary, Kwan Yin, the Mother, or the Void. The Divine is simply that which loves unconditionally and reflects the power needed to keep us safe.

Your prayer can be phrased in the form of an intention. A spiritually based work intention should be packaged as a request that the Divine bring about the best possible change in order for your gifts to be used ethically and wisely. You must then be willing to receive the inspiration and guidance necessary to bring about the plan or follow it as it unfolds. You must be willing to follow your intuition—your ability to sense, see, hear, feel, or understand the Divine's insight. One of the reasons we need clear and solid spiritual boundaries is so that we can distinguish intuition from interference; it's difficult to do so if these borders are cloudy, broken, or permeable.

A prayerful (or requesting) and meditative (or receiving) attitude can lead to the next step: healing our spiritual borders. Use the Spirit-to-Spirit process in chapter 4, concentrating on your work concerns. Now ask the Divine to access your intuitive faculties to reveal any cords, bindings, curses, or spells, from the living or the nonliving, that are penetrating your spiritual boundaries. If you want to better understand the origin of these attachments, ask for insight. If you want to better comprehend how these intrusions are affecting your spiritual work, ask for revelation.

The easiest, most loving, and most powerful way to clear the interference is to ask the Divine to release these bindings or negative connections from you and other parties involved, and to replace the cords with the healing streams of grace. There is no reason to tug at the cords or fight them, or to become scared or angry. Grace will replace all negative energies with positive ones of light, freeing you and the others involved in the spiritual pact to follow the correct destiny. These streams of grace can come directly from the Universal Field, cutting through all energetic interferences.

You can supplement this work with any or all of the techniques provided in this chapter. I encourage you to let your own intuition select physical tools, foods, beverages, and activities, but here are a few tips.

Any clear crystal quartz or diamond serves as a positive conductor of spiritual intent. An unusual stone, the cat's eye is an Indian gem also known as the "tail of the dragon." This "stone of success" protects us from negative energy forces, improves our intuition, and invites mystical experiences and divine revelation.[2]

The number 7 is one of the most mystical and invites divine assistance, while a 9 can move us off an old cycle. Be careful of the 6, which asks us to make a choice between good and bad—that is, unless we're willing to choose the good.

To the spiritually inclined, all of life is enlightened if we are willing to see and embrace it in a loving manner. To engage in our work and walk into our workplace with proper spiritual borders is to discover that the world is already good, and we are here, quite simply, to make it better.

||||||||||||||||||||||||||||||||||||||||||||||||||||||||||||||||||||||||||||

Safe Client Work: Boundaries for Caregivers

The most frequent question I hear from caregivers, especially those who work with clients one-on-one or in small groups, is, "How can I keep my boundaries?" How can you maintain your own energy when caring for, helping, or giving to others in some form is your work and calling?

Healers, consultants, health-care professionals, therapists, social workers, and similar professionals often experience caregiver burnout, the long, slow slide to exhaustion that comes from giving yourself away.

Caregiver burnout is at least partially an energetic issue. I know because I work with clients, but also because these are the types of complaints I hear:

"I only get the same type of client, over and over." "My clients don't pay their bills, complain all the time, never show up for appointments, take advantage, expect something for nothing" (Paper Doll Syndrome).

"My clients steal all my energy" (Vampire Syndrome).

"My clients expect me to do all the work for them" (Mule Syndrome).

"I pick up all my clients' issues, including their illnesses, entities, family-of-origin issues, feelings, and more" (Psychic-Sensitive Syndrome).

"I end up totally drained and doing all the processing for my clients" (Healer's Syndrome).

"I totally lose all my energy." "I can't tell what's mine and what belongs to my clients." "Sometimes I even speak, act, or think just like my last client, and I can't figure it out." "I can't separate from my clients." "Sometimes I want to get involved with my clients, even though it's wrong" (No-Boundary Syndrome).

"The setting must be absolutely perfect, or it interferes with my work." "I can't work on people who are wearing perfume or inorganic clothes or who just ate meat." "Cosmic energies interfere with my client work." "I keep getting messages from my clients' pets" (Environ Syndrome).

If you have any of these symptoms, figure out which energetic boundaries are most likely being violated and work on these boundaries. You can also draw from the following techniques I use every day in my own client work to guarantee that, at the end of a workday, I actually have more rather than less energy.

1. Preparation. Before work, I make sure I walk or exercise and set an intention for the day. I also pay attention to my clothing. Colors, as covered in chapter 4, are frequencies. I let my intuition select my wardrobe. I know if I'm reaching for red, I'm probably going to have to be pretty forceful and dramatic. If I'm going for a dark outfit, I might be dealing with a needy or angry client; the black or gray clothing might hide my personal reactions or my entire self so I can better assist the client.

2. Setting. I've set up my client room with my favorite objects, each of which holds meaning. For example, near the door is a lightning rod, signifying that I'm open to divine power. Over my client chair are two pictures from Peru: one represents the love of the Divine, the other, the release of negative energies and entities. A picture of dolphins invites joy, childlikeness, and healing. And throughout the room are different rocks and gemstones, each with a specific purpose.

3. Protocol. I start sessions with a short statement that verbally creates boundaries. I tell clients my intention, which is to invite healing and assist them. I also tell them that I ask the Divine to form parameters and boundaries, so at least I cause no harm and at best I can assist. Then I make sure they understand that I can't guarantee my work or information and that it's their job to decide what information is helpful and what is not. I also answer any questions they might have about what we're doing.

4. Physical boundaries. I keep a table between my client and myself. I pick up a lot of information from and for my clients through my physical energetic boundaries and need a physical barrier for filtering purposes. I only do hands-on healing if I feel like I'm safe and strong that day. Sometimes I recommend that hands-on workers employ a cloth, gloves, or special jewelry programmed to deflect negativity and boost the healing energies. I also take a quick break between clients to wash my hands, visualizing my previous client's energy being lovingly washed off as I do.

5. Emotional boundaries. I imagine a clear screen of energy between my client and myself. This screen filters the client's emotions from my own. Because my work relies on my ability to sense others' feelings and thoughts, however, I program this energetic screen to allow through others' emotions in a way that doesn't involve me taking in the emotions' actual energy. This way I can register my clients' emotions without taking them on.

6. Relational boundaries. Sometimes it's difficult not to get overinvolved in clients' problems. When a child is being abused, a talented individual fired, a spouse abandoned, our heart can't help but go out to the other person. This is when I make sure to intuitively pull back my heart, in addition to my other energy, when I'm done with a session. By sensing the outer edges of my relational or heart field, I make sure I've disengaged it before the client leaves the room. If it's not back around me, and attached to only me, I conduct a few deep-breathing exercises until it's intact.

Using holy water, I have also made the sign of a cross within a circle over all my doorways. When my client walks in, he or she is immediately blessed for a higher purpose. When my client walks out, my own energy stays on my side of the door.

7. Spiritual boundaries. I always employ the Spirit-to-Spirit exercise when working with clients. I use the same process when teaching classes. I also habitually ask the Divine to link my clients with any needed healing streams of grace at both the beginning and end of a session, and to do the same for me.

8. Dealing with your own issues. I ask the Divine to alert me when my issues are triggered during client work and to set the issues in a white box I keep inside my heart. At the end of the day, I spend a few minutes reviewing the contents of this box. More than a few issues have then made their way to my own therapist's office!

9. Coworkers. Though I usually work alone, I do have business partners, and I sometimes coteach classes. When working with others, I ask the Divine to "hold space" for our higher efforts, and I envision a white bubble of healing grace surrounding all concerned. This energy protects each of us from each other, keeps our issues from blurring, and enables a safe and loving connection.

10. Being done. At the end of the workday, I conduct the Spirit-to-Spirit exercise for myself, using Christ as my stand-in witness and calling upon the Divine to release me from my daily work. Very seldom do I obsess about my workday, which leaves me free for the rest of my life.

||||||||||||||||||||||||||||||||||||||||||||||||||||||||||||||||||||||

‖‖‖‖‖‖‖‖‖‖‖‖‖‖‖‖‖‖‖‖‖

Chapter 7

The Staff of Life:
Boundaries for Making Money

All our elements, with the exception of hydrogen and
helium, came from the dying throes of large stars.

CLIMATOLOGIST CHRIS POULSEN

Money is a physical tool for meeting our material needs, but it is also linked to our emotional and relational health and supports our spiritual pursuits. We need money to flourish, mature, and tend our spiritual gifts. We require it to sustain ourselves so that we can enjoy our purpose. Money can be considered a return on the investment of time and dedication it takes for us to achieve our life mission.

Money is also one of the greatest causes of the type of stress that leads to career, relationship, and health crises. There are a lot of reasons for money issues, but one unsung factor is energetic-boundary damage. Through my work, I've determined that ill-suited protective borders can cause or add to every single money challenge, including debt, lack of money, loss of income, financial disarray, tax problems, inconsistent earnings, overspending, dependency issues, and even poverty. Since everything is energy, think of all the twists and turns that could be caused by our physical experiences with, emotional confusion about, relationship mishaps with, and spiritual misperceptions regarding money. Any or all of the seven syndromes can erode our pocketbook and self-confidence, or even leave us living on the streets.

You can work on your money issues by applying the techniques described for energetic boundaries at work (in chapter 6). But money is also a stand-alone topic in that, as a concept, it's even more convoluted than career or spiritual purpose. I've heard people describe money as power, love, energy, an element, an exchange, an idea, an object, a measurement of success, evil, and even a gift from God. Money holds multiple meanings for all of us, and these multifaceted views only make our money issues messier.

I've determined that each of the four energetic boundaries actually represents a different concept of money. To examine one of the four main boundaries specifically for money concerns is to examine one particular facet of money. You may find that your money issues fall into one category more than others, but then again, you might need to evaluate each energetic boundary in relation to money.

On the physical level, money provides security—especially material security. It could (and should), therefore, be considered a substance. To reject money is to reject the nourishment life can provide; to receive money is to accept this nurturing. To hoard money is to mistrust our place with others, and to give all our money away is to forgo personal safety. On the emotional level, money, ideally, relays joy. If managing money isn't a joyous endeavor, we're stuck emotionally; our emotional boundaries are keeping us locked into shame or guilt. Relationally, money reflects the balance of love and power; spiritually, money is a means for fulfilling our spiritual calling.

Can we really experience a life of enough money to go around, with some extra? We can if we're willing to take the steps necessary to repair our physical, emotional, relational, and spiritual boundaries. Nourishing ourselves financially nurtures our souls, supporting the journey of our spirit from earth to sun, while giving ourselves a selection of fruits to enjoy on the way.

While you are establishing your energetic boundaries to ensure financial security and prosperity, I encourage you also to repair your boundaries to heal work-related issues, using the advice provided in chapter 6. Our work issues often parallel our money issues. If, for example, you are afflicted with the Psychic-Sensitive Syndrome relationally when at work, you are most likely suffering from the same problem with money. (This is a loose rule, however, so treat yourself as the unique being that you are.)

Making Money Via Rich Physical Boundaries

Simon couldn't keep a dime in his pocket if the coin were sewn in. Sooner or later, something—a contagious bug, his wife, one of his teenagers, or an unplanned catastrophe—would worm in and steal his coins away. While he earned pretty good money, Simon's income had decreased, and his knees were buckling under the weight of a first and second mortgage. The situation was so awful that he was considering bankruptcy. He felt so bad about his fiscal predicament that he was considering a divorce just to spare his wife and kids his problems.

I asked Simon what he thought was the core cause of his situation, a decent income peppered with high debt, and he looked at me teary-eyed. He had never known his father, who had deserted his mother at birth. For her part, his mother had cleaned houses for a living, enduring demeaning treatment from her employers. Unable to cope, she whiled away her extra cash on drugs and alcohol. Simon, therefore, associated money with pain, suffering, and abandonment, as well as straight-out abuse. A lack of money threatened his ability to survive, but having money created a security menace.

Energetically (through his physical boundaries), Simon sent mixed energetic messages to the world. Any vote of yes for financial security was cancelled out by a distinct no. The concrete world responded by letting him make a living—almost; by providing him his financial needs, kind of; and supporting him with financial rewards only inconsistently. His wavy, permeable physical energetic boundaries were a mess.

Our psyche recognizes money as material. It responds positively to behaviors and experiences that teach us that money will increase our security. It reacts negatively to situations and people that make us believe money decreases our sense of security or that the world itself is so insecure, money is insignificant. I've learned that the more extreme and life-threatening someone's money issues are, the more intense are their traumas related to money and, ultimately, to their well-being. In other words, physical-boundary issues often present the most shocking and obvious of money quandaries. These most typically appear as a series of acute financial predicaments, seemingly impenetrable impasses, or chronic money worries.

We could fill pages describing the financial disorders caused by mismanaged physical borders. They can include severe debt, constant underemployment, insecure investments, continual loss of income, or chronic underpayment. They might involve loss of money due to untreated addictions, such as gambling, shopping, drugs, or alcohol, or involvement in a relationship that threatens your life or livelihood. I've even worked with clients whose financial situation was critically wobbly because a loved one was frequently ill, mentally challenged, or physically abusive. Bottom line, if your monetary security is continually in upheaval to the point that your survival seems frequently threatened, you have experienced physical boundary violations and must repair this boundary if you want to fix your monetary health.

Like work issues, these physically based money problems are frequently caused by exposure to or participation in abuse, addictions, trauma, or other violating circumstances. I've worked with one client who, as a child, was sexually abused for years. As an adult, he never had any money. A bright man, he started businesses that usually reached a level of promise within a few short years, only to have them fall apart just when they were ready to jettison to the stars.

Physical boundary disorders can also be caused by more covert plights, which we can see energetically, but are not always obvious on the surface. These situations can include being raised in a financially deficient family, if this condition was accompanied by additional threats. Perhaps Dad was usually sober and employed, but as soon as he pocketed any extra money, he was off to the bars to get drunk. One of my clients was raised by a shopaholic mother, who hid every spare bit of cash in the dresser drawer until she could enjoy a secret spending spree; she'd always overspend, leaving the family without food for days. Maybe a parent was constantly overextended with credit cards or lost our school money paying off a gambling debt. Perhaps our parents spent all their money on a challenged child, and we received nothing.

Experiences like these—up-and-down, unpredictable situations—qualify as intermittent abuse. When the teeter-totter abuse is linked with money, our fiscal security will also rise and fall.

Any situation that links money with physically challenging circumstances or abuse will lead to at least one energetic syndrome. We might not even know what occurred to cause our problems. I worked with a man who was adopted by wealthy people. No matter how much his parents financially helped him, he could hardly pay his bills. After investigating his birth parentage, he discovered that he was the fifth child of a married couple who gave him up for adoption because they were shy of resources. He had unconsciously absorbed their energetic pattern, and as a result, his physical energetic boundary broadcast the energy of poverty into the world with such intensity that the world had no choice but to agree with him!

Scientific fields, including microchimerism, the inheritance of our mothers' physical cells, and epigenetics, the assumption of our ancestors' memories in our bodies (both discussed in chapter 2), underscore the fact that many of our most life-challenging money issues don't originate with us. Nonetheless, the more serious the violation or tragedy associated with money—regardless of whether it happened in our own or in others' lives—the more dramatic the effects will be on our fiscal bottom line. The best way to start enriching your physical boundaries is to set an intention or add a financial twist to the work intention you set in chapter 6. Use this intention to program your food, drink, and various objects. Wear the colors and use the shapes discussed in chapter 6, and do everything else you can to enhance your work life.

If money considerations are seriously affecting your physical survival, it is important to return money to its natural place in the physical territory. Contrary to your unconscious sense, money is not monstrous or a threat to your personal security. Rather, money is a physical object or substance. Putting money in its place takes the sting or sizzle out of it, effectively calming and initiating healing within your physical borders in relation to money.

Originally, money was a medium of exchange. Our ancestors traded a potato for a cob of corn or a few rocks for a neighbor's help. It was pretty easy to keep track of money when it was a solid object. Eventually, money became quantified in valuable substances, such as gold, silver, or copper. Paper bills were originally backed by real gold; now the copper penny is only coated with copper, and gold has long since disappeared from the reserves. Today, our paychecks, credit and debit cards, and checks aren't genuine coinage, but only symbolic representations of money. And the goods that money buys? We seldom stare at a couch or coffee cup and see dollar signs. Money has become separate from its physicality, which makes it easier to project our issues onto it.

To repair our physical boundaries, it's imperative to link money with our physical being again. Moreover, we must reclaim our need for money as a need equal to our need for air, food, shelter, and drink.

Start by remembering the material spin money held when you were a child. My generation enjoyed piggy banks, coins, and dollar bills. I remember saving upwards of ten dollars, which I would wad into my pocket and dole out at the local drugstore for Christmas presents. I was so proud of myself. Money wasn't scary; it was delightful.

Perceiving money as a physical object and need justifies our desire for it. Quantifying it as a material substance encourages us to use it wisely, to refrain from giving it away to abusive people or spending it dangerously. You let yourself breathe air, don't you? You'd never give all your air away to someone who is manipulating you, would you? As we become accustomed to seeing money as a touchstone for our well-being, it will actually transform into a bandage and medicine, cast and splint, balm and nectar, for our physical energetics.

How do you reeducate your subconscious about the true nature of money on the physical level? First, forgive yourself and others for believing that money can hurt. Instead, acknowledge that money is an object that holds the blessings of the world. Then begin carrying cash everywhere you go, even if it's only a few pennies. Intentionally program this cash, and every new bit that ends up in your wallet, for increased prosperity. Use your monetary or work intention, if you have one. Do the same with every other tangible sign of money, including paychecks and bills.

Next, start blurring the boundaries between money coming in and money going out. Both flows sustain and nourish you. Just as a plant takes in oxygen and releases carbon dioxide, we must both receive money and release it.

Now get as much money pulled together as you can and throw it in a dry bathtub. Program this money by holding it and sending your intention into it. You could even imagine it multiplying as you do so! Climb into the bathtub yourself and feel all that money. Imagine the abundance, the kiss of prosperity, as the energy of that money repairs your physical energetic boundaries and the parts of your past that forced you into a poor relationship with money.

As often as you can, use cash to make your purchases. Set aside a certain amount of currency for your pay-as-you go bills and purchase your groceries, haircuts, gas, and more with cash. Sometimes you'll have to give up something you desire for something else—sometimes not. Using cash will reestablish the necessary and healthy link between money and your needs.

Finally, I recommend thinking about the actual wounds that created monetary insecurity. Use the techniques in chapter 4 to uncover your storyline, but go a step further. Instead of concentrating on what didn't happen, think about what should have occurred. If your parents hit you every time they were low on funds, ask yourself what they should have done. Perhaps they should have discussed their worries with a financial planner or cut back on eating out. Maybe they should have hugged you and told you it would all be okay. Commit to giving yourself what you were never given and doing what the adults or authorities should have done: See a financial planner or reduce your dining out budget, if you're tight on funds. Ask a friend to comfort you when you're scared about finances.

I had one client who was consistently paid less than his coworkers. At home, he made sure everyone else's physical needs were met, usually at the expense of his own. The reason? He was one of five children when growing up. As the oldest, his share of the funds was reduced every time another child was born until, at age twelve, he was forced to work. The others were literally given more food, clothing, and money, and he was given nothing. This type of neglect qualifies as physical abuse, creates unworthiness (an emotional issue), and, in his case, affected his sense of value to the extent he didn't fight for equal pay. I had him take $50 cash out of his weekly paycheck and spend it only on himself—no one else. After a few months of nurturing the inner self who had been physically wounded, he started to gain a sense of deservedness. He looked for a better job and, even in a recession, got one. It paid 20 percent more than his last job did. He has since increased his own "under the table" take to $100 and is on his way to another promotion at work.

Physical energetic boundaries respond to physical activity, substances, and objects. Reward any gains you make in your money situation with a physical reward, even if it is just a walk in the park or a drugstore trinket. Treating yourself like you are worthy of having money opens the space for more money and less lack.

Emotional Boundaries for More Money

Years ago, I worked with a financial therapist who declared that almost all money problems originated with emotional issues.

At the emotional level, financial satiation is *not* about how much money we have or don't have. We might have millions of dollars in the bank, but still feel poor. Conversely, we might have only a few dollars in our pocket and consider ourselves the wealthiest person on this planet. Money itself isn't the issue. Instead, it's our emotions—our trained and programmed beliefs paired with our various feelings—that determine how we feel about money in general, specific money-related situations, our ability to face money strains or disasters, and our willingness to receive and respond to opportunity.

A strong emotional reaction connected to money, especially one that continually results in poor financial situations, covers up pain linked with money. Pain is our reaction to being treated wrongly. Maybe our mom never spent money on us, but did on our sister; maybe we were the only kid in school with goofy clothes because we were so poor. It doesn't matter what we experienced, only that we got trapped in the pain of being treated as less than worthy of financial support.

We might experience anger, fear, or sadness because of our money issues, but surrounding all of these is disgust, often in the form of shame or guilt, in our emotional field. Disgust both causes and is produced by a distorted emotional energetic boundary.

Shame says there is something wrong with us. It's the product of participation in a shameful or disgusting act, event, or relationship. When we're young, we don't create our own shame. It starts with someone around us doing something bad or disgusting. Of course, that person doesn't want to feel shameful, but the energy of that shame has to go somewhere. It ends up in us, interweaving through our emotional energy field.

For example, one of my clients watched his mother beg his father for money. Dad would call her and the four boys names when handing over a few dollars for food. One time, my client and his mother went to the local grocery store, where they had an account. Embarrassed, the shopkeeper said the account was so overdrawn, he couldn't give them any more food until the father came and paid up. That night, the family ate bread and butter for dinner. As an adult, my client hardly ever had a penny to his name. Why would he? He equated money with being embarrassed.

If the original event violating our emotional boundary involved money, we'll have money shame, which will prevent us from being happy when dealing with money. In fact, we'll believe having money should make us feel bad.

Guilt is closely aligned with shame. We are supposed to feel guilt when we do something wrong. That way, we can mature the guilt into true, healthy disgust, which tells us we need to change our actions or our relationship with a certain person or substance. We'll then make the change and avoid repeating the same error. If we're shame prone, however, we'll feel overly guilty, developing what I call false guilt. Maybe every time we have money and someone else doesn't, we'll feel guilty or so bad that we'll take on others' debt or work. Maybe we'll let spirits guilt us into making stupid money errors, or we'll let others steal our money. If we have a weak or damaged emotional boundary, we can easily pick up others' money guilt, too, compounding our problems.

When our emotional boundaries are bound up in shame or guilt—ours or others'—our feeling of unworthiness grows like mold on old bread. We are also unable to mature any of our feelings (anger, sadness, or fear) to their true destination, joy.

To shift our emotional boundary, we have to be willing to take these five steps:

1. Feel the hidden pain.
2. Release the disgust that doesn't belong to us.
3. Empower our original disgust.
4. Cleanse our emotional field.
5. Take action to create joy.

1. Feel the hidden pain. Using the technique for uncovering your storyline (see chapter 4), return to the situation that created dissonance with money. Feel the pain and hurt and love yourself through it.

2. Release the disgust that doesn't belong to you. Continue nurturing yourself through the pain of the original situation until you can feel the disgust you had for the person who created the negative association with money. As long as you're blaming yourself, you haven't yet arrived. Wait until you can pinpoint a person, situation, culture, religion, or institution that is not you. We don't willingly adopt negative monetary beliefs. Now ask the Divine to sort the disgust, dividing it between you and the original owner of at least some of the disgust or shame. (I often ask the Divine to actually tell me the percentage split, such as 20 percent mine, 80 percent theirs.) Request that the Divine free you from the disgust that was never yours. Know that the Divine will deal with this disgust and its rightful owners in a loving way.

3. Empower your original disgust. Give it power by forgiving yourself for repressing it. You don't have to forgive the other parties, at least not yet. You must only release yourself from the chopping block of shame and guilt by understanding that, at that moment, you had no choice but to adopt a detrimental emotional belief and deny your deservedness of prosperity. Remain in this stage until you know that you did no wrong at that moment and can, therefore, forgive yourself for what you have done with your money fears since then.

4. Cleanse your emotional field. Now visualize yourself washing your emotional field of the gray, blotchy, shadowy energy of unhealthy disgust. You don't need it anymore. You have no reason to hide from abundance, love, or money. You have no reason to punish yourself by withholding monetary joy. Continue this cleansing until you sense that your emotional boundaries are whole and open to healthy monetary rewards.

5. Take action to create joy. Ask yourself, what will bring you joy in regard to money? Let the answer pop into your head. Do you need to pay off debt? Cut up your credit cards? Start spending money on yourself rather than everyone else? Ask for a raise? Listen to the answer and respond. Now for every day of the rest of your life, ask the same question. Watch as the money flows in—and remains!

In general, a healthy emotional boundary links money with joy, resulting in monetary transactions that increase our joy. Orienting our emotional health toward joy encourages financial wholeness. Once you've cleansed long-held disgust and felt any outstanding pain, you can process other feelings. This often-used therapeutic phrase means feeling all of your feelings, discovering their meaning, listening to their messages, and doing what you need to do to make effective and positive decisions. Remember that all emotions lead toward joy, as discussed in chapters 5 and 6 (specifically in regard to work in chapter 6). That means that within your emotional reaction to every money issue, opportunity, debt, bill, or challenge is an opportunity to find joy.

Alarmed by those overcharge drafts you incurred? First, shift your original fear into joy by being grateful that you have a bank account. Now pay attention to the message of fear, which says that it's time to take action. What can you do to produce more joy? Change banks? Move money from one account into the other earlier in the month?

Upset by a demotion and salary decrease? Shift the anger into joy at still having a job, and then listen deeper. Does remaining in this new, downgraded position make you sad? Then you must seek a more loving monetary situation. Maybe it's time to buff up your resume and start job hunting.

If at any point you uncover disgust, pay attention. Analyze for a syndrome and start the five steps over.

You've dealt with your feelings. Now what about your beliefs? Ideally, we will operate from mature beliefs underscoring our worthiness, deservedness, powerfulness, value, essential goodness, and lovability. These types of beliefs enable us to stare down our financial woes and solve problems appropriately. They also help us avoid bad financial situations in the first place. For instance, we won't marry that gambler because we believe we deserve better than having to pick up someone else's money messes.

How can we replace negative monetary beliefs with more rewarding ones? First, we can examine our major syndromes or money issues to figure out what we wrongly believe. From there, we can mature our belief into a more appropriate and healthy one.

Are you constantly broke? Then you believe that life has broken you. Instead of thinking "I am broken" or "I am whole," create an intention such as, "I am inviting more money into my life in order to embrace my inherent wholeness."

Are you usually in debt? Then you most likely believe that the world owes you. Affirm that you are now learning how to give and receive abundance.

Do you often need others to rescue you monetarily? Let yourself know you are powerful enough to accept money for good work performed.

Do you struggle to stay with a budget (as all good no-boundary individuals do)? Know that you deserve the safety of structure and can trust your own limits.

Do you constantly rescue others financially? Let yourself know it's safe to receive.

Transform your repetitive money issues by reducing them to their core misperceptions and then start telling yourself the truth. This truth can also be programmed as an intention into objects, food, or beverages, such as discussed in previous chapters.

Relational Boundaries and Financial Woes: What's a Girl or Guy to Do?

The couple sitting before me was arguing about money—or so they thought. The truth is, they were both stuck in relational-boundary issues, which reduce to these two ideas regarding money:

• Power versus love
• Mom versus Dad

Our monetary beliefs are encoded into our relationship boundaries in early to mid-childhood. Around age four, we emerge from our families as social creatures. Our tromping ground is school. For the next several years, we're unconsciously deciding how to replicate our home instruction in the greater world of people. Our relational boundaries carry what we've learned into this new environment and get added to.

What's the main medium of social exchanges, even at school? You've got it: money.

We are a tribal people, and we earn our place in a social continuum through the things that money can buy. The most popular and encouraged children are usually the ones whose parents can best tend to them, and it takes money to do this. The boys and girls with the cool technology, the latest haircuts and fashions, the resources to buy equipment for and participate in sports or other popular organized activities are automatically elevated in the school social strata. Money essentially bestows power, lovability, or both.

I wasn't one of those girls. I still remember moving from Huntsville, Alabama, to Edina, Minnesota, a wealthy suburb of Minneapolis, and being the only second-grade girl who had brown instead of red boots. It would be years before my family had enough money for any new clothes, much less boots. So my mother decided to sew our school clothes. I showed up in elementary school wearing green-and-yellow flowered dresses fashioned from our old muslin bedroom curtains. I looked like an escapee from a horticulture experiment. I wasn't well received by my classmates or teachers.

I internalized this rejection, which was linked to money, and had money challenges for years. It took me decades to work out the issue, even when I became therapeutically aware of it, because relationship issues imprint in our energetic field, informing people about our status, level of perceived power, and receptivity to all things financial.

Money as power means we get to make financial decisions. This is true within businesses, government institutions, religious spheres, and, of course, coupledom. For thousands of years, most legal systems gave men ownership to a woman's money, property, children, and decisions. This is still the case in many cultures and religions. Money equates to relational power.

Money as love implies that the most lovable will be provided for financially. Most religious institutions underscore this philosophy, emphasizing that good financial stewards are rewarded with prosperity. For thousands of years, the most valued or lovable women won the richest men.

We're all programmed to link power and lovability with money and to think that the most wealth is given to the most powerful and most desirable people. After all, don't "good people" live in the "good houses" and "bad people" live in "bad houses"?

We carry this program into our romantic partnerships. This template says that men are supposed to make more money than women and be the boss, while women are supposed to make less money and take care of the home. Powerful men earn their wives' care and high positions within society and work arenas; lovable women avoid the worldly messes and are taken care of. Money and financial care are the rewards for how well each gender plays its assigned role.

But the realities of modern life conflict with this conditioning. Women now work outside the home and earn their own income, and men participate in home affairs. The number of single mothers (I am one) also throws a wrench in the system. Many women currently run households, wielding both power and love, even while lacking funds and time. These days, no one knows how to deal with money within relationships, because no one has enough power (resources and authority) or love (time for care).

Our relational boundaries haven't shifted from the old notions because we inherit our relational beliefs about money from Mom, our love expert, and Dad, our power guru. Their streams of consciousness lock into our energetic system, and away we go.

How do we release ourselves from the narrow idea that money equals power and love? How can we clear up these relationship dynamics and live a healthier fiscal life? There are a number of techniques that work through the relational boundary.

The starting point is changing our inappropriate idea of money as power versus love to an appropriate one equating money with empowered love. We make this change by playing sleuth in our own back yard, the one we grew up in. We need look no further than Mom and Dad, or the figures representing them, to uncover our relational assumptions about money. We must then cleanse our relational field of the effects and open to the flow of affluence. At this point, we'll be able to block relationships that create monetary drains.

Think back to your early school days. Let your memory wander, remembering how you felt at the ages between four and eight. Recall the effects of money and affluence. Start with your peer group. Which kids were more powerful or the natural leaders? Which ones had the most friends? What were their families' economic situations? More important, how did your perceptions of their privileged circumstances influence how you looked at yourself?

Whatever your social perceptions, they originated in your home. Focus on Mom or Dad, or whoever served those roles. Think first of your mom or the feminine influence. What did she believe about money? What did she teach you about money? What did her money behaviors instruct you about the feminine aspects of yourself or of women? How did her money issues formulate your ideas about how finances relate to power (the ability to get things done; authority) and love (giving of time, care, and compassion)?

Now ask the same questions about your father or the male figure in your life, concentrating on what he showed you about the masculine within or about men.

After reviewing your parental monetary beliefs, reduce your conclusions to the responses to these questions:

• I believe the following about the feminine in relation to money:
• I believe the following about the masculine in relation to money:
• I believe the following about power in relation to money:
• I believe the following about love in relation to money:
• The role of money in relationships is:

Can you see how your relationships issues have affected your monetary situation? It's time to substitute a healthier belief for your unhealthy ones and package this new idea in an intention. For example, you might create new beliefs such as "I participate in loving relationships that share power, love, and money," "I give and receive generously," and "I love myself and others enough to be empowered financially." Start working with your prosperity intention as suggested in chapters 4 and 5.

It's not enough to simply think differently. The relational money beliefs you adopted during childhood and that were furthered by your perceptions and behaviors are woven throughout your relational energetic boundary. After performing the inner work, you have to fix your energetic field, or your worldly patterns will continue.

To work on your energy field, enter a meditative state and ask to intuitively see, know, sense, or be told by your inner spirit how the false beliefs affected your relational boundary. Specifically check for indications of the seven syndromes. Too thick boundaries prevent you from receiving from others. Leaky holes indicate syndromes that are draining you of money; you are frequently in situations where money flows from you to others, but not in return. Two-way holes, through which energy both comes in and goes out, suggest the Healer's Syndrome: you give away your money and take on loved ones' monetary problems. Gaps through which energy pours into you can indicate hypersensitivity to others, such as occurs in the Psychic-Sensitive or even Environ Syndromes.

If you are ready to really give up your old relational beliefs about money, make that decision and then ask the Divine to help repair your relational boundary. Intuitively watch as they are shifted and changed. Now you can use the techniques for either career support in chapter 6 or relationship healing in chapter 8 to support and further your work.

Spiritual Boundaries and Monetary Satisfaction

Spiritually, money is a measurement of our relationship with the Divine. Most of us are conditioned to use money as the yardstick to answer the question, "Does God value me or not?"

Many spiritually based institutions, entities, and systems, intentionally or unintentionally, take advantage of this inherent question by implying that money given to them will increase our standing with God. We'll give to them if we think it gets us closer to God. This belief is one of the reasons so many of us develop weak, rigid, or poor spiritual boundaries in terms of money.

Reduce your religious programming, and you'll usually find two opposing spiritual views, both of which completely corkscrew our spiritual boundaries:

• Money is the root of all evil.
• Money is the reward for being a good person.

We usually gravitate toward one side of the continuum rather than the other, based on our natural personality, upbringing, and monetary success. If we're on the leaner side of wealth, we might prefer the first belief. Being broke makes us good. If we have plumper pocketbooks, we probably prefer the second statement. Some of us might ricochet between the two, and our earning results follow.

If we buy into the first statement, but we have money, we'll feel shameful about being prosperous. Maybe we'll make sure we spend more than we make or lose all our savings. Perhaps we'll let ourselves be vampirized, or we'll assume others' problems and work to prove our goodness. If we're on the poorer side, we might feel sacrosanct, but also secretly angry and resentful.

Believing the second statement can cause the wealthy to feel either egotistical or undeserving. If we have less money yet believe the second statement, we'll feel shame and envy. These reactions, or a combination of them, underlie spiritual-border problems. The resulting vulnerability can have devastating effects on both our bank account and our spiritual health. We might feel resentful toward the Divine. How can we trust a god that wants us broke or, conversely, trust a god that rewards only the rich? The consequences to our spiritual borders are devastating and sometimes supernatural. Violated spiritual boundaries can cause susceptibility to entities, ghosts, or other types of spiritual interference.

I worked with one individual who was always flat broke. His other family members started and sold companies and were extraordinarily wealthy, but not him. I perceived an energetic cord or contract between him and his whole family system. He was being completely vampirized through his spiritual energetic field. He truly believed it was better to give than receive, that money was the root of evil, and he couldn't bear to see his family suffer. Consequently, his spiritual abundance was pouring out through his spiritual field and entering the spiritual fields of family members.

After releasing this cordage, he started a new business. It succeeded almost immediately. The businesses run by his family members? While they didn't go belly up, their growth rate slowed and then stalled. On the upside, one of his sisters decided that she didn't want to be in business. She sold her business and went to art school. On the downside, the other two siblings intuited that their brother was responsible for the downward shift in monies and stopped talking to him. When we release intrusive energetic connections, those who have benefited from these cords often try to reengage us or break off contact altogether.

Personally, I believe working on your spiritual boundaries is a must if you desire monetary success. Foremost, accept your spiritual calling. As discussed in chapter 6, you are here for a vital purpose that only you can perform. To accomplish this goal, the Divine has guaranteed you the material and monetary resources you need. Some of us might require ten million dollars to fulfill our mission; others might require a sizeable salary. Yet others are to be provided for through donations. The crux is that what you need will be provided.

To heal our spiritual borders, we have to replace spiritual misperceptions with divine truth. This isn't as hard to do as you might think. Ask yourself, yes, right now, what is your essential truth about money?

Now picture yourself taking that belief and holding within a fluid stream of white, liquid light. Ask the Divine to flush your spiritual field and your heart with this wash of truth. Notice that any cords, entity attachments, and inaccurate beliefs simply flow out of you. Notice how free you feel. Notice that you now perceive money as a gift freely given by the Divine. As with any gift, the Divine will tell you how to open to it and what to do once you obtain it.

Now employ healing streams of grace (introduced in chapter 4). Ask the Divine to insert a stream of grace into your spiritual field where needed, and pay attention to how connected and loved you feel.

Do you doubt your ability to maintain this new way of being in everyday life? Call a friend or a support person. Ask him or her to hold faith, or any of the virtues, for you. Faith, hope, truth, love, and abundance—these are concrete energies and emanate straight from the Divine. When we're down, we can trust another to hold the energy we need to be held up.

You can also try the following exercise, a guided meditation for spiritual wealth, which helps you assume an attitude of gratefulness and which in turn opens your spiritual boundaries to monetary guidance and prosperity.

Exercise: Gratitude in God's Room

As discussed in earlier chapters, concentrating on a positive spiritual emotion in our heart shifts our neurology, cardiovascular system, brain functions, and, therefore, our behavior. In other words, when we are more altruistic, when we embrace our birthright of goodness and invite the Divine to support us, the world will respond in kind. When we insert the *kind* back in *humankind,* we'll also be more willing to allow a flow of money into our lives and seek the spiritual guidance necessary to direct the outflow.

This guided meditation can be done anytime and for any reason to affirm the connection between you and the Divine; the latter is your true source of spiritual and monetary wealth.

Enter a meditative state and take a few deep breaths. Now imagine your spiritual boundaries, the field farthest away from your body, filling with a white and golden light. You sense the boundaries between heaven and earth, your own spiritual borders and the Divine's presence, dissipate and disappear, and the strange, wonderful feeling of unconditional love swims into and through you. Rainbows flood your space before the colors separate into distinct forms and images. Do you see angels? Spiritual guides? Beings of nature, love, and help?

You know that this is the way the world really is and that your spiritual borders are designed to enable this sensation all the time.

Gratitude emerges from your heart—gratefulness that the Divine loves you so much that it has created a room, a mansion, a home that continually revolves around and through your spiritual field. Anything unsuitable is simply and easily whisked away by divine helpers, and you experience the full safety of being held by the Divine.

Within this divine place, focus on money. Ask the Divine how it wants to provide for you. What must you believe or do to accept what the Divine wants to give? What does money mean, from the Divine's perspective? How can you let the Divine evolve your sense of money into the acceptance of empowering divine love?

Let the answers soak into you. When you're ready, take a few deep breaths and return to your everyday consciousness, knowing that heaven and its blessings remain around and within you.

||||||||||||||||||||||||||||||

Chapter 8

Love, Relationships, and Romance: Energy Boundaries That Create Heart

Simply pushing harder within the old boundaries will not do.

PSYCHOLOGY PROFESSOR KARL WEICK

L ove is perpetually creative because it starts in our hearts, which disperses goodness throughout our bodies and our energy fields. While we desire loving relationships, seeking especially that special soul mate with whom we feel we should need no boundaries, the truth is that we'll never achieve any real love without healthy boundaries.

We've spent our life operating under relational boundaries. As a child, you couldn't tattle, or a friend would drop you. If you showed up at Grandma's with a nose ring, you'd be grounded. At my house, if you didn't eat two helpings of Great Aunt Hannah's horribly dry strawberry shortcake, your allowance was eliminated for a month. As adults, we realize that we'll never get a second date if we chew with our mouths open on the first go-around, and even the most loving spouse probably won't tolerate us cheating. But do we understand the vital role our energetic boundaries play in attracting, creating, shaping, enjoying, and even ending relationships?

If we are serious about love, we have to get serious about establishing energetic boundaries that clearly reflect what we're willing to endure, experience, enact, or enhance in the dance of love and relationship. Included in that dance are not only our unique soul mate, but also relatives, friends, coworkers, and others. Lacking healthy energetic boundaries, we'll be prone to the seven syndromes. To create healthy energetic boundaries, on the other hand, is to formulate whole relationships.

Special note: That very important relationship between parents and children has earned its own chapter. Chapter 9 discusses how parents can help children develop their four main boundaries while parents continue to develop their own.

Sex, Touch, Sleep, and Other Physical Boundary Plays

Who gets closest to us but the people who touch us physically? The first people who touched us were our parents or equivalent figures, and maybe our siblings and relatives.

When school age, we innocently exchanged hugs and wrestled with our peers. Then when we reached puberty, touch suddenly held an entirely different enticement—one invoking our sexuality. Sex became linked with romance, intimacy, and our ideals about a one, true love. Sex is also tied with physical touch. Even though one can certainly enjoy physical touch without being sexual, it's hard to be sexual without physical touch.

If you examine your past, you'll most likely discover that some physical touches benefited and supported you, while others hurt or damaged you. Pain and pleasure became so intertwined, it's now hard to separate the two sometimes, isn't it? Every sort of touch, even suggested touch, is under the rule of our physical energetic boundary. It performs several big jobs: staving off others' harmful energies, welcoming loving touch, and ironically, completely dissolving when it's safe for us to bond with another human being.

It will fulfill all these roles if you've experienced enough healthy relational touch: if, as an infant, you were held and cuddled with care; if your mother or father held your fingertips when you first were walking; if your school nurse tended your playground wounds with empathy; if your friends patted you on the back when you needed encouragement; if you, as an adult, swathed children with comfort and care and gave of your heart to your loved ones. Your physical boundary won't operate as well if you were physically or sexually abused or exposed to violating behavior. You might attract people who aren't physically safe and repel those who are. You'll certainly have developed one or several of the seven syndromes and be really confused, especially in the arenas of sexuality and romance, sleep, and trust—three strange bedfellows, to be sure, but ones that share important links.

I want to talk first about sex because it's such a vital life area. If our physical energetic boundary is healthy, our sexual life will be as well. Even if we're abstaining from sex, we'll love ourselves, invite healthy intimacy of every sort, and feel good about our bodies. But if we've been damaged by sexual hurt, our sexual boundaries will either be too rigid, rejecting partners or the love they can share through sexual play, or too permeable, causing us to lose our life energy or take on others' negative issues.

When we have sex, we exchange psychic, vital life energy with our partner. Our psychic energies flood in and out through the mouth, vagina, or penis, or any other orifice, as well as the skin. If each of us is lovingly motivated, we'll give and receive love, whether our sexual acts include intercourse, kissing, fondling, oral sex, or just touch. Both partners will leave the process having gained positive energy. If either party is stealing energy from the other (vampirism) or sending undesirable and unaddressed issues into the other, both will leave hurt and damaged.

It can take years to clear out all the psychic imprints from an unhealthy sexual lover. In fact, if sexual abuse or use is involved, I don't believe the toxic energy leaves our body or our physical boundaries repair until we consciously work on cleansing. If you were sexually abused, others' shame, dirtiness, guilt, and terror are in your body and physical field; your beautiful, bountiful, innocent energy might be held captive in their body and physical boundary. What if, as an adult, we were used for sex or used someone else for sex? The user walks away with the victim's healthy energy; the victim is left with the crud.

In situations involving multiple partners or someone who is cheating on his or her spouse, everyone's energy is exchanged. If a man leaves his wife's bed and has sex with a lover, the lover ends up with the wife's energy, and the wife with the lover's. But the man doesn't usually feel a thing. Why? Because he just dumped all his dissatisfaction about life into the women.

Sex is a big part of our lives. According to the Kinsey Institute, a well-reputed research organization, eighteen- to twenty-nine-year-olds have sex around 112 times a year; thirty- to thirty-nine-year-olds, 86 times a year; forty- to forty-nine-year-olds, 69 times a year. Women have about four male sexual partners in a lifetime, and men have six to eight. This is a lot of energy exchange.[1] If we have sex twice a week, on average, for seventy years, we'll have around 5,000 sexual acts—5,000 energetic exchanges—per lifetime.

Now let's look at the shadowy side of sex. At least one in four girls worldwide are sexually abused, as are one in six boys. I believe the internal damage is matched by the energetic damage, which leaves us exposed for repetitive treatment. Just as bad, U.S. porn revenues exceed the combined revenues of the big media companies, including ABC, CBS, and NBC. Over half of all spending on the Internet is related to sex.[2] Viewers don't have to touch the porn star or youngster on the computer screen to absorb and participate in the violence, dirtiness, and perversion. Whatever the viewer picks up energetically clings to his or her physical field and is deposited into the fields anyone he or she is around—and, especially, touches—in life. This includes the viewer's spouse and children, who are potentially vulnerable to the same physical energy warping the porn watcher experiences.

I worked with one man who had cheated on his born-again Christian wife by watching porn and engaging in several affairs for several years, during which time he also did drugs and drank. He went to therapy, changed his behavior, and entered a loving relationship after a time, having figured out that his abuse pattern started with being sexually violated by a relative in the home. But he couldn't at first figure out why his only daughter ended up with a severe drug and alcohol addiction, which she sponsored by sleeping with pimps. She finally admitted she had started this behavior at age sixteen, the exact age she was when my client had started cheating on his wife. The daughter's physical field had shaped itself to the father's. "This is apparently how, as a woman, I'm supposed to get my needs met," she had unconsciously decided.

Sometimes our physical field's programs affect our sleep, in addition to our physical and sexual safety. At least once a week, someone calls me claiming that they can't sleep with their bed partner. As one woman said, "I lay awake all night. I can literally feel his negativity slime me." The unclaimed energy from a partner with poor physical fields can and does enter the boundaries of the partner physically closest to them. At night, our bodies automatically let their guard down. If your sleeping partner's energies keep you awake, you'll know it. And you'll be nodding your head right now, wondering what to do about it.

Both physical and sexual violations to our body distort our physical energy fields. Besides affecting our relationships through sex and sleep, these hurts lead to trust issues. Even if a friend hugs us, are we able to let the love in through our physical field, or do we tense up and reject the reassurance? Do we remain calm in the presence of someone who scares us, embracing the safety of our physical borders, or do we freak out, looking for the open door? We deserve to trust that our physical energy borders are up, erect, and blinking away, always functioning, assessing situations and individuals for safety and, ultimately, the likelihood of love and respect. If this isn't the case for us, it's time to work energetically.

If your boundaries have been violated to the extent that you are continually subjected to one of the seven syndromes in your relationships, your first step is therapeutic. You deserve to get underneath your behavioral and energetic reactions. Know that these patterns didn't start with you. If you have undertaken therapy and still find yourself subjected to one of the syndromes, I encourage you to add energetic processes to your toolkit.

No matter which syndrome affects you, I suggest you begin or further your healing by releasing the energy that isn't your own—energy deposited by an abusive person, system, or entity—from within and around your body. Consider working with a therapeutic or energy professional. The following exercise can be used to supplement this process.

Prepare yourself for a meditative state and make sure you won't be disturbed. Now breathe deeply into your heart and ask that the Divine conduct a cleansing process. Think of the syndrome you most relate to or the pattern you most frequently experience. Now shift your focus from your heart to your physical energy field, which emanates from and immediately surrounds your skin.

As you sense this field, ask the Divine to connect you to a healing stream of grace and directly into the Universal Field, as discussed in chapter 4. When we are dealing with relational issues, especially those caused by violations, the most effective way to truly cleanse is through the spiritual forces provided directly by the Divine. You do not need to plug this stream into any particular part of your body. Instead, allow the Divine to swirl it around you, washing clean every part of your physical field.

While this occurs, ask the Divine to help you remember or recall the event or type of situation that underlies your relational syndrome.

Keep breathing. Go through the terror; don't stop until you discover the wounded self underneath your own behaviors and others' traumatic treatment. Now ask the Divine to connect the healing stream of grace to this wounded self. Watch as he or she is purified, healed, cleansed, and separated from whatever and whoever caused the injuries.

Now invite this wounded self into your heart. Allow the Divine to cleanse the rest of your current self internally with this healing stream of grace.

At this point, it's important to establish a new intention for the physical aspect of your relationships. What is it? What might the Divine suggest? As you focus on this intention, ask the Divine to mold your physical energy field so it will support this intention and no other.

You can repeat this cleansing exercise as many times as you need to, until you feel like your physical energy field is rehabilitated and actually working for, not against, your love life. It will be important to move your intention into concrete reality, which can be accomplished through energetic techniques. ?

This energetic layer monitors your primary partner or mate, sexual intimacy, and primal connections. The reason you first cleared your physical field is so that you can shift your current relationships, if they require a change, or attract better ones. To shift a current primary relationship, further develop your intention so it is clear. It's unethical to establish an intention to change someone else. You can't say, "Please make my partner stop using me sexually," or, "Make my spouse want more sex," or even, "Strike my living partner with the desire to clean the house day and night." What you can do is program yourself for change.

I had one client with the Mule Syndrome who decided to write statements all over her skin with toxic-free paint. Her intention was, "I am accepting intimacy freely, no strings attached." After a month or two, she noticed that her spouse started picking up his share of the bedroom. (Most likely, her intention encouraged her to stop performing his labor for him.) He then began doing his own laundry, to her amazement.

Finally, his romantic attention increased; he even spent more time titillating her sexually than having her attend to him.

We can also program almost any physical item to help us modify our physical field and, consequently, our subtle and measurable behavior in an existing major relationship. I recommend using gemstones and various metals for this. Use the techniques described in chapter 4 to program these tools. Pink quartz will assuage a too-intense sexual relationship, whether it involves someone who steals your energy through sex or a no-boundary looseness of your own. Amethyst, obsidian, or hematite will repel psychic entities or cords, and garnet will encourage your own or another's sexual desire. Turquoise, especially worn near the neck, enables you to receive guidance from the Divine and enhances higher communication; it is especially useful in argumentative relationships. Silica can help resolve sexual dysfunctions, such as if you are shut down because of being used or ignored; tourmaline can do the same. If you want to increase your fertility or sacred connection through sex, try carnelian, especially to balance the feminine energies.

Silver will repel cords, entities, and others' energies, and gold will help us attract another's affection. Gold will also empower us if we've tended to give ourselves away, such as those with the Healer's and Vampire Syndromes might do. Do *not* use gold if you've had a no-boundary or psychic-sensitivity problem, or you'll attract more of the same unwanted energies.

Colors and clothing also mitigate our physical fields. Wearing red will initiate excitement, especially anger, but isn't recommended if your relationship is already too dramatic or flamboyant. Avoid black if you absorb others' energies or problems, and add hints of pastels to soothe riled up relationships.

If you feel disconnected from a loved one, envision circles in your energy field. If you feel endangered relationally, situate a square or rectangle all the way around your physical boundary. To formulate new responses to old problems, put a triangle into your physical border.

Do you have a hard time sleeping with your partner? Surround the entire bed or your side of the bed in particular with limestone, water rocks, or granite. These stones fortify physical boundaries. Wear a cap to bed if you pick up on entity activity or your partner's thoughts, and wear slippers or socks if you sense environmental energies or your partner's past. Never sleep in red. You'll be up all night. Instead wear underwear or pajamas that have a glint of silver in order to deflect another's energy.

Want to attract a relationship? Be careful what colors you wear or envision around your energy field. I once told a client who hadn't had a sexual partner in years to picture red around her field. She had nine men show her interest, but none of the men was the type a woman would want to date.

The best way to generate true interest is to show your real self. One way to do this is to wear or carry a small bag of gemstones that represents your truest nature, enables you to release your syndromes, and affirms the qualities most desirable in another. A few stones that might do this are:

- Agate: to attract love
- Amazonite: for a trustworthy mate
- Amber: for a loyal partner
- Aventurine: for a compassionate mate; also attracts mature, rather than immature, love
- Blue sapphire: for a faithful love
- Chalcedony: for unconditional love
- Charoite: for someone who accepts you
- Emerald: for a marriage relationship
- Jade: for someone who is generous
- Moonstone: for an empathetic partner
- Pink tourmaline: for a devoted love
- Prehnite: for helping forgive yourself for not having picked the right person before

- Rhodonite: attracts true love, not fantasy
- Rose quartz: for highest love
- Topaz: for romance[3]

Environmental modifications, especially in the bedroom, can enhance a lagging intimate life and draw in a lovely partner. Start by decluttering and removing all technology. You want your bedroom to be conducive to love, not work, and you want nothing in it that will grab your mind—only things that grab your soul. Hang dreamy and romantic paintings that feature couples in love, and make sure you have two nightstands, especially if you don't have a partner and want one. Who knows who might show up to fill the empty space? Set your bed in a diagonal position across from the door, but still facing the door, so you feel safe and open. This will help you sleep, at the very least.

Finally, be careful whom you kiss. Studies show that the closer people are, the more blurred together their auric fields become. Kirlian photography shows that when two individuals are kissing, their boundaries lose their borders and seem to almost disappear. If this occurs during a kiss, think what happens during sex. Select your sexual partners knowing that you might potentially exchange every single bit of your energy with them. Better yet, ask if you'd like to wake up in the morning having become him or her—or his or her other sexual partners. Asking yourself these questions will help you discern who to have and not have sex with.[4]

Friendly Love: Relating Through the Emotional Boundary

What do you suppose Alice thought about mirrors after visiting Wonderland? When peering at her reflection, did she imagine she was seeing her real self or a dream image? Did she see the Alice from the looking-glass world or a trickster?

Once you really understand the nature of emotions in relationships, you'll find yourself constantly asking these types of questions. What's my feeling, and what's someone else's? <u>Do I love or hate this person because I believe I'm supposed to or because I really do</u>? This confusion occurs because emotions can stray through the looking glass of our emotional field. This isn't wrong; it's what is supposed to happen to create empathy.

As emotional expert Daniel Goleman explains, people with rich relationships, including a spouse and close friends and family, are healthier and live longer than those without. Connections with other people, via emotional interactions, are formed through mirror neurons, a widely dispersed set of brain cells that act like Wi-Fi. These cells track emotional flow and intention and, through an incredibly quick recognition of the other's posture, vocal pacing, and movement, create what's called entrainment.[5] Studies at the Institute of HeartMath have also shown that the heart is able to entrain at a distance through the heart field.[6]

Entrainment occurs when one person's emotions blur with another's until both people share the same emotional state. In the body, we measure emotions chemically, but the sharing occurs through the emotional field. We know this because couples don't have to be touching to experience synchronized feelings. Goleman explains that the created emotional circuit is so strong that one person's strong negative emotions will almost immediately appear in a close friend or loved one, as will a person's strong positive emotions.[7]

We can understand how this friendly empathy keeps us bonded and ready to soothe, enjoy, and help each other. The problem is that unless our so-called negative emotions are "grown up," or matured, a process discussed throughout this book, we'll be emotionally stuck or stunted. So will our relationships.

Certain syndromes cost us emotions, depriving us of the emotions' powerful motivational force, while other syndromes flood us with others' emotions, creating exhaustion, overwork, and even physical problems. I've determined that people who read books like this one are more likely to absorb others' emotions, especially those of their immediate family and significant others. Plagued by permeable and gaping boundaries, they are also apt to attract love partners who could be termed emotionally dissociated, or devoid of emotions. In syndrome language, they attract individuals similar to those with the no-boundary syndrome. Unlike the no-boundary people, however, emotionally dissociated partners push their issues out through their weak boundaries instead of absorbing others' energies. These people are separated from their internal emotional sensations, but have wide-open emotional boundaries, through which their feelings and beliefs flow out unabated. These individuals don't usually know they are out of touch with their emotions; they feel only empty or incomplete. They don't know that deep within them are unresolved and unfelt hatred, grief, rage, pain, and undeservedness. They think they are fine. Aren't they saying the right things? Aren't they calm under pressure, reserved during a fight? What they do know is that their partner (this would be you) is overly emotional and crazy.

Other individuals with permeable emotional boundaries, such as those with the Mule, Healer's, or Psychic-Sensitive Syndromes, and individuals with no boundaries at all, constantly pick up others' emotions and act them out.

With so many emotions getting passed between people like a baton between relay runners, what can you do to eliminate boundary invasions, overarmoring, or leaks? As discussed in previous chapters, emotions are constructed of feelings, all of which can lead to joy, and thoughts are constructed of beliefs that can elevate us to love. When you are aware of an emotionally based syndrome, do everything you can to stop and be quiet for a moment. Imagine a luscious orange or white color washing through your emotional boundaries and purifying your body, cleansing you of others' emotions or any emotional attachment. Concentrate on your belly or abdomen, and invite your own emotions forth. Then isolate the emotion causing your current difficulties before separating the feeling from the thought.

Your intuition will provide you with the insights needed. You might sense, feel, hear, see, or even simply know which feeling has been conjoined with a certain thought. Now ask to intuitively picture or sense the person, group, or system that stimulated your emotional response in the first place. What might have been a healthier way to respond? What would have been a more mature way to feel or think?

Examine your beliefs for misperceptions such as, "Family sticks together no matter what," "If you love someone, you'll let them treat you any way they want," "You can't expect too much out of emotionally wounded people," or, "Someone has to feel all these feelings." How about substituting ideas like, "Family are the people who treat each other with respect," "I deserve to give and receive honor," "Everyone has the right to choose who to be close to or not," "It's important to let everyone feel their own feelings, or they won't learn what their feelings mean," or "Internal peace is my own responsibility."

To further heal your emotional boundary, get creative. Emotions are closely aligned with creativity; in fact, creativity equals emotions come to life. Whether drawn on a canvas, sung in song, danced on tiptoes, or inscribed on scroll, emotions expressed through creativity form joy, build healthy beliefs, and engineer healing.

Use color through clothing, drawing, sketching, imagining, or energetic practices such as colorpuncture, which is acupuncture that utilizes light. Aware of certain stuck feelings? Try the following:

- When you're *angry,* eliminate reds and soothe with blues.
- When you're *sad,* avoid brown, gray, black, or white, and excite with soft reds, oranges, or yellows.
- When you're *scared,* strike out red, yellow, or too bright colors, and go for browns, russets, navy blue, or deeper hues of other colors.

- When you're *happy,* avoid all startling colors to prevent mania; lock in joy with bright pastels.
- When you're *disgusted,* form a gray bubble in your mind and energetically jettison into it disgusting energy or issues, asking the Divine to dispose of them. Avoid wearing grays or blacks, but consider whites or very soft pastels.
- If you are highly susceptible to taking on others' issues, consider black. Even though it's an absorbing color, others won't notice you when you're wearing it.

Two colors and their related stones are especially helpful for enhancing the emotional qualities of a relationship. Coral activates joy and happiness and encourages loving bonding. Turquoise accesses higher wisdom and allows emotions to flow appropriately.

If someone constantly attacks you emotionally, either psychically or directly, imagine yourself inside a pyramid with black-mirrored scales on the outside, pointing upward. This pyramid is interwoven through your emotional boundary. The black effectively hides you from others' projections, the mirrors deflect negativity, and the upward-pointing shingles assure that anything negative making its way to you is returned to the heavens or the other person's higher self for processing.

If this emotionally charged person is one you see often, keep the black-mirrored pyramid up whenever you're around him or her. Then line the inside of its walls with colors that feel comfortable and supportive to you. Consider using pink, which represents love, coral for emotional support, or turquoise for receiving divine guidance. Also concentrate on sensations of joy and beliefs encouraging positive emotional relationships, such as one you might have formed if using the process described at the beginning of this section. To take this process a step further, imagine filling the inside of the pyramid with joy, as if you were pumping in joy with bellows, and then psychically write your intention on both the inside and outside of the pyramid.

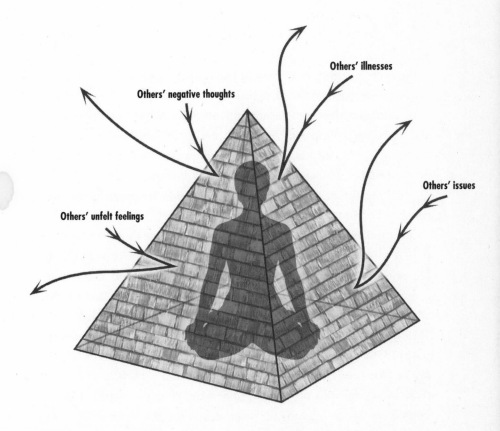

Figure F. *Want to energetically protect yourself from others' emotions? Insert the image of a pyramid into your emotional field. Picture black-colored, mirrorlike scales or shingles pointing upward to deflect others' negativity to their higher selves.*

Music is ideal for releasing others' emotions, soothing your own raw emotions, and creating a space for emotional health. Music, songs, toning, chants, and all other sounds are received by not only the ear, but also the greater body, especially the skeletal system. Your nerves disseminate the music as electrical energy, which is received by the brain. The brain then generates various brain waves. Beta waves are active during focused and active thinking, alpha during relaxation and inactive creativity, theta during meditation and pre-sleep, and delta during dreams and dreamless states of sleep. Via the brain waves and electrical impulses, the music passes down your spine and alters your autonomic nervous system, affecting your heart rate, blood pressure, pulse, skin reactivity, and more.

The body interprets others' emotionally hurtful or abusive statements, behaviors, or even psychic thoughts as "bad" music. Their effect is the same as that of heavy metal music, which raises our blood pressure and heart rate (compared to calming music, such as lullabies, which decreases our blood pressure and heart rate). You can counteract the negative effects of others' erratic emotions by chanting, toning, listening to, thinking about, or humming beautiful music, or simply breathing the sound of *Om* in through your heart.

Om is the most ancient of spiritual sounds, the one the Divine is said to have uttered to begin the universe. If you aren't alone, you can chant Om without making a sound. Think and sense the sound as it enters through the back of your heart, washes through your heart, and finally emanates through the front side of your body into your emotional field. This is a simple way to transcend the moment and reach your higher state of knowing. (Also refer to the chart "Sound Healing: The Songs of the Gods" in chapter 4, and select the Hindu syllables or octave tones most related to your issues, to heal this or any of your energetic boundaries that are creating dissonant relationships.)

You might also benefit from meditation, yoga, or deep-breathing exercises. Mindfulness meditation is a highly accessible way to quickly enter a state of calm and gain emotional sobriety. I encourage you to read books or watch videos by Jon Kabat-Zinn, who analyzes mindfulness meditation from a neuroscience point of view. I've developed my own quick and simple version of mindfulness meditation to apply to the emotional energetic boundary:

1. In a quiet place, sit straight, but not stiffly.
2. Set aside stray thoughts about yesterday or tomorrow, and concentrate on the moment.
3. Pay attention to your breathing, feeling every part of your belly, lungs, and mouth respond to your inhales and exhales.
4. Envision every thought or worry flowing away on your exhale. Watch also as these, along with others' emotions, release from your emotional boundary.
5. Keep returning to the awareness of release and the acceptance of your natural feelings and true thoughts, which focus on love and worthiness. Invite these healthy feelings and thoughts back into your body and life with each inhalation.
6. End this time with a sense of gratefulness for yourself and the Divine in your heart.

||||||||||||||||||||||||||||||||||||||||||||||||||||||||||||||||||||

For Really Difficult People

Sometimes we're involved with really toxic people. They might be parents, friends, or bosses, but the really challenging situations usually involve our primary other—or our almost or already ex-other.

At least three times a week, I'm asked to counsel a client or friend dealing with the abusive spouse or ex. Usually traditional therapeutic tips help, but not if we're dealing with an addict, abuser, or borderline-narcissistic personality.

The third type is especially difficult, because such people can appear quite lovely to the world, even to judges in the court system. We know better, but we often can't prove that they are fundamentally imbalanced and manipulative.

A technique I use when dealing with demonic attachments or fallen angels is also useful in these situations. "Fallen angels?" you ask. Yes. There are such beings, and they cause everything from social phobias to major illnesses. I used to try to establish energetic boundaries around the individuals affected by these dark entities, but I found it did little good. The entities could simply go around my client or friend and energetically, or sometimes even physically, interfere or injure a loved one. For example, one such entity couldn't get through to my client, so it made everyone she came in contact with sick until my client would do this being's bidding.

Finally, I asked the Divine for a solution, and I was told to establish a Wall of Truth around the fallen angel. This silver-white bubble of shimmering energy, made of strands from healing streams of grace, forced the demon to act and speak with honesty. It didn't hurt or injure this soul, but forced it to turn to the Divine, rather than my client, for energy. Inevitably, the demon left my client's presence, allowing the Divine to assist it to a higher place.

If someone is really difficult, I suggest asking the Divine to create this Wall of Truth, or bubble of containment, around this person, according to divine will. I had one friend do this for an ex-wife who had turned his children and the court system against him, even though she had been cheating on him for several years. Worse, everyone he engaged to help him battle in court was stricken ill, lost their notes, or was similarly detained, or stopped in their efforts to help. As soon as the Divine formed the bubble around his ex, my friend's luck turned. He received a fifty-fifty custody arrangement, and his ex finally went into treatment for borderline personality disorder.

You can ask the Divine to fashion a bubble of truth or love, but always ask that it be done according to divine will. It's not for us to intrude on another's destiny, but neither is it someone else's right to step on ours.

|||||||||||||||||||||||||||||||||||||||||||||||||||||||||||||||||||||

Expanding Only Love: Healing Your Relational Boundary

At the center of our relationships is our relational boundary. It emanates from our heart and expands outward through our heart field, the most potent generator of our electrical, magnetic, and auric fields. As discussed in previous chapters, the heart perceives others' needs, emotions, and even actions through this surrounding field long before we are consciously aware of the energies received. It pulls this information into our body, tells our brain how to react, and formulates a response, even before we've thought a thought.

There are actually two levels to the heart energy center and field. Understanding their differences is the key to healing and maintaining your relational boundaries, and to attracting and conducting loving relationships. Inside your heart and lining its related energy field is your spirit, or indwelling essence that knows it is imminently and eminently connected to the Divine. This *spirit field*, as I call it, continually evolves, yet is programmed with all the truths inherent in your own spirit. These truths could be considered a unique set of genetics or codes that instruct your body, mind, and soul about the types of relationships the Divine wants for you, which are great ones. The key to loving relationships is to emblazon the entirety of your relational field with the energy from your spirit field. To surrender to this loving energy is to invite destiny, not tragedy.

The other level of your heart energy center and field isn't bad; it simply doesn't function for your highest good. It is programmed with family-of-origin beliefs, cultural imprints, religious dispositions, and your own relational experiences. It is also encoded with soul patterns and karma. I believe that we have lived before. During our past lives, we formed relational and other energetic patterns based on our experiences, many of them negative. When we enter a new life, we often form contracts with the very same souls, thinking that this time, we'll do it right. We often don't.

I once worked with a man who wanted an intuitive reading, but wouldn't provide any information about what was occurring in his life. I saw a past life in which he was an African chieftain with two wives: his legal wife and a concubine. I gave him thorough descriptions of their personalities and appearances. The two women hated sharing him. His mother of that time appeared to me in spirit form and told me she was extremely angry, vehemently ending her diatribe with a prayer I'd never heard before. When I related what I'd heard and saw, my client turned ashen. In this lifetime, he was married and had a mistress. Both women displayed the same traits today as they had during the African lifetime. Both were mad that he wasn't choosing between them. His current-life mother had discovered his affair and uttered the same prayer over him before she died.

This situation is a clear example of karma, an invitation to repeat a situation until we get it right. Patterns such as this are deeply ingrained, not only in our soul, but also in our neurology. At birth, all the issues and experiences of our soul are uploaded into our energy system and, through it, into our nervous system. Our energetic boundaries are, therefore, inscribed with three sets of programs: those from our soul or past lives, those of our current life, and those of our spirit.

You can use any of the tools provided in the other three sections of this chapter to assist your relational boundary, but the single most important activity for the relational boundary is this: *activating the spirit center of your heart (or your "spirit heart") and the spirit field of your relational boundary.* Other tools can be useful, but this action is imperative.

How do you do this? Start by assuming a quiet stance within your heart, connecting with your own inner spirit. Feel the Divine breathe in and out of your heart center and sense the oneness you have with this higher presence, this unconditionally loving All.

Now intuitively sense the karmically programmed areas of your heart and in your surrounding relational field. Can you feel any cords, shadows, holes, rigid barriers, and attachments? You might even drift into a sense of a past life or early childhood memories as the Divine helps you perceive the repetitive nature of your relationships. Decide to forgive yourself and all others. You don't have to forget; you don't want to. You want to remember what doesn't work so you don't repeat it. To forgive is to release, to surrender what wasn't and isn't supposed to be to a truer destiny.

Refrain from actually fixing these energetic issues. Instead, ask the Divine to stimulate your spirit heart and spirit field, the latter transforming into a beautiful haze of light clearing and cleansing the programmed field. Every karmically programmed molecule of your heart and relational field is gently healed, assuaged, and transformed by the living consciousness of the Divine.

You can ask the Divine to continue this process far beyond this brief interlude and to guide you, through the communication apparatus of this field, toward making relational changes.

This is really the only activity you need undertake to transmute your relational field, besides committing to following the divine guidance you receive. There are many forms of intuition that can help you open to divine revelation. I suggest you read some of my other books, including *The Intuition Handbook, The Subtle Body,* and *The Complete Book of Chakra Healing* for intuitive tips. To remind yourself you are committed to this shift in total consciousness, I suggest you program some physical object as a talisman. Jade, tourmaline, pink quartz, and diamonds are ideal, especially if they're circular. Also consider wearing jewelry or a watch with platinum, a higher element for conveying spiritual energies.

The Spirit of Relationships: Your Spiritual Boundaries

Deep inside, we long for relationships that are spiritually sanctioned and fulfilling. If we have boundary problems (and most of us do), many, if not most, of our relationships are inferior to this ideal. We enter them to learn a new way to love, but usually end up repeating our old, unloving patterns.

Healthy relationships should always support our spiritual mission. You don't have to be completely clear about your purpose to engage in relationships that support it. In fact, relationships assist us with our destiny by helping us clarify our purpose.

Ironically, to assume our destiny, we must be willing to release bad relationships and negative patterns—those that keep us trapped in fear and unable to courageously embrace our authentic selves. Inaccurate assumptions about our value as a spiritual being and the nature of the Divine often force us to settle for incomplete relationships. We might read the Bible verse telling us to honor our father and mother and believe this means we're not supposed to tell someone we were sexually abused. We might be told how important it is to convert the world to our religion, be it Christianity, Judaism, or Islam, and decide that means we can bomb people unlike ourselves or that our spiritual leaders can attach dynamite to our child's chest.

There are unending numbers of spiritual beliefs that might undermine our relationship health, as I witnessed first hand when meeting a pastor who felt called to work in the inner city. He believed that God protects his own, so he moved with his two teenage daughters into "the hood," the worst section of town, to conduct his ministry. I cautioned him, but he insisted that God watches his flock, as the Bible says. Within a year, both daughters had been raped and borne illegitimate children. He still refused to move.

I believe that this pastor's spiritual boundaries were rife with holes and that his children's spiritual boundaries mirrored his own. How would his daughters have known, unconsciously or consciously, that they deserved true protection if their father didn't provide it? The man's error was that he didn't model the loving safety of the Divine, and so neither did his children's spiritual fields.

My mentor, Cindy Libman, a Sufi therapist, taught me the easiest and most effective way of clearing spiritual boundaries for healthy relationships. Though I consider myself a Christian, I believe that the Divine is bigger than any religion and that all spiritual paths present a different facet of truth. The Sufi path acknowledges God as Allah and asserts that there are ninety-nine qualities of Allah, each of which is a unique truth of the living God. This approach and Cindy's practical application of it have gone further than any other to heal my spiritual boundary and help me focus foremost on a relationship with the Divine. If we are in union with the Divine, our spiritual boundary will automatically regulate our relationships.

Whenever I'm in a relational quandary, such as when my issues have been triggered or I'm scared, I breathe deeply into my heart and chant, tone, or think *A-lah* from the back side of my heart to the front side. I then ask the Divine to send me the quality I need for this particular circumstance. That quality floods through and around me, much like healing streams of grace (discussed in earlier chapters) do. These divine qualities differ from streams of grace in that they are composed of the Divine itself. You can research the ninety-nine qualities in books or on the Internet, or do what I do: I invite the Divine to bring me what I need.

Exercise: Shifting the Path Under Your Feet

Poor relationship choices and distorted boundaries can lead us off our spiritual path. We might feel so stuck, mired in brambles, thorns, and pain, that we give up hope.

There is always hope. In fact, there's more than hope—there's help.

We don't always have to walk to get somewhere. The Divine is perfectly capable of moving our spiritual path, our destiny, from a far-off locale to the land we're standing upon. This guided meditation will assist you in inviting this change. Be aware, however, that you will be different when you're standing on your own two feet and on the wings of the Divine. Old relationships might break down. You might find your voice. Others might resist the alterations; still others might appreciate you more. The cost of being true might be great, but being inauthentic is even more expensive. When we're genuine in our relationships, our genius can emerge.

I recommend this exercise as a way to invite the Divine to get you on path, especially in reference to relationships, if you're stuck in any of the seven syndromes, no matter which of the four main boundaries are off. It will set you exactly where you are supposed to be—where you are now, but in full connection with the Divine. If there are past lives to understand, issues to clear, or answers to receive, you'll be able to do so.

Begin in quiet. Then:

1. Acknowledge that where you are relationally is the only place you've known how to get.
2. Forgive yourself for not being able to get farther.
3. Now imagine that you are standing at a crossroads, in the middle of several lanes. Ask the Divine to erase all paths except for the one that the Divine approves and sanctions as highest for you. If necessary, know that the Divine will actually move a far-off path or lane and bring it directly underneath you.
4. Stand in this place, your path of destiny, until you are clear about why the relationships you've had have been in your life.
5. Ask the Divine to tell you what to do to more forward, and when. Agree to listen.
6. Enjoy the resulting shift in consciousness.

Chapter 9

Parenting (and Inner Parenting): The Pleasures of Teaching Boundaries

It is easier to build strong children than repair broken men.

FREDERICK DOUGLASS

There was a study conducted years ago with school-age children on the playground. In this study, the fences guarding the schoolyard were removed. When the children came onto the playground for recess, they huddled in the middle of it, anxious and insecure, rather than rush to the limits of the schoolyard to laugh and play as they usually did. When the fences were returned the next day, the children returned to normal, roaming and interacting as usual.[1]

Limits help children feel safe, secure, and loved. It's our job as parents to provide boundaries and instructions on updating them when necessary.

We require the same type of borders for ourselves. Within each of us are the children we once were—scared inner children trapped in time, usually due to trauma or neglect. But there are also bold, shy, loving, resourceful, innovative, and resilient child selves that need encouragement to grow and progress. All of these inner selves should be promised the safety provided by solid boundaries. In my opinion, the intangible boundaries are just as and sometimes more vital than concrete or behavioral boundaries, because they constitute the home a child or inner child has when he or she isn't home.

As a parent, you can't serve border-control duty all the time. I have two sons, and as I watch them grow, I am grateful I worked so hard to help them develop the energetic borders and protections necessary to survive and thrive in this world. They are fine young men. They aren't perfect; there isn't a plant that grows straight without first sending its roots downward in unpredictable directions or its tendrils and branches upward at odd angles toward the sun. But they know themselves, which is the gift of boundaries. To separate yourself from others is to distinguish who you are from who you aren't, and this is the key to making suitable life decisions.

This chapter is laid out a little differently from chapters 5 through 8. It still discusses the four main types of energetic boundaries, but I've described the seven syndromes in tangent with another personality descriptor: **spiritual personality.** I believe there are five main types of spiritual personalities on this planet right now. Understand which describes your child (or inner child), and you'll be better able to customize boundary healing and development and personalize the process of parenting.

For you, as the reader, an adult who comes into the parenting process ready to love, but also needing love, this chapter is aimed at helping to heal the wounds of childhood. Every child has them; every adult has inner children inside. To repair our past is to add wings to our future. We can then rise like a phoenix from the ashes and, strengthened where we'd been weakened, mended where we'd been broken, be happy for the days to come.

Our Soul Tendencies

Children need energetic boundaries, and it's our job as parents to provide them until our children are mature enough to create their own. We provide boundaries for them by caring and through modeling, but also by deliberately assessing their needs according to their personalities.

For instance, my son Michael is extraordinarily kind hearted and devoted to goodness, especially in relationships. Consequently, he lowers his relational energetic boundaries when he loves. This establishes the basis of intimacy, but if his partner lacks decent boundaries, he'll be used. He's had to learn to keep up his relational boundaries long enough to gauge the nature of a relationship before dropping them.

Two interwoven typologies can help us decide which types of energetic boundaries need to be developed in our children or inner children. The first of these areas is the seven syndromes; the second is our soul grouping. We each tend toward certain syndromes rather than others, based on our spiritual essence, basic personality, upbringing, experiences, and more. But we are also each positioned within a soul group. The soul is the part of us that moves through time and experience, gathering both wounds and wisdom. Many cultures throughout time have postulated that certain souls enter life at the same time or in waves in order to advance the planet and humanity, as well as themselves. This idea gained popularity a few years ago with the introduction of books on *indigo children,* a term describing children who exhibit a certain set of supernatural or unusual traits. I believe there are several types of souls alive today and that each tends toward a certain set of energetic syndromes, spiritual purposes, and energetic needs.

As you read these descriptions, pay attention to which ones best portray the children in your life and the child within yourself. While these groupings tend to be age related, the divisions aren't clear-cut. Our soul types are all mixed up right now, so stay open minded. Know, too, that you might fit two or more of these descriptions, although each of us tends toward one more than others. These depictions can help you determine which energetic boundaries to nourish.

The Main Soul Groups

What are the major soul groupings on this planet right now? What is unique about each, and which syndromes are they most prone to? The following is my own understanding, developed through my client work, studies, parenting two children, and self-parenting my own inner children.

Construct Souls. Here are our builders, souls devoted to the creation and sustenance of institutions, organizations, communities, and "members-only" clubs, which can include religions, ethnic cultures, and more. If you're a construct soul, you embrace systems, seeing the strength and power they provide members.

Systems can assure safety. Unions, for instance, have ensured their members security and equitable pay for decades. In many big cities, ethnic groups cluster in their own neighborhoods and, as groups, are able to assert their needs and rights, in addition to caring for each other. Unfortunately, systems can also foster prejudice, like the Nazi party did, and create the opposite of what's promised: insecurity, rather than security, at least for people who aren't welcomed into the given system.

Today, in the early twenty-first century, most members of the construct-soul group are middle aged to elderly, as they were maturing in an era where humanity's development required stability and form. No matter what your age, a devotion to tradition, hard work, and systems indicates you are a construct soul or have elements of one.

Construct people are prone to having too-rigid energetic boundaries or syndromes that guarantee them the lion's share of any work. Contract souls suffering from the Paper Doll Syndrome will follow rote behaviors that don't always serve them. Does your child become terrified at the thought of changing schools or moving homes? Has she developed obsessive-compulsive behaviors to guarantee safety? Does he freak out if everything isn't exactly right? While any extreme behaviors require therapeutic help, these sorts of reactions can also hint at a construct soul who needs stronger energetic boundaries in order to feel safe regardless of circumstances.

Construct souls often become the worker bees, a behavior that, when taken to the extreme, can make them Mule Syndrome victims. Children (or inner children) are so responsible they have no fun. I have a great deal of construct in me. By age five, I was cleaning the house and taking care of my sisters. I still struggle to not pick up every burden and carry it on my own shoulders. I often have to work on this syndrome by relating to the little girl inside me who gets scared if she isn't working all the time, sure she'll be punished if she lets others down.

The trick for transforming construct conditions through energy-boundary work is to highlight one's uniqueness, specialness, and individuality, opening the often too-rigid boundaries for a flow of love, emotion, personalized care, prosperity, and grace.

Bridge Souls. Bridge souls connect people, cultures, ideas, or approaches. These souls excel at linking the old with the new, tradition with innovation. Most baby boomers (born between 1946 and 1964) are bridge souls. Born into a world reliant on institutions, corporations, major religions, and rigid family definitions, they are, even now, struggling to incorporate values like freedom, creativity, and expressiveness into life. Often bridge souls work from the inside out, changing themselves through therapy or organizations by adding creativity.

Unfortunately, bridge souls feel so strongly compelled to connect people, places, or ideas, they don't know when to let go. Because they don't like to see anyone hurt, scared, or left out, they are often at risk for giveaway syndromes. They'd rather lose their own energy than leave someone sad or lacking (Vampire Syndrome) or take on others' issues and lose their own energy (Healer's Syndrome). If environmentally sensitive, they are the ones who adopt every stray dog, homeless cat, or injured bird. In other words, they're set up for codependency, an inner trait made worse by bad energetic boundaries.

Indigo Souls. These unique and exceptional individuals are seekers of a new world order, one run on humanitarian rather than systematic terms. Dedicated to the development of their distinctive personalities, they work toward a world that not only recognizes global consciousness, but also welcomes personal satisfaction. Their inner struggles involve changing the world through love-based rather than power-based values. To work through these conflicts, they often turn to holistic or even mystical pursuits, sometimes to the chagrin of their parents, who might be bridge or construct souls. Most of today's indigo souls are between the ages of fifteen and thirty-five, although they can be younger and older.

As children, indigos can be affected by any number of syndromes, but the most likely is the Healer's Syndrome. In their journey to change the world, they often take on the world's problems, offering their contributions, resources, and heart energy in exchange. They are also prone to the Environ Syndrome because of their drive to save the planet. This short list doesn't rule out the other syndromes, which indigos can develop with flair, depending on their personality.

For indigos, the key to healthy boundaries is to balance borders that are sometimes too rigid and other times too fluid, and to infuse their internal spirit into all the fields, but especially the relational one.

Crystal Souls. In kid form, these psychic, sensitive individuals reflect their name. Brilliant in personality, as multifaceted as diamonds, they can be so complicated it's hard to figure them out, much less help them achieve energetic balance.

This category tends to be made of the very young to people aged twenty-five or so, but I personally know a number of older crystal souls. They are usually called "New Age" because they gravitate toward the spiritual rather than anything construct.

In a way, the phrase "New Age" sums up the crystal personality. These souls are new; I believe they are actually pretty new to this planet and haven't incarnated many times before. Lacking experience in dealing with life's hard edges, they don't have many hard edges. In fact, different types of crystal kids can be missing most or all of their physical, emotional, or relational boundaries. Without these boundaries, they respond to life events in ways that cause society to label them sickly or hypersensitive; afflicted with Asperger's syndrome or autism-spectrum disorders; or suffering from ADHD. These three main types of crystals are discussed in the crystal-kids section later in this chapter, along with their tendencies toward Psychic-Sensitive and No-Boundary Syndromes.

Assisting the crystal child requires the methodical and ongoing construction of all energetic boundaries. He or she will need more work on the physical, emotional, and relational boundaries, as crystal kids are naturally more spiritual. But even the spiritual boundary will require assistance; because it's been trying to do the work of all four boundaries, it will be full of holes or, conversely, overly rigid.

Spirit Souls. Just who are these little ones, or maybe big ones, with big spirits and hearts? From my perspective, these beings are angels come to earth. More equipped to cope with our challenging, everyday reality than crystal souls, they are already ignited with their spiritual purpose and are usually quite clear about it.

One of the reasons they are more fortified energetically is that they have rich physical, emotional, and relational boundaries, in addition to the spiritual field that is so accessible to the crystal children. I think the reason their first three boundaries stay largely intact is that they have already lived a few past lives in which they achieved joy and peace with self, or they've actually been guardian angels and learned a lot by observing humanity. Whatever the case, these are typically the youngest of today's children, although individuals such as Mother Teresa and the untoasted that give willingly in the world are also spirit souls.

Spirit souls can exhibit any of the seven syndromes, though often to a lesser degree than others of the soul groups, simply because they arrive with better energy boundaries and are willing to receive assistance from both the spiritual and human realms for their problems. The development of a permanent syndrome often depends on how well their parents are able to customize their parenting to suit the child.

Loving the Children, Setting Their Boundaries

You might already recognize your own children (or inner children) in the descriptions. What might you do to assuage the challenges of each soul group or the ones your inner children are still experiencing? Here are a few tips for each of these soul groups, emphasizing the boundaries and syndromes that are most likely to be affecting them.

Construct Children: Building with Building Blocks

Construct kids are serious, knowledgeable, and dedicated to the systems that provide for them. One of my favorite construct-child clients was an eleven-year-old boy who knew he was going to grow up and be an engineer. Jason proudly discussed the various Lego sets in his room and ways I could lift my front steps so they could better accommodate physically challenged individuals.

What emerged through our discussion was a dismay with the other children his age. "They aren't mature," this young man explained. "They make faces at the teacher and don't turn in their homework." His home situation was a duplicate. Far more responsible than his older and younger siblings, he stopped just shy of threatening to run away from home. To compensate, he made life easier for both his teacher and his mother, who was a single mom, by performing as many extra duties as possible, in addition to maintaining a straight-A average. You can imagine what the kids at school thought of him.

Some adults might have considered this boy the perfect child. Fortunately, his mother and teacher were wiser than that. They had both agreed that he needed help loosening up. His mother suspected he was scared of losing control and so had adopted his own form of perfectionism to compensate. Jason was seeing a therapist, who suggested a session with me to work on the energetics of the situation.

I immediately knew that Jason was afflicted with rigid boundaries, most likely all four fields, but especially the physical field. His perfectionism was a form of a Paper Doll Syndrome, and his over-responsibility was a clear indication of a Mule Syndrome. Not only did he welcome work, but he also rejected love. He refused to cuddle with his mother, welcome affection, or even consider the presence of a higher power. Jason was already a man unto himself, and I felt sad about it.

You can't and shouldn't try and make a child something he or she isn't. In my vocabulary, Jason was a construct child—a builder, a little person who dreamed big. But he was growing himself up too fast. Consequently, his physical boundaries were exhausted, too open to work energies, and his emotional, relational, and spiritual boundaries both too thin and too armored, rejecting all good things.

With construct kids, I like to use exercises that appeal to their kinesthetic and visual gifts. A good mixed practice might use coloring, sketching, or computer graphics to explain what's happening in their energetic fields. With Jason, I first drew a really thin band around a figure of a body on paper. This is your physical field, I explained. I then drew symbols of what was coming into his field, like lots of work, and what he was keeping out, like hugs, more play, and good sleep.

I next sketched his orange emotional boundary, which was way too thin, and showed how its outer layer was reflective silver, which deflected happy feelings. I revealed that it, too, had the same problem as the red field and was keeping friends away. This depiction invited a discussion on feelings, like loneliness and sadness.

I then illustrated his spiritual boundary and talked about how opening it might help him feel safer, helping him realize there were adults and even angels that could alleviate some of his burdens. He felt relieved, pointing out that he had thought he needed to be the man of the family because his father had deserted them. Maybe it would be nice to have help.

We next redrew these pictures so they looked the way they were supposed to. After a year of envisioning himself wearing these "coats of color" every morning, and working with a therapist, he proudly announced that his life included friends and fun.

This exercise can also be done kinesthetically. Take out a huge tub of blocks or widgets, whatever the construct kids are into, and illustrate that way. Whichever technique you use, it's important to have them visually or kinesthetically rewrite, redesign, and reconfigure their boundaries.

I also encourage construct kids to use physical-boundary techniques that involve programming stones, objects, or more. They are so physical that they often respond to practices for repairing physical energetic boundaries, such as those covered in chapter 5. Because they are actually quite scared inside, they like to have something to hold onto: a blessed blankie, a blessed stone, a special reminder note, a bracelet they can play with to remind them of their parents or their new and improved physical boundaries.

Know that these energetic techniques are supplemental to actual therapy. Children will need to discuss their newly recognized emotions, talk about friendships and feelings, and learn how to make all spiritual things real and positive. Being a listener and teacher is your job as a parent, and that job is easier if first you help your children set their energetic boundaries.

Bridge Kids: Between Forever and Today

Bridge kids worry a lot. They stress about what's happening around them and check for what might occur tomorrow. In their spare time, they peruse yesterday, wondering what might have gone wrong, and then they make sure what went right keeps going right. There are so many areas to be concerned about, too! Even their home life is affected by what occurs outside of the home—like parents, who always seem to be fretting about work, money, health, or how to drive kids everywhere.

Being a bridge is a stressful position, fraught with potential disaster—or at least, that's how it feels. A bridge kid feels pulled in two or more directions all the time, but the center subject is seldom the self. That's why it's such a set-up for the giving conditions, including the Vampire and Healer's Syndromes. Any, some, or all of the four main boundaries might be weak and full of holes or cords through which the self's energy pours out and others' energies flow in. You can cull healing techniques from chapter 8, on relationships, for strengthening all four fields, but the most necessary place to start is in the relational boundaries. Basically, bridge kids are about relationship.

The primary goal is to teach bridge kids that it's good for them to put themselves first. You'll never convince true bridgers to cancel others out, so you don't have to worry they'll become narcissistic. Set this objective, and you'll be lucky to get them to fifty-fifty: putting themselves first half the time, and others first half the time. If you make it that far, it's pretty good.

I have two favorite energy techniques for bridge kids. The first is kinesthetic and requires three small bags and twenty or so marbles or small stones. Make sure these bags are different colors. Every day, hand your bridge kid a full bag of marbles and two empty bags. These marbles need to be spent on kindnesses. One empty bag is for *Self;* the other is for *Other.* Every time the child does something good for someone else, he or she slips a marble in the Other bag. For self? The Self bag. At the end of the day, the marbles from the full bag should be emptied into the Self and Other bags in equal numbers. If there are more marbles in the Other bag, the child has to give extra marbles or kindnesses to him- or herself the next day. If, for a week, these bags are even, Mom or Dad does something *really* fun both for the child and for someone the child cares about.

Can't bring a bag of marbles to school (or the office)? Provide your child (or inner child) with a tiny pencil and pad to keep score, then transfer the appropriate number of marbles to each bag at home later.

The second technique is totally energetic and has two stages. The first involves breathing in pink energy through the backside of the heart toward the front, and then exhaling this pink energy into the world. Tell the child that pink is love. If you're religious, you might say this is love from God, Allah, Christ, the Buddha, or the Spirit. This pink energy must first fill the child's heart, being given first to the self, before being offered to others on the exhale.

After your child has become versed on this first stage, you can move on to the second: encourage him or her to start filling the relational energy field with the pink light and letting the love glitter and shine out through the relational field. Bringing in pink love energy encourages even more self-love, and this rosy light will now be able to heal the two fields underneath and the spiritual field atop.

Indigo Kids: Painting the World Mystical

My oldest son is a combination of a construct and indigo soul. His practical, down-to-earth nature is constantly tweaked by an advanced sense of changing the world for the better. Know what he does for a living right now? He works for a U.S. senator, helping to change the world. Yup, that's an indigo for you. (And he works *all* the time, as constructs often do.)

Some indigos work within a system, but only if they can change it or if it's a transformation system. Others operate outside systems. But they all seek to catalyze this world to a higher place of functioning. Their talk is peppered with words like *ethics, goodness, sustainability,* and *love.* Indigos are nearly always affected by the Healer's Syndrome. Those who are earthier in consciousness often exhibit the Environ Syndrome. Other syndromes are usually salted in quite liberally.

Indigos are great kids, but they never feel like they've arrived, because they can't. You simply can't fix as many problems as humankind has—not with just your own energy, anyway. This is why for indigos, I work the relational and spiritual fields, emphasizing the communication capabilities of the relational. I then link the relational field with the heavenly aspect of the spiritual field to alleviate the indigos' sense of over-responsibility.

It's important to teach indigos how to open to intuitive and inspirational guidance, so they don't think they have to do everything themselves. Receiving input from their higher selves, the angels, the Divine, even a trusted mentor, takes the pressure off. Filling up these two outer fields also builds a strong filter system, slowing down the indigos' sometimes overly emotional and overly eager responses to harmful or old-fashioned systems. The best technique is to teach an indigo child how to pray, meditate, and contemplate, in that order.

Prayer is any process that sends a message to the Divine, usually in a request form. It can involve writing down a need in a journal, speaking a desire aloud, thinking or chanting a communiqué under one's breath, sending a mind-made picture up to the heavens, or even writing an e-mail addressed to God. Prayer also includes the more traditional forms of contacting the Divine, such as kneeling with folded hands by the bed or attending a church service. But many indigos are edgy, so never force your method of prayer on them.

Meditation is a process of quieting the mind and heart to receive messages from the Divine. The incoming information might be a response to the prayer request, but it could be a freely given revelation. You can certainly see if your indigo wants to practice traditional meditation, which usually involves closed eyes, deep breathing, and either mindfulness or an emptying of the mind, but you might need to customize the method to an indigo's individual style. Some indigos are open to chanting and mantras, and respond to humming the Hindu chants or octave tones presented in "Sound Healing: The Songs of the Gods" (chapter 4).

You can always encourage fourth-chakra chanting, as the heart shares its knowledge with all other chakras.

Have a skateboarder on your hands? Tell your indigo to ask the Divine to send a message while she is skateboarding. How about a moviegoer or bookworm? Tell him to look for messages within what he's watching or reading. Messages can come in through any vehicle.

Contemplation is basking in the loving presence of the Divine. For an indigo, the easiest way to engage in contemplation is to first consider the spiritual field a sacred space. Then reaching a contemplative state is a two-fold process.

First, help your indigo settle into a quiet and comfortable state, breathe deeply, and connect with his or her spiritual field, which lies about six to eight feet away from the body. Ask the indigo to simply sense the loving presence of an angelic or divine being and to enjoy it. Now tell your indigo to reconnect with this field and its ensuing sense of peace anytime he or she is stressed out or frenzied.

After this state becomes comfortable and automatic, teach your indigo to link this spiritual field and its band of light with the next layer down, the relational field. He or she might want to imagine the spiritual field as iridescent white and the relational as blue, for the part of the field that represents communication. After this linkage becomes comfortable and soothing, let the indigo experiment with prayer and meditation while in this bubble of blue-white light. Over time, your indigo will almost immediately access this double-field bubble when seeking spiritual assistance, receiving guidance, or dealing with a life stress.

A psychically visual indigo will notice that the colors of this bubble shift and play. This dual field will open as white and blue, but eventually also fill with purples, greens, yellows, oranges, reds, and more—the colors of all the fields. At this point, those additional rainbow hues will color in the two remaining fields, the emotional and physical.

Attuning the Crystal Child: From Discordance to Chords

The crystal child is like a beautiful crystal bowl, resonant and redundant with sweetness and grace. Unfortunately, these higher angelic tones usually fall on deaf ears. The world is more an out-of-tune and scattered orchestra lacking a conductor than the harmony of the spheres it is supposed to be.

The strongest boundary surrounding a crystal soul is the spiritual. This field tinkles like silver bells. But unsupported by the underlying boundaries, which usually lie fallow, the spiritual field is unable to filter invading energies, creating unusual amounts of strain in the weakest of the three other fields.

If the physical boundary is weak, the crystal kid or adult will be markedly ill, unable to screen others' primary needs or illnesses, and often stricken with monetary or resource issues. I once worked with a crystal child who was sick every other week, always with a different illness. That same week, I saw a grown woman who was also constantly ill. Though much older than the child-client, this fifty-year-old single mother had been struck with different types of terminal cancer five times in as many years. While the chemotherapy always worked, nearly instantly, her body was wearing out. Despite their difference in age, both individuals were crystal souls. Both were cloaked in a glowing spiritual field and were two of the kindest persons I had ever met. But neither had sustainable relational or emotional fields, and their physical energetic boundaries were almost nonexistent.

In both cases, the crystal soul was being attacked by dark energies. Each had an alcoholic father and the entity attachments that often accompany substance abuse; entities ride in on the frequency of a substance being used to cover pain and attach themselves to the user. Both clients became better almost as soon as we released the cords and repaired the physical energetic boundary. For this work, I suggest applying the practices described in chapter 5.

A wounded physical energetic boundary, partnered with an overemphasized spiritual field, usually results in allergies, environmental sensitivities, and other indications of an overactive immune system. I always suggest that children with these conditions work with a holistic food allergist, nutritionist, or naturopath, and also consider programming food, drink, and beverages as described in chapters 4 and 5. If you can isolate the most challenged chakras and related auric fields, also consider chanting the corresponding Hindu syllable or octave note, even under your breath, when putting your child to bed or when he or she needs calming. These sounds produce almost instant positive effects. (The syllables and notes are outlined in chapter 4's "Sound Healing: The Songs of the Gods" on page 108.)

A child with these susceptibilities can often learn to treat him- or herself energetically through the imagination. I suggest that parents help the crystal child reach a quiet state, perhaps by playing music with a heart-rate tempo, which is sixty to ninety beats a minute, or music featuring nature sounds, such as ocean waves or raindrops. Then show your child pictures of any natural plants or roots suggested by your nutritionist or naturopath. For instance, if the holistic practitioner has recommended a dandelion tincture to clear out the liver, present a picture of a dandelion and ask your child to imagine that the spirit of this plant is filling out his or her physical boundary. This process is called spirit-plant medicine, and crystal children are especially responsive to its effects.

These children are also often affected by shifts in barometric pressure, planetary movements, sunspots, and sometimes geofield shifts and electromagnetic pollution. To alleviate negative reactions to these disturbances, decorate your crystal child's room with care and insight. For instance, I recommend gluing images of a galaxy, or at least our planetary system, on the ceiling or hanging a mobile with all the planets and the moon. Representing the cosmos in its correct formula will alleviate a crystal child's reactions to real universal changes. If your child reacts to geofields, ley lines, or electromagnetic pollution, make sure you have pink felt or wool somewhere in the room. Pink felt absorbs these electrical energies. A blanket is easiest, as you can wash it once a week or so. Also make sure the room is free of all electrical devices; even use a battery-operated rather than electrical clock.

Some crystal children have heavily damaged emotional boundaries, yet true to form, their spiritual boundaries are strong. Unfortunately in these cases, the spiritual field isn't of much use because the weakened emotional field determines the child's well-being. In some crystal children, the too-thin emotional boundary is stronger mentally, but weaker in terms of feelings. In extreme cases, this disparity can cause the crystal to have (or appear to have) Asperger's syndrome or autism-spectrum disorders. It can also cause an over-reliance on certain mental ideas and a decreased sensitivity to feelings. I believe that these behaviors reflect a combination of the Paper Doll Syndrome, in which certain beliefs cycle over and over, and an odd version of the No-Boundary Syndrome. The spiritual and emotional boundaries are leaking the crystal child's feelings, but seem to block others' feelings from entering.

In true Asperger's or autism situations, the spiritual field is actually inverted. It is inside out. This means that the crystal child's true spiritual nature is facing inward, and the dark, mirrorlike quality of the field is facing out. The field is literally sending others' feelings back to them and imprisoning the child within his or her own kindly nature.

The causes of such conditions are highly complicated and could occupy their own book. Think about this, though: How would you feel if a part of your skin were inside out? Wouldn't you be hypersensitive—so sensitive that you would flinch at bright lights, strange sounds, strong emotions, and other abrasive stimulation? If you are a parent to a child like this, whether the child is outside or inside of you, be very gentle. I suggest learning color and geometric-symbol healing techniques. Look up the colors, geometric shapes, and their meanings in chapter 4. In general, you can psychically envision the outside of the spiritual field covered with soft green, pink, or pearl gray colors, which will encourage neurological healing and provide a much-needed cloaking. As time goes on, work on intuitively picturing the reversal of this spiritual field. In fact, you can put (or have your child put) your child's clothes on inside out and then reverse them every morning, at the same time imagining the same reversal happening to the spiritual field.

Then consider using chapter 5's techniques for healing the emotional and relational boundaries for physical well-being. (While you can use the techniques outlined in chapters about the other life areas, those used for physical healing are the most powerful. A crystal child needs all the empowerment he or she can get.) While the emotional boundary might be the most injured in shut-down crystal kids, the relational boundary is usually almost as damaged.

Other crystal children have the opposite problem. While their spiritual boundaries are normal, they lack a healthy emotional boundary, or their emotional boundary represses their personal feelings and lets in deluges of mental energy from the outside world. The resulting condition? ADHD.

The relational boundary is usually off in these situations as well. Have you noticed that your ADHD child (or inner self) has a hard time adapting to the slower thinkers around him or her? In comes the data, and off goes the ADHD kid, wild and unruly in thought and sometimes behavior. Quite simply, these kids don't notice their impact on others. This is because the relational boundary is being flattened by the incoming gush of mental energy. Neurologically, this influx causes brain activity to exceed spinal activity; ADHD kids literally can't keep up with themselves.

There are many therapeutic and nutritional, as well as energetic, assists for ADHD. I suggest reviewing my advice for the latter in chapter 8, about relationships. My favorite energetic exercise for crystal children is designed to help them smooth out their entire energetic field and perform what I call a cross-check maneuver, which sets up more fences while helping them bond internally and externally.

To begin this exercise, help your child become calm and think of his or her feet. This is very important, as hyper-data kids usually think of their heads, not the other end of the body. Once your child is settled (a bit), have your child focus on his or her spiritual boundary. Crystal kids are often disconnected from their bodies, so your child might need to visualize rather than sense this field. It should look like a wide band of white light about six to eight feet away from the skin. Now ask your child to leave the outer rim of this field where it is, but to pull the inside of the bubble right next to his or her skin. Keep at the exercise until your child feels this inner layer like a warm, slippery, or light towel or blanket. Ask your child to lock the spiritual boundary into the physical energetic boundary, maybe by pretending to tie a boat to the dock. Now ask your child to send energy from his or her heart back out to the outer rim of the spiritual self.

After your child gets good at this process, which evens out all the fields, you can start to work emotionally, asking your child questions about daily life, such as, "How did you feel when your friend did this or that?" Or even, "What's your favorite food? Why? How does it make you feel?"

The other important activity for all crystal children is releasing others' energies. Since this process is also vital for spirit kids, I'll cover it in the next section.

Spirit Children: With Wings to Fly, Walking the Ground

Spirit children are better equipped for this life than almost all the other soul personalities because they come into this three-dimensional world with better energetic boundaries and a clear sense of mission. But they are also vulnerable to any or all of the syndromes, especially if they are misunderstood.

I met one spirit child who was a little boy with huge blue eyes and even bigger glasses, which kept falling off his face. Since he had become old enough to talk, he had eaten only three foods: yogurt, oranges, and nuts. He said he remembered having been alive before and didn't believe in killing another living being just for food. Did he have a paper-doll pattern? No, he was sharing a conviction, which was an extension of his spiritual purpose. At age six, he clearly knew that he was here to help save this planet.

Spirit kids often have an inherent sense of calling, as I've seen in my son Gabriel, who is a spirit child with crystal-soul tendencies. When he was four years old, his daycare provider looked me in the eyes and thanked me for the honor of allowing her to know Gabriel, saying he was one of the world's greatest humanitarians, his heart was so big.

The challenge for spirit children (and their parents) is that they can become locked into their calling, injuring or further damaging the energetic boundary that serves the mission, but failing to develop the others. The little boy with the big glasses could start to over-identify with animals' emotions, thus warping his emotional boundary. Maybe he'd establish a lifeline to the natural world, initiating a Vampire Syndrome. Gabriel could easily slip into a Healer's Syndrome—and has. One day, I was thinking an angry thought, and he suddenly developed a headache. My angry thought disappeared. He had taken on my energy and sent me healing.

Spirit children are not immune to the syndromes, but they are bright enough to tell you what they need when you ask them. The one thing I've found most challenging for them is releasing others' emotions, mainly because these children are here to help. Isn't taking on others' emotions helping? Spirit children must learn that others need to deal with their own problems because problem solving brings wisdom.

To help spirit children release others' energies, teach them to close their eyes two to three times a day and ask the Divine to shower them in a waterfall of light. Tell them that this waterfall is cleansing them of all energies not their own. Be picturesque. Help them pretend they are actually standing under a waterfall, being purified. Point out the cords that attach them to things they don't like, and have them observe these cords washing away. Finally, they emerge onto a lovely stretch of grass, where they dry off in the sun. Everything of nature reconstitutes their boundaries: the red and brown of the earth shore up their physical field; the oranges and yellows of the flowers and sun contribute to their emotional field; the greens of the grasses and blues of the sky bolster the relational field; the white of the clouds heals the spiritual field.

Some kids (typically boys, but you never know) love shields. Have your spirit kid imagine a silver mesh all the way around his or her body; this mesh reflects dangerous energies back to the heavens. Build a story around this image, if you can. When I taught it to my son, I told him that the Norwegian gods used the deflected energy to make thunderstorms. Some kids (often girls) might like to paint their energetic boundaries with every color under the sun or wear a color that will keep them safe, a strategy covered in this chapter's exercise.

Above all, enjoy whatever type of soul your children are! The best gift we can give our children is to like them.

|||||||||||||||||||||||||||||||||||||||||||||||||||||||||||||||||||||||||

The Troubled Child—From a Distance

What can we do for a troubled child, especially if the child is now an adult? We don't have any authority over him. We have no mechanism for control or maybe even access to her. We have only concern and love.

Remember the quantum-physics rule? If two people connect at some point, they forever remain interconnected. Your children can still feel and sense you; they can still receive care packages from your heart. There are two keys to influencing stuck children from a distance.

The first is to do your own work. This is a hard statement to make, but I must, and I do so as a parent who has spent years in therapy and working energetically to correct some of the mistakes I made with my own children. Some of our children's problems are bound to have originated with us. Whatever we didn't deal with, feel, understand, or work through flows downward, to the next generation. The same was true of the generation above us. Didn't we inherit our tendencies and a lot of our issues from our own parents? This is the nature of the human condition. We become heirs to that which is unhealed, and that which we don't transform is passed down to our heirs.

This also means that whatever we do in the present to heal these issues will help our children. I once worked with a man with four adult children, each of whom had at least one addiction: sex, alcohol, shopping, and more. They also shared a panoply of mental health issues, including depression, anxiety, bipolar disorder, and borderline personality disorder. He himself exhibited most of these conditions, while his wife was a religion addict with severe attachment disorders. But he entered therapy and began to change. He also used several of the energetic techniques I teach, mainly focusing on setting energetic boundaries where he didn't have any. Slowly, over several years, his children began to grow and progress. Three of the four children are now living functional lives, although they are on prescription medicines and in therapy. The fourth has entered a rehabilitation treatment center. Yes, they still struggle. They are stuck religiously, and their spiritual boundaries remain confused, because their mother hasn't changed. But they are transforming.

One incident was telltale. When my client threw away his marijuana, his oldest daughter called to say that she was admitting herself into treatment to quit pot and methamphetamines. This is a clear sign that what we do positively transfers to our children.

The second key is to remember that our children enter this life with a soul and as a spirit, a being who has lived or experienced before, and a child of the Divine, fully connected and loved. You watched your children when they were infants. They aren't really you, are they? They enjoy fully formed personalities. This means that they will suffer and learn through challenges unique to them—challenges that you can't necessarily help them with.

Love, however, permeates all walls, all boundaries, and all fears. You can always ask the Divine to help your child. You can always initiate a healing stream of grace. You can always love. Love is free, and when freely given, it heals.

||||||||||||||||||||||||||||||||||||||||||||||||||||||||||||||||||||||||

Exercise: Colors in the Kid World

Instinctively, kids love color. I tell children that the different colors, if pictured, worn, or carried as a stone or marble, can help them do almost anything. Here is a short list you can use to explain the benefits of various colors to your children. Have them add their own ideas, as if they're doing an experiment, and you'll be amazed at how their boundaries grow.

- **Red:** Red makes you strong. It will help you win races, get over being sick, make bullies go away, and do chores faster, so you get your allowance quicker.
- **Orange:** Orange makes you feel better if you are sad or angry. It also makes coloring, painting, drawing, dancing, writing stories, or anything else that's fun even more fun. This is the color to wear if you want to have a great time. You can imagine an orange bubble in front of you, put happy thoughts into the bubble, and send the

bubble to Mom or Dad. This will stop you from taking on Mom and Dad's sadness or other feelings.

- **Yellow:** Yellow will make you smart and help you do well in school and on tests. If you feel confused or can't think of something, pretend you're in a yellow balloon, and the answer will come. If you are thinking too much, picture a yellow flashlight shining on you and sending the worries away.

- **Green:** If you're worried about someone, send the person green thoughts. Create a green bubble in your mind and fill it with your wishes for the other person. Now blow this healing bubble at him or her, like you are blowing on a dandelion puff. Green also makes pain go away and makes things and people grow strong and healthy.

- **Blue:** When you have to say a lot of things, think blue. Talk blue words and sing blue notes and write blue words, and you'll sound really smart and make sense, too. Pretend you are colored blue when you're scared about what others think of you, and you'll know exactly what to say.

- **White:** White makes everything good because it brings in angels. White is the color of their feathers. Ask an angel to send an invisible feather to make bad thoughts stop. You can also ask an angel to give you a hug, keep your parents' arguing from hurting you, or help you think of what to do when you're scared.

- **Black:** Black can hide you if you don't want someone to see you at the bus stop or if you don't want to answer a question at school. Wear only a little black, though, because you don't want to hide all of yourself.

- **Silver:** Silver sends bad energy away so it can't hurt you. Wear or think of silver to feel safe from others' mean thoughts or make bad ghosts go away. Also wear silver if you want to talk with God and ask a question. Take all your bad thoughts or those bad things that people tell you, and put them into a nickel or dime. Then bury the silver coin. That can help end all that badness.

- **Gold:** Gold will make big changes. It will help the angels and God come and take care of you and your problems. Think about God sending you a big beam of gold light to help you out of trouble.
- **Pink:** Pink is love. Think or wear pink if you're feeling kind of bad about yourself, if kids are teasing you, or if Mom and Dad are having trouble. Think of a nice message, put it in a pink bubble, and send it to anyone who needs it, instead of taking care of everyone else and getting too tired.

Conclusion

ılıllıllıllıllıllıllıllıllıllıllıllıl

It's a slippery slope, Carrie.
Without boundaries, you never know what might happen.

MIRANDA HOBBES (PLAYED BY CYNTHIA NIXON), *SEX AND THE CITY*

There are no energetic-boundary police on our city payrolls. Psychologists, medical doctors, social workers, parents, and community experts aren't trained in the existence of, much less the need for, such boundaries.

Lacking energetic boundaries, we'll be confused about who we are, what we're here to accomplish, and how we can best express our true selves in the world. We'll become prey to any number of the seven syndromes and their symptoms: repetitive patterns, loss of energy, overwork, being overwhelmed, psychic intrusions, codependency, mixed-up behaviors, and environmental sensitivities. We'll struggle with health, work, money, relationships, and parenting—or maybe all of these life areas. We'll lack the energy required to live the authentic, bountiful, and rich life we're supposed to be enjoying.

Conversely, conducting the rewarding, but sometimes challenging work of diagnosing, cleansing, and healing our energy boundaries invites love, prosperity, and wealth. These riches might be financial, but equally important, if not more important, are the treasures of joy, truth, and satisfaction.

The entire world is composed of energy. This means it's logical to assume that shifting the energy inside of you, around you, or even in your food, drinking water, thought processes, environment, or objects, can produce wildly effective changes. Programming intention into a simple stone can repel another's negative force. Imagining a circle around your body really can encompass you in a sacred space that encourages monetary rewards, loving exchanges with others, or a revelation of a truth needed to cure our self-hatred. Even deeper issues, such as addictions, abuse, poverty, and major illness, are energetic traumas. Whatever undesirable circumstances appear in our physical world started as rips or ruptures in the energetic realms. To make a small change in the fabric of the universe is to potentially birth a new star, to call to us a comet of transformation.

This book is intended to serve as an ongoing resource for meeting the challenges of a sometimes hostile yet lovely world. It is an explanation of the beauty that creates us and a compendium of suggestions for evolution and progress. It presents techniques for growing your soul, the brilliant you that is learning how to be more yourself, no matter what ups and downs you face.

Is addressing our energetic issues mandatory? Is it necessary to thoughtfully assess and weave our physical, emotional, relational, and spiritual boundaries so that they keep us and others safe? No, but it is wise. It is wise to know all of ourselves and to feel compelled to become more of the same.

It is also wise to create within ourselves the change we desire to see in the world. David Starr Jordan, a leading educator and peace activist in the early twentieth century, said, "Wisdom is knowing what to do next; skill is knowing how to do it; virtue is doing it." As you make your energetic repairs, may your wisdom ever increase, and your joy along with it.

Notes

Chapter 1

1. "Kirlian Photography Research," web page (kirlian.org/kirlian2.htm) produced by Energy Works, a maker of Kirlian cameras.

2. Hans Brugemann (ed.), *Bioresonance and Multiresonance Therapy* (Brussels: Haug International, 1993), 231–239. Cited by Steve Gamble, "Healing Energy and Water," article online at Equilabra (equilibrauk.com).

3. Lynne McTaggart, *The Field* (New York: HarperCollins, 2002).

4. Jim Oschman and Nora Oschman, "Science Measures the Human Energy Field" (last revised April 30, 2009), article online at the International Center for Reiki Training (reiki.org): "Reiki Articles."

5. Nenah Sylver, "Healing With Electromedicine and Sound Therapies: Part Two" (2008), article online at the Qi Gong Institute (qigonginstitute.org): "Scientific Papers."

Chapter 2

1. Ethan Watters, "DNA Is Not Destiny," *Discover Magazine* 27, no. 11 (November 2006). Available on the website Living Aryurveda (living-ayurveda.com).

2. J. Lee Nelson, "Interdisciplinary Research in Chimerism" (2008), article online at Microchimerism (microchimerism.org): "Research."

3. j_philipp-ga, response to question by qpet-ga, "Thoughts Per Day" (February 1, 2003), Google Answers (answers.google.com/answers/): "Relationships and Society: Cultures."

4. HeartMath, LLC, "Solutions for Stress: Quantum Nutrients: Energy Out, Energy In," article online at HeartMath (heartmath.com). Rollin McCraty, Mike Atkinson, and Dana Tomasino (eds), "Science of the Heart: Exploring the Role of the Heart in Human Performance; An Overview of Research Conducted by the Institute of HeartMath" (Boulder Creek, CA: Institute of HeartMath, 2001), e-book available on the website Institute of HeartMath (heartmath.org): "Research."

5. Rollin McCraty, "The Energetic Heart: Bioelectromagnetic Communication Within and Between People," in *Clinical Applications of Bioelectromagnetic Medicine,* edited by P. J. Rosch and M. S. Markov (New York: Marcel Dekker, 2004) 541–562.

6. Rollin McCraty, Mike Atkinson, and Dana Tomasino, "Modulation of DNA Conformation by Heart-Focused Intention" (publication no. 03-008, Boulder Creek, CA: Institute of HeartMath, 2003). Available at the website Institute of Heartmath (heartmath.org): "Research: Research Library."

7. McCraty, Atkinson, and Tomasino, "Science of the Heart."

8. "41 Random Facts About Stress" (posted February 19, 2010), article online at Random Facts (facts.randomhistory.com).

9. Steven P. Brown and Thomas V. Leigh, "A New Look at Psychological Climate and Its Relationship to Job Involvement, Effort and Performance," *Journal of Applied Psychology* 81, no. 4 (1996): 358–368.

Chapter 4

1. Hilary Hart, "Holy Cacao! Science Adds Love to Chocolate," article online at It's a Healthy New Age (healthynewage.com). Accessed November 17, 2010.

2. "Experimental Research" (2010), Princeton Engineering Anomalies Research: Scientific Study of Consciousness-Related Physical Phenomena (princeton.edu/~pear): "Experiments."

3. Lia Scallon, "The Healing Power of Sound," article online at Sounds of Sirius (soundsofsirius.com): "Articles: Articles by Lia." Accessed November 29, 2010.

4. Scallon, "The Healing Power of Sound."

5. "Scientific Validation of BioGeometry: The Agricultural Research Projects," article online at BioGeometry: Dr. Ibrahim Karim (biogeometry.com): "Research Projects." Accessed November 29, 2010.

6. Fiona Petchy, "Bone," article online at radiocarbon WEB-info (c14dating.com), a website about radiocarbon dating, Tom Higham, Radiocarbon Laboratory, University of Waikato, New Zealand: "Pretreatment: Bone." Accessed November 29, 2010.

7. Lauren D'Silva, "How Do Crystals Work?" article online at BellaOnline: The Voice of Women (bellaonline.com): "Religion & Spirituality: New Age." Accessed November 29, 2010.

8. Rumi Da, "The Legacy of Marcel Vogel," transcript of a paper presented at the 1996 2nd Annual Advanced Water Sciences Symposium and the 1998 United States Psychotronics Association Conference, available online at Vogel Crystals (vogelcrystals.net): "Articles."

9. Da, "The Legacy of Marcel Vogel."

10. B. Stone, Maria Rippo (ed.), "The Healing Properties of Metal in Ayurveda" (August 16, 2010), article online at Bright Hub: The Hub for Bright Minds (brighthub.com): "Health: Alternative & Natural."

Chapter 5

1. Gia Combs-Ramirez, "The Importance of a Vital Energy Field" (April 14, 2007), article online at The Science of Energy Healing (scienceofenergyhealing.com).

2. Combs-Ramirez, "The Importance of a Vital Energy Field."

3. L. W. Konikiewics, "Kirlian photography in theory and clinical application," *Journal of the Biological Photographic Association* (1977) 45, 115–134.

4. Randle Russell, "Aura Photography" (posted January 2002), paper available online at Triune-Being.com (triune-being.com): "Kirlian Photography: Research Papers."

5. "Russians develop dynamic Kirlian-type process," *Brain Mind Bulletin* 3, no. 10 (April 3, 1978). Cited in Swami Shankardevananda Saraswati, "Prana Shakti," *Yoga Magazine* (October 1980), available online at Yoga Magazine (yogamag.net): Archives.

6. "Electronic evidence of auras, chakras in UCLA study," *Brain Mind Bulletin* 3, no. 9 (March 20, 1978). H. Motoyama, "Yoga and Oriental Medicine," *Research for Religion and Parapsychology* 5 no. 1 (March 1979): 1. H. Motoyama, "The Mechanism Through Which Paranormal Phenomena Take Place," *Religion and Parapsychology* (1975), 2. All cited in Swami Shankardevananda Saraswati, "Prana Shakti," *Yoga Magazine* (October 1980), available online at Yoga Magazine (yogamag.net): "Archives."

7. Russell, "Aura Photography."

8. Robin Kelly, *The Human Antenna* (Santa Rosa, CA: Energy Psychology Press, 2007), 65–67.

9. Stephen Harrod Buhner, *The Secret Teachings of Plants* (Rochester, VT: Bear & Co., 2004), 86–87.

10. Robert K. Adair, "Analysis: The Physics of 'Alternative Medicine': The Fear of Weak Electromagnetic Fields," *The Scientific Review of Alternative Medicine* 2, no. 1 (spring-summer 1999). Available online at The Scientific Review of Alternative Medicine (sram.org): "Online Articles."

11. Buhner, 85–88.

12. Buhner, 107.

13. Rollin McCraty, Mike Atkinson, Dana Tomasino, and Raymond Trevor Bradley, "The Coherent Heart: Heart-Brain Interactions, Psychophysiological Coherence, and the Emergence of System-Wide Order," *Integral Review* 5, no. 2 (December 2009). Available online at Integral Review (integral-review.org): "Back Issues."

14. Don R. Powell and the American Institute for Preventative Medicine, "Minding Your Mental Health: Section II: Mental Health Topics: Anger" (last reviewed August 9, 2010), online content at Navy & Marine Corps Public Health Center (www-nehc.med.navy.mil): "Healthy Living: Psychological Health: Minding Your Mental Health."

15. Desiree Despues, "Stress and Illness" (spring 1999), student paper, California State University, Northridge. Available online at the website California State University, Northridge (csun.edu), homepage for professor Donna Fitz Roy Hardy, "Courses Taught," Psychology 691B: Seminar in Emotion and Motivation, Graduate Student Papers on Human Motivation.

16. Buhner, 124.

17. William Tiller, *Science and Human Transformation* (Walnut Creek, CA: Pavior Press, 1997), 211–212.

18. Valerie Mellema, "Laughing for Stress Relief," article online at StressDen.com (stressden.com). Accessed November 29, 2010.

19. Marianne Schnall, "Interview With Buddhist Monk Thich Nhat Hanh," article online at Our Inner Lives (feminist.com/ourinnerlives): "Features." Originally published in *The Huffington Post*, May 21, 2010.

20. Robertson (no first name given), "The Power of Your Inner Smile," *WellBeing* (December 23, 2009). Available online at the website WellBeing (wellbeing.com.au): "Features, Soul Health."

Chapter 6

1. "What the Ancient Egyptians Knew and Modern Science Can't Explain" (August 5, 1993), article online at Vesica Institute for Holistic Studies (vesica.org): "Biogeometry, Articles on Biogeometry." Accessed November 29, 2010.

2. "Crystal and Gemstone Therapy," article online at Peaceful Mind (peacefulmind.com): "Crystals, Metaphysical Properties." Accessed November 29, 2010.

Chapter 8

1. "Frequently Asked Sexuality Questions to the Kinsey Institute" (updated November 29, 2010), The Kinsey Institute for Research in Sex, Gender, and Reproduction (iub.edu/~kinsey/index.html): "Resources, Facts and Statistics."

2. Ibid.

3. "Using Gemstones and Crystals to Create Positive Relationships," online content at Emily Gems (crystal-cure.com): "The Reading Room." Accessed November 29, 2010.

4. Russell, "Aura Photography."

5. Daniel Goleman, "Friends for Life: The Emerging Biology of Emotional Healing," *New York Times* (October 10, 2006). Available online at The New York Times (nytimes.com).

6. Rollin McCraty, Mike Atkinson, and Raymond Trevor Bradley, "Electrophysiological Evidence of Intuition: Part 2. A System-Wide Process?" *Journal of Alternative and Complementary Medicine* 10, no. 2 (2004), 325–336. Available online at Institute of HeartMath (heartmath.org): "Research, Research Library, Research Publications, Intuition Research."

7. Goleman, "Friends for Life: The Emerging Biology of Emotional Healing."

Chapter 9

1. Jim Cunningham, "Children Want Boundaries," article online at Early Childhood News and Resources (earlychildhoodnews.net). No date. In response to reader questions, Cunningham posted a June 26, 2010, comment saying the study is from James Dobson and Focus on the Family.

Further Reading

||||||||||||||||||||||||||||||||||||||||||||||||||||||

In addition to the sources cited in endnotes, here are some books I recommend for more information about energetic boundaries.

Beattie, Melodie. *Codependent No More.* Center City, MN: Hazelden, 1992. Not specifically for energetic boundaries but an excellent guide for healing the issues underneath certain energetic vulnerabilities.

Bloom, William. *Psychic Protection.* New York: Fireside, 1997.

Bradshaw, John. *Healing the Shame That Binds You.* Deerfield Beach, FL: Health Communications, 1988. Not specifically about energetic boundaries, but an excellent guide to healing family-of-origin issues, which create boundary problems.

Brennan, Barbara Ann. *Hands of Light.* New York: Bantam, 1988.

Craig, Gary. *The EFT Manual.* 2nd edition. Santa Rosa, CA: Energy Psychology Press, 2011.

Eden, Donna, with David Feinstein. *Energy Medicine.* New York: Jeremy Tarcher, 2008.

Eden, Donna, David Feinstein, and Gary Craig. *The Promise for Energy Psychology.* New York: Jeremy Tarcher, 2004.

Emoto, Masaru. *The Hidden Messages of Water.* David A. Thayne, translator. New York: Atria, 2005.

———. *The Miracle of Water.* New York: Atria, 2007.

Evans, Patricia. *Controlling People.* Avon, MA: Adams Media Corporation, 2002. Not specifically about energetic boundaries, but a helpful guide to dealing with difficult people.

Hall, Judy. *The Art of Psychic Protection*. York Beach, ME:
Samuel Weiser, 1996.

Heller, Sharon. *Too Loud, Too Fast, Too Tight*. New York: HarperCollins,
2002. Not specifically for energetic boundaries, but an excellent
guide for assisting with sensitivities.

McLaren, Karla. *Energetic Boundaries*. Boulder, CO: Sounds True, 2003.
Audiobook.

———. *The Language of Emotion*. Boulder, CO: Sounds True, 2010.

Myss, Carolyn, and Norm Shealy. *The Creation of Health*. New York:
Three Rivers Press, 1988.

Myss, Carolyn. *Defy Gravity*. Carlsbad, CA: Hay House, 2009.

Orloff, Judith. *Emotional Freedom*. New York: Harmony Books, 2009.

———. *Positive Energy*. New York, Three Rivers Press, 2004.

Roman, Sanaya. *Personal Power Through Awareness*. Tiburon, CA:
HJ Kramer, 1986.

For children and the child within, I recommend several books by Marcella
Landsdowne, including:

The Adventures of Patty and Annabel: The Monsoon and The Auric Field

The Adventures of Patty and Annabel: Apache Lake and the Chakras

The Adventures of Patty and Annabel: The Javelinas and Releasing the Cords

(Publication information at marcellatheauthor.com and purchasing through
Amazon.com.)

Acknowledgments

||||||||||||||||||||||||||||||||||||||||||||||||||||||||||||

To acknowledge the thousands who have sat in my office or in chairs in my workshops would be to count the words in the dictionary. These are the people whose questions—*Why am I so sensitive? How come I always feel others' feelings as if they were my own? How can I set boundaries when the invading forces are invisible? How can I figure out who I am when I sense so much that is not my own?*—have prompted me to discover answers.

I thank you all, in addition to specific individuals who have taken the threads of this book and woven them into reality: Anthony J. W. Benson, my business manager and helmsman; Amy Rost, editor and friend; and Haven Iverson, Sounds True editor. May the energy be with you all!

Index

ancestors
Environ Syndrome and, 81
healing, 134
inherited memories from
(epigenetics), 21,
25, 133
Psychic-Sensitive Syndrome
and, 69–70
angels, 231, 248
fallen angels, 218
anger, 2, 27–28, 29, 139
red color and, 137, 213
Vampire Syndrome and, 53
animals, energetic conversation
with, 9
anorexia, 30
anxiety, 2, 38, 40, 128, 148
bridge children and, 234–235
Mule Syndrome and, 58
Psychic-Sensitive Syndrome
and, 68
yellow color and, 137
arthritis, 30
Asperger's syndrome, 76, 231,
241–242
asthma, 124, 128
attention deficit disorder (ADD), 43
attention deficit/hyperactivity
disorder (ADHD), 76, 136,
231, 242
attracting
function of energetic
boundaries, 17
gold (metal) and, 156, 208
needy or hurtful people, 37–38
the same people (Paper Doll
Syndrome), 48–51
supportive people, 35

auric field, 7–10, *8*, 18
activation of layers throughout
life, 10, *12*, 18
chakras and, 103, 104
twelve layers of, 10, *11*, 19
autism-spectrum disorders, 43, 231,
241–242
autoimmune disorders, 128
aventurine, 209
Ayurveda, 119

B
bacteria, replication stopped by
shapes, 110
bad behaviors, 170
bad feeling/belief, 141, 148
Baule, Gerhard, 10, 13
Beaulieu, John, 107
beliefs, 33–34, 138–141
about money, 180, 187–189,
191–197
changing/reframing, 140–141
emotions and, 26–27
immature/negative, 33–34,
139–141
maturing, 137–138, 162,
191–192
messages within, 138–141
misperceptions in, 139–141,
162, 213
religious beliefs, 60–61, 196–197,
222–223
separating from feelings,
137–141
workplace and, 161, 162
beta waves, 216
beverages. *See* drink
bindings, 63

BioGeometry™, 110, 159
biomagnetic field, 10, 35–36, 126–128, 142. *See also* electromagnetic fields
disease and, 13
bipolar disorder, 43, 148
black, 102, 134, 155, 214
anger and, 137
cautions for use of, 208, 214
children's use of, 248
depression and, 137
protective quality of, 214, 248
black-mirrored pyramid, 214, *215*
black opal, 150
blame, releasing, 88
blessings. *See also* intention
blessing an object, 90–91
blessing food and drink, 154, 162, 167
blue, 96, 100, 213
children's use of, 248
energy loss and, 137
sadness and, 137
for work objectives, 156
blue opal, 144
blue sapphire, 209
body areas, chakras and, 103, 104
body cells. *See* cells and organs
body's fluids, 153–154
borderline personality disorder, 148, 217–218
boundaries, energetic. *See* energetic boundaries
boundaries, energizing. *See* energizing your boundaries
boundary syndromes. *See* syndromes (energetic-boundary)

brain
activity, electromagnetic field and, 13
brain waves, 216
electromagnetic field of, 35
stimulation by sound, 107
brainwashing, 41
breathing
Divine breath, 221
emotional boundaries and, 163, 216
intentional, 166
physical boundaries and, 154–155
relational boundaries and, 166, 216, 221
releasing toxins through, 154, 163
bridge children, 234–236
bridge souls, 229
Brown, Steven P., 38
brown (color), 99
anger and, 137
in red boundaries, miasm and, 63–64
Vivaxis and, 134
bubble of containment, 218–219
Buddha, 151
Burnett, Mark, 47
burnout, caregiver, 173

C
calcite, pink, 164
Campbell, Don, 107
cancer, 30, 32–33, 124
healing of, 33
cardiovascular system, crystal network involving, 126

damaged or lacking boundaries, 2–4.
See also specific boundaries
danger, alerting to, 20
dead people. See also ancestors;
entities
communication with, 7, 95
connection through cords, 170
déjà vu, 68
delta waves, 216
demons, 170, 218
dependence, 30. See also addictions
depression, 40, 128, 135, 148
black color and, 137
diabetes, 124, 128
diagnosing
with chakras, 105
with colors, 96–97
of disease, with energy fields,
124–125
with Kirlian photography,
8, 125
with sound, 105
diamond, 132, 172, 221
diet. See food
disconnection, from self, 135
discounted feelings, 28–29
discrimination, 41
disease. See also health problems;
illness
curses and, 63
detection by magnetic fields, 13
diagnosis with energy fields,
124–125
diagnosis with Kirlian
photography, 8
patterns (miasms), 63–64,
133–134
psychic/physical toxins and, 30

disgust, 137, 139, 187
colors and, 214
empowering original, 189–190
money issues and, 187,
189–190, 191
releasing, 189
disillusionment, 169
Divine
asking for help
calling on Allah, 223
emotional boundaries
and, 189
energetic boundary
healing, 56, 88,
98, 130, 132–133,
134, 138, 149
with money issues, 189,
196–197,
198–199
prayer, 150, 171
relational boundaries
and, 196
spirit field, stimulat-
ing, 221
Spirit-to-Spirit exercise,
94–96, 122
transformation through,
221–222
using intention to bless
and object, 90–91
Wall of Truth/bubble
of containment,
218–219
work boundaries and,
150, 161, 171
breathing in and out, 221

feeling gratitude (provided for),
198, 199–200
healing stream of grace from.
See healing stream of
grace
Divine love, through Universal Field,
120–122, *121*
DNA, 9, 25, 36, 128
dopamine, 146
Douglass, Frederick, 225
drink (beverages)
abstaining from certain,
162–163
blessing/intention and, 131,
154, 162
healthy, 163
Dunne, Brenda, 87
dysfunctional families, 31

E
earth
electromagnetic frequency
of, 107
magnetic field of, 124
earth tones, 155
eating disorders, 30
Egyptians
colors and, 102
shapes and, 110, 159
Einstein, Albert, 120
electrical field, 126–127
electricity, 7
conduction by water, 9
magnetism and, 10
electromagnetic energy, 9–10, 34
as light, 9
electromagnetic fields, 6, 7, *8*,
126–128

external, 80, 124, 127
of head, 10–13
healing with, 13–14
of heart, 10–13, 34, 35–36,
126–128, 142
Kirlian photography of, 7, *8*
measuring, 10–14
mother's, 127
shape of, 126–127
electromagnetic frequency of the
earth, 107
electronography, 125
EMDR (eye movement
desensitization and
reprogramming), 136
emerald, 132, 144, 168, 209
emotional abuse, 23, 31–33
emotional chakras, 104, 108
emotional energy boundaries, 26–34.
See also relationships
assessing/visualizing, 125,
137–138, 161
beliefs, misperceptions from,
139–141, 213
caregiver work, tips for, 175
clearing/cleansing, 164–165,
190, 212–213
colors and, 135–136, 137
bright colors, 163
grey in, 190
orange color, 26, 99, 135
compromising factors for,
28–34
environment and, 163–164
feelings, major groupings of,
138–139
healing of, 161–165, 189–191,
212–216

H

Halpern, Steven, 107
hand washing, 164, 175
hands-on healing, 159, 175
happiness, color use and, 214. *See also* joy
harmonics (sound), 106–109
harmony, boundaries working in, 44
head, electromagnetic field of, 13, 35
headaches, 124, 135
healers
    boundaries for safe client work, 172–177
    coworkers, 176
    dealing with own issues, 176
    relational boundaries and, 37–38
    spiritual boundaries and, 43–44
    techniques for energetic work, 174–177
Healer's Syndrome, 70–74, 81
    bridge souls/children and, 229, 235
    emotional boundaries and, 136
    indigo souls/children and, 230, 236
    signs of, 72–73
    spirit children and, 244
    using numbers for, 116–117
    Vivaxis and, 134
    vs. Mule Syndrome, 72, 81
healing, 123–150. *See also* energizing your boundaries; specific energy boundaries
    with chakras, 105–106, 131–132
    with colors, 96–102. *See also specific energy boundaries*
    examples of results of boundary healing, 3–4
    forgiveness and, 129–130
    hands-on, 159, 175
    heart and, 126–127
    intentions and, 86–91
    with magnetic fields (externally-applied), 13–14
    meaning of, 123
    natural (qi, chi) energy and, 13–14
    with numbers, 115–117
    programming intention into a substance, 90–91, 131–132
    with shapes, 109–114
    with sound, 106–109
    with stones and metals, 117–120
    through emotional boundaries, 135–141
    through physical boundaries, 128–134
    through relational boundaries, 142–147
    through spiritual boundaries, 147–150
"Healing Power of Sound, The" (Scallon), 107
healing stream of grace, 65–66, 122, 130, 136, 144, 150, 172, 199
    relational healing and, 206–207
    Universal Field and, 172, 206
    Wall of Truth and, 218–219
health
    energetic boundaries and, 123–128
    heart and, 36, 126–128

I

IBM, 118

illness. *See also* disease; health problems
  catching energetically, 24, 123,
      124, 126
  childhood injuries and, 143
  emotional abuse and, 33
  neglect during, 32–33
  physical energy boundaries
      and, 21
  spiritual energy boundaries and,
      40, 42–43
  witnessing, 21, 24

immune system
  laughter and, 146
  mother's cells and, 26
  overactive, in crystal
      children, 240
  Psychic-Sensitive Syndrome
      and, 69
  Vampire Syndrome and, 54

in utero experiences, 106, 107,
    127, 129

indigo color, 96, 100

indigo children, 227, 236–238

indigo souls, 230

infection, 128

information exchanges, through
    energetic fields, 7–9

infrared energy, 9

inherited factors, physical energy
    boundaries and, 21, 25–26,
    183–184, 186

inhibiting contracts, 61–66
  payoff of, 64–65

injuries/violations, physical, 21,
    22–23, 128–129, 182–183,
    203–206

inner child, 143. *See also* parenting
    and inner parenting

insomnia. *See* sleep

Institute of HeartMath, 33–34, 36,
    38, 211

intention, 86–91
  acknowledging original
      intention, 88–89
  believing in, 90
  clearing out current, 88–89
  effects on mechanical
      objects, 87
  for emotional boundaries at
      work, 162–163
  frequency of, 87
  green color and, 168
  intentional breathing, 166
  for physical boundaries
      money and, 184, 185
      relationships and,
          207–208
      work and, 153–154, 155,
          156, 158
  power of, 86–87
  programming into any
      substance, 87, 185
  programming into food and
      drink, 131, 156, 162,
      184, 240
  programming into stones and
      metals, 87, 117–119,
      131–132, 156, 164, 234
  for relational boundaries at
      work, 166
  setting with the heart, 89
  for spiritual boundaries at
      work, 171

transformed into physical, 30
Sufi path, 223
suicide, 130
supernatural beings. *See* entities
supernatural traits, in children, 227
swastika, 114
symbols. *See* shapes
syndromes (energetic-boundary), 47–
    84. *See also specific syndromes*
    children and, 226–227
    determining, exercise for,
        82–84
    Environ Syndrome, 78–81
    Healer's Syndrome, 70–74
    journal exercise, 82–84
    Mule Syndrome, 57–61
    multiple or all at once, 48, 82
    No-Boundary Syndrome,
        74–78
    numbers and, 116–117
    Paper Doll Syndrome, 48–51
    physical boundary violations
        and, 22, 23, 26,
        128–129
    Psychic-Sensitive Syndrome,
        66–70
    similarities and differences in,
        81–82
    storyline leading to, 91–94
    Vampire Syndrome, 51–57

T
T-cells, 146, 147
tai chi, 155
talisman, 221
tea, 153–154
    baths with, 159
    green tea, 167

terrorism, doctrines of, 41
therapy, recommendation for, 88,
    89, 136, 143, 206
theta waves, 216
thoughts
    as energy, 6
    negative, 33–34
    number per day, 33
    yellow color and, 26, 97, 248
Tiller, William, 142–143
Tomatis, Alfred, 107
topaz, 210
torus shape, 126–127, 132
touch
    physical boundaries and, 155,
        159, 202–203
    sex and, 202–205
tourmaline, 144, 208, 209, 221
toxic dumpsite, 78
toxic people, 217–219
toxins
    disease and, 30
    environmental, 78–79
    jade and, 156
    psychic, transformed into
        physical, 30, 73
    releasing, 133, 154, 159, 163
trauma
    physical, 21, 22–25
    relational, 24–25
triangle, 113–114, 158
    healing with, 144
    in heart chakra, *145*, 146
    relationship issues and, 208
    work issues and, 165
troubled children, 245–247
trust, 205–206

truth
blue color and, 100
silver color and, 102
Wall of Truth, 218–219
turquoise, 168, 208, 214
twelve-step programs, 143

U

ultraviolet energy, 9
uncovering your storyline, 91–94,
    129, 149, 165–166
    someone else's storyline, 134
undeservedness, 140
unhappiness, transforming, 138
Universal Field, 120–122, *121*
    healing streams of grace from,
        172, 206
unlovability, 140
unmet needs, 21
unworthiness, 140
    messages of, 41
    thoughts of, 33, 43

V

value, feeling lack of, 141
Vampire Syndrome, 51–57
    bridge souls/children and,
        229, 235
    client's story, 55–57
    emotional boundaries and, 136
    otherworldly interference,
        55–56
    signs of, 53–54
    spirit children and, 244
    using numbers for, 116–117
vampires, deflecting with
    amethyst, 119
Vesica Institute, 159

victim syndromes. *See* Healer's
    Syndrome; Mule Syndrome;
    Vampire Syndrome
violations. *See* injuries/violations
visible light, 9
vitamins, 131, 163
Vivaxis cords, 133–134
Vogel, Marcel, 118–119

W

Wall of Truth, 218–219
water
    blessing/intention and, 154
    conduction of electricity by, 9
    crystal use with, 118–119
    crystals (water crystals), 110
    energetic field of, 9
    fountains/running water, 157
    as information-storage system,
        118–119
wavelengths, 9
Waynbaum, Israel, 147
Weick, Karl, 201
weight issues, 44, 124
white, 98, 101
    boundaries. *See* spiritual energy
        boundaries
    children's use of, 248
    denoting innocence, 98, 101
    in spiritual boundaries, 39,
        101, 147
    tones/hues of, 96, 101
witnessing
    children's experience of, 23
    physical abuse or illness, 21, 23,
        24, 128
women, absorbing emotions of
    others, 29–30, 31

About the Author

‖‖‖

Cyndi Dale is known and respected worldwide as an energy healer, intuitive counselor, and author of bestselling books, including *The Subtle Body* and *New Chakra Healing* (republished and expanded as *The Complete Book of Chakra Healing* in 2009). Through her company, Life Systems Services, she provides intuitive assessments and life-issues healing, as well as inspiration, for thousands of clients a year, both by phone and in person. She especially enjoys helping people awaken their spiritual gifts and live their destinies.

Having studied with healers from all parts of the world, including Peru, Belize, Costa Rica, Japan, Iceland, Mexico, and across Europe, Cyndi now conducts workshops, training sessions, and college classes across the globe. Her enthusiasm, care, and down-to-earth teaching style make her wisdom and techniques accessible to everyone. She lives in Minneapolis, Minnesota, with her two sons and five pets (at last count).

More information on Cyndi's products, classes, and services is available at cyndidale.com.

About Sounds True

|||||||||||||||||||||||||||||||||||||||||||||||||||||||||||||||||||

Sounds True is a multimedia publisher whose mission is to inspire and support personal transformation and spiritual awakening. Founded in 1985 and located in Boulder, Colorado, we work with many of the leading spiritual teachers, thinkers, healers, and visionary artists of our time. We strive with every title to preserve the essential "living wisdom" of the author or artist. It is our goal to create products that not only provide information to a reader or listener, but that also embody the quality of a wisdom transmission.

For those seeking genuine transformation, Sounds True is your trusted partner. At SoundsTrue.com you will find a wealth of free resources to support your journey, including exclusive weekly audio interviews, free downloads, interactive learning tools, and other special savings on all our titles.

To listen to a podcast interview with Sounds True publisher Tami Simon and author Cyndi Dale, visit SoundsTrue.com/bonus/Cyndi_Dale_Energy.

sounds True
many voices, one journey

Personal Power Chakra (1. Root, 2. Sacral,
3. PP) Closed + Throat Chakra (4. Heart,
5. Thrt) Closed. Rest are strong (6. Intuitive,
7. Crown, Cnctn to Divine)